Blood Work

Blood Work

Imagining Race in American Literature, 1890–1940

SHAWN SALVANT

Louisiana State University Press *Baton Rouge*

Published by Louisiana State University Press

Manufactured in the United States of America
First printing

Designer: Michelle A. Neustrom
Typeface: Livory
Printer and binder: Maple Press

Library of Congress Cataloging-in-Publication Data

Salvant, Shawn, 1974–
Blood work : imagining race in American literature, 1890–1940 / Shawn Salvant.
pages cm
Includes bibliographical references and index.
ISBN 978-0-8071-5784-8 (cloth : alk. paper) — ISBN 978-0-8071-5785-5 (pdf) — ISBN 978-0-8071-5786-2 (epub) — ISBN 978-0-8071-5787-9 (mobi) 1. American literature—History and criticism. 2. Race in literature. I. Title.
PS169.R28S26 2015
810.9'355—dc23

2014034963

The paper in this book meets the guidelines for permanence and durability of the Committee on Production Guidelines for Book Longevity of the Council on Library Resources. ♾

CONTENTS

ACKNOWLEDGMENTS

While writing this book, I truly learned more than I ever imagined I would. I am grateful for every lesson learned and every person I met during this journey. Sam Otter at the University of California at Berkeley got me started, and I cannot thank him enough for his time, expertise, advice, and humor. The project could not have been completed without the friendship and support of the faculty, staff, and students in the University of Connecticut's Department of English and Institute for African American Studies. I am especially grateful for the collegiality and generosity of the Americanist Reading Group: Martha Cutter, Sharon Harris, Cathy Schlund-Vials, Jerry Phillips, Kate Capshaw Smith, and Chris Vials. I will also never forget the kindness, brilliance, and support of my friends from the Vanderbilt English Department, particularly Deak Nabers, Janis May, Jonathan Lamb, Natalie Baggett, Jay Clayton, Paul Young, Polly Case, Sam Girgus, Sean Goudie, Teresa Goddu, and Tina Chen. Special thanks to Dana Nelson, whose numerous acts of kindness helped me to move forward. Margaret Lovecraft at LSU Press expertly and efficiently shepherded this book through its final stages. I appreciate her professionalism, and I am thankful for all of the work done by the readers and staff at LSU Press in bringing this book to fruition. Thanks to Gary Von Euer for his patient, diligent, and marvelous copyediting. Nathan Grant, Aileen Keenan, and all the good people at *African American Review* kindly published this book's third chapter as an article in *AAR* 42.3–4 (2008). Finally, I am especially thankful for the patience and support of my family—my mother Patricia, brother Bryan, stepfather Dewey, Sonia, all of my family back home, and my grandmother Marlin Cook, who completed her work before I could complete mine. We miss you, Ma.

Blood Work

INTRODUCTION

Race, Blood, and the American Racial Imagination

Following the work of anthropologists and sociologists, recent literary and philosophical critiques of the concept of race have revised the definition from biological category to social construction, ultimately going so far as to suggest that race is largely an effect of language. According to these critiques, race itself should no longer be considered a biological reality but rather a metaphor or system of metaphors, or in Henry Louis Gates's formulation, a "trope of ultimate, irreducible difference between cultures, linguistic groups, or adherents or specific belief systems" (Gates, "Writing 'Race'" 5). Consequently, if race is a problem, then the problem of race is in some measure a problem of figuration, a language problem with vast social significance. If race is a figure or a metaphor, then the problem of race (when considered through the classic Aristotelian explanation of how metaphors create meaning) is a problem of misnaming.[1] As Gates himself explains, to speak "in metaphors" of "'the white race' or 'the black race,' 'the Jewish race' or 'the Aryan race'" is to speak "in biological misnomers" (4). Current critiques of racialism thus shift toward focusing on race not as an essence but rather as a function: race stands in for something it is not. When considered "like all other concepts, constructed by metaphor and metonymy," Anthony Appiah explains, race "stands in, metonymically, for the Other; it bears the weight, metaphorically, of other kinds of difference'" ("Uncompleted Argument" 35).

These recent reconceptions and redefinitions of race necessarily alter the field upon which race and racialism can be critiqued and contested (a shift in jurisdiction with certain intellectual and disciplinary, not to mention professional stakes). For approached as the problem of figuration or metaphor, the problem of race is no longer the problem that once occupied anthropologists such as Franz Boas, Ruth Benedict, and Ashley Montagu or evolutionary biologist Stephen Jay Gould, those who marshaled scientific counterarguments to rebut popular misconceptions about the division of the human species into racial types and racial varieties. Those efforts were motivated by the premise that more accurate scientific information about the biology of human difference could ameliorate racial animosities. "Social prejudices themselves may be refractory," admits Stephen Jay Gould in the coda to *The Mismeasure of Man*, "but particular biological supports for them can be dislodged" (322). Yet despite a century of advancement in genetics and various robust campaigns to make known the nonexistence of biological races, racial thinking of course persists. Moreover, scientific counterargument becomes even less effectual given the terms through which postmodern critiques are redefining race itself as a discursive rather than a biological concept. Race survives by slipping beyond the jurisdiction of the scientific method that has turned against it. The geneticists and anthropologists have done what they could to dismantle the biological race concept, but their work, as difficult as it has been, may ultimately prove more manageable than the work that lies ahead for the next generation of antiracialist warriors, those confronting the metaphorical conceptualization of race now gaining ground.

After all, the modern biological concept of race, the invention of eighteenth-century European natural philosophy, has run its course partially because this previous concept of race was mercifully sown in the soil of its own destruction. As a scientific claim, race was born from a discipline whose methodological commitments would ultimately (albeit with much resistance and far too gradually) guarantee its undoing. But this new, metaphorical concept of race will, once fully installed, become much more intractable in comparison with what was an always unstable biological notion of race. Race as metaphor is here to stay because, unlike its biological predecessor, race as metaphor is by all means a "real thing." The various post-structuralist critiques that have unmasked race have also revived it in a form more frustratingly real than ever. By recasting race as a form of figurative language, critical race theorists and literary critics ultimately conserve race. This conserved, discursive form of race becomes even more powerful and more persistent than the biological form it supersedes. Because now, as Gates warns, even to speak of "race" is "to engage in a pernicious act of language, one which exacerbates the complex problem of cultural or ethnic difference, rather than to assuage or redress it" ("Writing 'Race'" 5).

The metaphorical conception of race will persist because, as theories of metaphor itself have demonstrated, metaphorical figuration is not only an occasional practice but rather a mode of thought that governs (if not makes possible) the very negotiation of everyday life, "a pervasive, irreducible, imaginative structure of human understanding that influences the nature of meaning and constrains our rational inferences" (Johnson xii). As metaphor or trope, race gains the advantage of such pervasiveness as a way of thought. No longer under pressure to justify itself scientifically, race can enjoy all of the luxuries of being an effect of language. Now the problem with race is not that it pretends to exist when it does not (while still inflicting tremendous damage in this process of pretending); the problem with race as metaphor is merely its lack of a denotative referent, which, for a form of language at play, is no problem at all. As Appiah writes, "Even if the concept of race *is* a structure of oppositions . . . it is a structure whose realization is, at best, problematic and, at worst, impossible. If we can now hope to understand the concept embodied in this system of oppositions, we are nowhere near finding referents for it" ("Uncompleted" 35). If race is merely language, merely metaphor, then race can enjoy doing what all metaphors do: not being what it claims to be, being both more and less than what it says, and standing in for something else. Post-structuralist critiques of race defer the demise of race by dismissing it from the field of scientific inquiry and relocating race within the field of language at play. Indeed, being recognized as metaphor may be the best thing that ever happened to race.[2]

There are no referents for race, because race (like all metaphors) is not referential but rather constructive. As Michael Omi and Howard Winant argue in their reconceptualization of race through the concept of "racial formation," race works not by assuming the terms and conditions of some other category (Omi and Winant specifically reject previous efforts to reduce race to nation, class, or ethnicity) but rather by conducting its own unique and constructive project. Omi and Winant describe race as an ongoing, ever-changing "sociohistorical process by which racial categories are created, inhabited, transformed, and destroyed" that unfolds through "a process of historically situated *projects* in which human bodies and social structures are represented and organized" (55–56).[3] Omi and Winant explain that, as a formation, race is not a single concept that can be applied but rather a strategy that the racialist employs opportunistically in the moment of historically contingent occasions. "The effort must be made to understand race as an unstable and 'decentered' complex of social meanings constantly being transformed by political struggle" (55). And because the particular circumstances that give rise to race are integral to its function at the moment, race, like all metaphors that are contingent upon the circumstances of their use, resists simple paraphrase. Race cannot be summarized or paraphrased in general terms that are divorced from the specific context of its usage. There can be no definitive answers to questions such as "What is race?" or "What do we really mean when we speak about race?" Race *means* what it happens to *do* in the moment of its historically and socially situated application; race means whatever it is being used for now. The only question that can be posed toward definition is "What is the work of race here and now?"

Blood Work studies a particular discursive project within the American racial formation: the work "blood" performs as an image and concept in the construction of American racialism in late nineteenth- and early twentieth-century American literature. According to Omi and Winant, "*A racial project is simultaneously an interpretation, representation, or explanation of racial dynamics, and an effort to reorganize and redistribute resources along particular racial lines.* Racial projects connect what race *means* in a particular discursive practice and the ways in which both social structures and everyday experiences are racially organized, based upon that meaning" (56). *Blood Work* treats racial blood rhetoric as a racial project within the process of American racial formation and examines how "social structures and everyday experiences are racially organized" based upon the meanings that "blood" imparts to race. Working as both an image and as a concept, blood provides the conceptual basis for various legal and psychological strategies within the formation of American racialism. As such, blood remains among the most persistent, prevalent, and powerful devices in the "interpretation, representation," and "explanation" of race in America and is a term used most effectively to "reorganize and redistribute resources along particular racial lines." If race emerged out of European Enlightenment thought as a way of thinking, seeing, and making sense of human difference, blood has been perhaps the most significant device by which American racialism has made sense of its own historically contingent racial projects.

The literary readings in *Blood Work* are thus motivated by the premise that the concept of blood, as the core image of American racial rhetoric, signifies a uniquely American racial formation characterized by particularly American cultural, legal, rhetorical, and literary constructions of the relationships between race, identity, and society. To suggest that American racial rhetoric is characterized by a particular emphasis on the concept and imagery of blood is not to suggest that an investment in blood is wholly unique to the American context. Uli Linke (*Blood and Nation: The European Aesthetics of Race*) has comprehensively traced the "visions of blood in European history" and the development of European blood symbology, which moved toward the biological conceptualizations of race that provided the naturalizing racial discourse of Nazism (vii). As well, George Mosse (*Toward the Final Solution*), Ivan Hannaford (*Race: The History of an Idea in the West*), and other historians of the idea of race and the ideology of racialism have demonstrated how the history of European racialism is replete with mystic, nationalistic conceptions of blood origins, of native genealogies identified through nefarious and pseudoscientific claims, protected and purified through inquisition and violent epic purges of unwanted blood mixture.[4]

But while American racial blood rhetoric develops from such European racial ideology, it is not expressive of the conditions that gave rise to that ideology. As Betsy Erkkila explains, there is a particular "metaphorics of American blood," stemming from the different functions played by racial difference in the contexts of the New and Old Worlds and the different conceptualizations of blood required to represent them: "Whereas in the Old World blood served to mark off the aristocratic body and the distinctions of a hereditary class system, in the New World blood assumed other and more mobile socially symbolic meanings as a signifier not only of class but also of bodily, sexual, racial, and cultural difference" (Erkkila 7). The images of blood deployed by American racialism thus articulate the unique historical and ideological contingencies of American racial history. *Blood Work* seeks to examine the implications of this premise: that while blood has been employed as a metaphor for race in many other race-nationalist contexts, the blood of American racialism is a particular substance, the product of American slavery and American race riots, the American Revolution and Civil War, American legal race discourse, American "racial science," and American racial violence. In order to consider the function of blood in the construction of race in the American context, this image as it is employed in American racial rhetoric must be considered within the context of the scientific, legal, and religious discourses from which it is drawn. In doing so, what we find is that American racial rhetoric has developed as a particularly bloody rhetoric because blood connotes so much of what race has meant here and so much of what America has asked race to be. In America, race has been a particularly bloody business both rhetorically and in practice, and it has been bloody in particularly American ways.

Although *Blood Work* focuses on the late nineteenth and early twentieth century as a period with particularly significant literary and cultural stakes for the use of blood as a device in the service of American racialism, the development of an American ideology of race and blood can be traced to early American history and culture. "During the very years when Americans were proclaiming the rights and liberties of the British colonies and the universal rights of man," writes Betsy Erkkila, "they began to deploy a metaphorics of blood to mark a boundary around whiteness, purity, virtue, intelligence, and beauty" (7). In *Mixed Bloods and Other Crosses*, Erkkila describes the coalescence of a sacrificial, honorific, and exclusionary form of blood that "saturates the literature of the American founding and the years of ongoing political and cultural struggle over the Revolutionary ideals of freedom, equality, justice, rights, and citizenship" and that comes to constitute a "national dialectics of blood union" characterizing the formation of citizenship during the early republic (1, 5). In this dialectic, the blood spilled during the Revolutionary War becomes imagined as the substance of collective sacrifice through which the segmented colonial population came to conceive itself as one (to the exclusion of Native Americans and black slaves). The sacrificial blood of the Revolutionary War dead effectively becomes the substance of an American blood covenant in a process of amalgamation that forges the lineages of disparate European genealogical and cultural histories within the crucible of a blood-saturated American soil. From this generative narrative of American identity and American family, the blood that binds is significantly the blood of war. Neither a substance nor symbol to be wasted, this blood is consecrated by virtue of its violent and sacrificial spillage, figuring the very meaning of the war as an event that formed a new nation *ex nihilo*, irrespective of the Native American and African blood with which it would inevitably become "mixed" in the soil of the national battlefield.

The image of blood remained central to the concept of American race citizenship based upon a narrative in which the nation earned its own *sui generis* origin through painful collective sacrifice, and this blood would be rearticulated as the shared carrier of the incipient American soul. Invested in an evolving calculus of value drawn from various forms of genealogically and racially motivated violence, this imagined essence of American identity would serve as the constant reminder of the sacrifices that brought American identity into historical flow. Embedding a "real or imagined threat of blood violence" with "anxious appeals to blood kinship," this American conceptualization of blood "underwrite[s] the language of the founding documents" and overcasts American political discourse with a paranoia over constant threats to this sacred national kinship (Erkkila 2). As Erkkila argues, American colonists devised a system of race laws whose appeal to the language of blood was by no means wholly derivative of the concept of blood as employed in European racial rhetoric, nor restricted to suggestions of biology alone. Instead, from its outset, an American racial discourse of blood paid special homage to the nation's own Revolutionary War dead by constituting a rhetoric of American exceptionalism that spoke its appreciation for the sacrifice of literal blood made by the martyrs of the Revolution. "These founding appeals to the blood sacrifice of the American Revolution would become part of an ongoing national dialectics of blood union," writes Erkkila, "a need to repeat the blood sacrifice of the founders as a means of consecrating the national union, the blood kinship of Americans, and their continuing commitment to the sacred ideals of liberty and independence" (5).

This sacred blood must, of course, remain distinct (legally, scientifically, ideologically, and rhetorically) from the blood of those groups that populated the landscape before colonization as well as the blood of those transported during and after settlement. That is, it must be kept separate from the blood of those peoples who (while undoubtedly sharing the family lineages as well as the sacrifices of the colonists) were deemed unfit to share in the benefits of this national investment in blood, namely Native Americans, African slaves, and subsequent European and Asian immigrants and their descendants. "As a practice of remembering and constructing history, American genealogy inevitably has signaled exclusion," writes Russ Castronovo in *Fathering the Nation*, "it identifies rightful members within ancestral paths, even as it omits those denied the originary authority of a patriarchal ancestor" (15–16). Thus the concept of an exclusionary blood flowing from the sacrificing "founding fathers" figured the essence of an American racial identity that was also a prerequisite for full American citizenship regardless of the criteria articulated by the protections of Constitutional amendments. Although the Fourteenth Amendment would eventually guarantee citizenship to "all persons born or naturalized in the United States," this Constitutional extension of citizenship would operate in a tense subordination to the required narrative of origination from mythical "first families," a narrative in which, as Castronovo puts it, "Some have descended from [founding] fathers and therefore have a citizen's blood running in their political and social bodies; others lack a legitimate ancestor within the nation and can claim no prior authority to act as citizens" (16).

And so, while they inherited previous European ideologies of nationalistic blood, the American colonists and their descendants constructed what would become a unique discourse of national blood born from violence and committed to violence in the name of preserving this rather deliberately defined form of citizenship. It was a discourse that underwrote the nation's contradictory combination of egalitarian principles and its history of harsh brutalities through Indian removal, racial enslavement, Civil War, race riots, and postwar enforcement of white supremacy by exclusive immigration acts against unwanted blood and acts of anti-immigrant and antiblack violence such as lynching, practices that would make real blood visible. As the perfect image for encapsulating the full breadth of this project of American racialism, blood speaks with equal dedication to the most sacred and profane elements necessary for the construction and maintenance of American citizenship.

American slavery and the Civil War extended the nation's commitment to blood as the visual sign of its commitment to racial ideology. American racial discourse invested in the image of blood to capture the unique interracial intimacies of both American slavery and the war it engendered; the violence inherent to both cast the nation's project of racial exclusion in an imagery of intermingled, broken black and white bodies. Yet, as Saidiya Hartman explains, the honored violence of the war overwrote the meaning of the violence done to enslaved black bodies. "The blood of warring brothers and mothers' sons that stained the war-torn landscape . . . granted the enslaved freedom, but the blood regularly spilt at the whipping post or drawn by the cat-o'-nine tails in the field, the 200,000 black soldiers who fought for the Union, or the hundreds of thousands of slaves who contributed to the defeat of the Confederacy . . . failed to be included in these accounts of slavery's demise" (130). In this fashion, the violence of the war brought an end to slavery while also recontextualizing the meaning of the black blood spilled during slavery within a larger narrative of the sacrificial acts required for the nation's moral progress, a narrative that privileged the blood of white Northern and Southern combatants over that of black slaves and black soldiers.

In addition to this history of shared violence, the blood of American racialist rhetoric always bespeaks the particularly volatile intimacy between black slaves and white masters that characterized American slavery and the institution's ever-present tension between forbidden interracial sex and the violent enforcement of racial sex codes.[5] While physical instruments of torture decimated slave bodies and spilled literal blood, an ideology and legal rhetoric of forbidden blood mixture sanctioned some sexual unions while enveloping others with threats of imprisonment, brutal physical punishment, and death. In this manner, racial blood discourse not only provided the terminology by which Americans codified and legislated the color line (not only, that is, a language for determining race), but, even more critically, this discourse provided the terminology for constructing this division between blackness and whiteness through the invention and enforcement of punishable acts of interracial sex. As Winthrop Jordan explains in *White over Black*, "The use of 'blood' in connection with miscegenation represented, especially before the advent of knowledge about genetics, much more than a convenient metaphor. . . . [A]t least from the time of the Greeks it had been intimately and explicitly linked with the concept of human generation" (166). To speak of racial categories in terms of "white blood" and "black blood" emphasized not only a static differential in racial identity but also a particular narrative of the generative roles of masters and slaves in the perpetuation of the slave regime; this would be a rhetorical inflection of particular significance after the outlawing of the Atlantic slave trade in 1808 made the continued proliferation of the slave population and thus the slave economy dependent upon "natural increase."

The rhetoric of blood thus worked to associate racial status with sexual history in a way that a discourse of skin color (with its own visible racial aesthetic) could not fully connote. The singular emphasis upon blood in American racial discourse speaks to the importance that the American racial imagination places not only upon racial identification and inheritance but also upon imagined (and literary) narratives of interracial sex: its genealogical permutations, situational possibilities, and prohibitions. As Leon Higginbotham has discussed, this strategy of sexualizing racial difference lurked behind the appeal to blood made by the nation's earliest race-based statutes (written in Virginia during the 1660s). Beyond essentializing race for the purposes of New World slavery, "the statutes also have another meaning that is equally important"; while the statutes certainly "grounded the precept of inferiority firmly in biology" (as Higginbotham explains), their references to "blood" also connoted "the legislators' rather compulsive preoccupation with interracial sex" (41). Blood, as the essence of race, was not only the sign of racial identity (like visible skin color) but also the residue of often illicit sexual acts that were intended to be imagined and whose meanings became inextricably linked with the racial status imparted to the inheritor. "If black blood was the mark of inferiority," writes Higginbotham, "sex became the instrument by which it was transmitted. Since sex for blacks was licentious and savage, there was a certain perverse logic to this theory that anyone born of such an act would inherit the very characteristics of the act itself" (41). (The image of blood in such statutes constituted some of the earliest efforts to codify what would by the late nineteenth century become the system of laws comprising the so-called "one-drop rule.")

For African Americans, this image of blood, by virtue of its sexual connotations, worked to construct a particular form of American blackness that would never be considered "pure" but always tinged with the assumption of a history of illicit sexual conduct. In 1903, even W.E.B. Du Bois lamented the persistence of a "burden" implicit in the African American male's "red stain of bastardy, which two centuries of systematic legal defilement of Negro women had stamped upon his race . . . not only the loss of ancient African chastity, but also the hereditary weight of a mass of corruption from white adulterers, threatening almost the obliteration of the Negro home" (14).

Higginbotham's analysis of some of the more implicit connotations conveyed to American racial identity through the use of racial blood rhetoric in these early statutes in Virginia anticipates some of the central arguments of *Blood Work*: that the full insidiousness behind such metaphorical language as the "one-drop rule" can only be gauged when the complete range of connotative work performed by blood is taken into account, that the meanings associated with the substance figuratively composing the one drop in the "one-drop rule" make a substantive difference in the ideology of race that this language articulates (and the fictional and real-world narratives it engenders), and that the work of blood in American racial discourse extends well beyond the relatively simple concept of biologism. In contrast to a rhetoric imaging black and white skin, the American rhetoric of racial blood images a much more salacious narrative of violence, sex, and intrigue. American racialism's commitment to a metaphorics of blood indicates the nation's commitment to cultural and literary narratives of racial tantalization. This metaphorics of blood speaks to American racialism's commitment not only to a practice of inclusions and exclusions but also occlusions. It is a racial rhetoric that emphasizes the existence of that for which a complete narrative can never be provided: each racial subject's share in the nation's uniquely and profoundly muddled interracial genealogical history, each subject's particular place within a history of interracial sex whose details will, in all likelihood, never be fully illuminated.

The tantalizing occlusions suggested by this rhetoric have become one of the defining characteristics of American race literature. In addition to its generative and sexual connotations, the drop of blood figured in the one-drop rule (for example) mobilizes a project of racial determination that is always beset with the problem of hiddenness, the defining dynamic of America's romance with race. Blood works to insure that American racial identity will always be a matter of obfuscation and revelation and that the project of racial determination will always entail a narrative of mystery and detection. Through its connotations of illicit, forgotten, and hidden sexual acts, blood has thus been crucial for constituting the romantic and Gothic narratives of incest and miscegenation that populate American literature (not to mention American history). It is this particularly American connotation of racial blood that energizes so many of the nation's narratives of racial identity with what Toni Morrison describes as the "thrill of discovery" (74). Speaking of the formal and thematic energy drawn from the narrative of racial discovery in Faulkner's *Absalom, Absalom!*, Morrison describes this energy as particularly characteristic of modern American literature and admires the novel's technical achievement of simultaneously insisting upon yet eliding race through the use of this figure: "As a reader you have been forced to hunt for a drop of black blood that means everything and nothing. The insanity of racism" (101).[6]

Blood Work focuses on the period of the late nineteenth and early twentieth century, a period in which the work of blood in American racialism becomes particularly visible and consequential. During this period, the saturation of blood in the nation's founding documents that Betsy Erkkila describes, becomes visible in the context of renewed political agitation and increased real violence over the unfulfilled ideals of universal liberty. As racial violence escalated, American race law witnessed a reinvestment in the ideology and rhetoric of racial blood through manifestations such as the "one-drop rule" and the proliferation of "scientific" racialism that justified prohibitions against interracial unions by both law and custom. "In the aftermath of emancipation, miscegenation acquired a political currency that was perhaps unprecedented," writes Saidiya Hartman of the increased attention to racial blood lineages during this period. The passage of stricter miscegenation statutes during Reconstruction "disclose[d] the obsessions of the state with pure blood, procreation, and legitimate union and the emergent antipathy and anxiety attendant to the new terms of interracial association now that slavery no longer provided the guidelines or rules for such interactions" (Hartman 185). The dialectic of blood identified by Erkkila (consecrated through making violent sacrifices and fostering kinship and national citizenship) becomes resurgent during this period in several forms: the language and imagery of legal and scientific definitions of race, with their emphases on visible admixtures of blood; the legal system's deepening investment in the "one-drop rule" as a mechanism for legislating a blackness that was becoming increasingly invisible; and the bloody practice of lynching, the heinous form of extralegal terror designed to interrupt advancements in African American social and civil rights. While blood had been used as a metaphor for race throughout American racial history, the late nineteenth century witnessed the construction of a particularly American complex with regard to this relationship, as the meaning of racial blood transcended simple essentialism in the wake of increased scientific knowledge of heredity and became ramified into blood's expression of America's racial past and the violence seen as necessary to protect it.

Du Bois's reference in *The Souls of Black Folk* (1903) to the irrepressible "red stain of bastardy" through which blackness had come to be imagined in the wake of slavery underscores the new exigencies of racial blood rhetoric arising during the post-Reconstruction moment, when antiblack racial attitudes were being preserved in segregation laws, discriminatory labor contracts, discriminatory sentencing, and the infamous "Black Codes," all used to circumvent the protections of the Fourteenth Amendment. Collectively, such efforts constituted the construction of a post-emancipation form of blackness, no longer aligned with slave status but nevertheless premised upon black inferiority. The concept of black blood had become inextricably linked with the interracial sexual intimacies of slavery and the blood sacrifices of the war. A drop of black blood was no longer regarded only as the presence of a deterministic biological essence but also as a reference to an irrepressible historical and cultural narrative. For the purposes of discrimination and segregation law, the manner by which black blood conveyed inferiority became increasingly less mechanical (as in the biological sense) and more associative; post-emancipation laws could not discriminate against blackness per se (expressly forbidden by Constitutional amendment), but they could effectively construct a host of negative social and economic corollaries to this blackness.

The 1896 decision in *Plessy v. Ferguson* culminated the construction of this emerging brand of American racialism, a racialism loosely guided by the principles of scientific racism but more committed to blood as a malleable, serviceable metaphor. It is in this context that Du Bois's reference to the "red stain of bastardy" echoes the logic of Albion Tourgée's argument on behalf of Homer Plessy in 1896: "What else but a badge of servitude is imposed and perpetuated . . . when a person, seven-eighths white and one-eighth of colored blood, or a person fifteen-sixteenths parts white and one-sixteenth part of colored blood, is subjected to fine or imprisonment by authority of State law, for insisting that he or she, as the case may be, should be classed as a white person . . . ?" (*qtd. in* Lofgren 46). The significance of Tourgée's objection to the unnatural illogic of blood supported by *Plessy* lies in his drawing of a relationship between the deterministic claims of racial blood derived from scientific racialism, the fears of miscegenation underlying racial segregation, and the bend toward post-emancipation racial violence that *Plessy* tacitly endorses. As Justice Harlan made clear in his dissenting opinion in *Plessy* (when he objected that "'the interests of both [races] require that the common government of all shall not permit the seeds of race hate to be planted under the sanction of law'"), one of the key outcomes of the case would be to codify this illicit blood in a manner that reconstituted what Du Bois called the "red stain of bastardy" as a "badge of servitude" that would in turn "promote racial violence" (Lofgren 194). As a moment in the development of the American ideology of racial blood, *Plessy* exemplifies the post-Reconstruction period's abandonment of a relatively simple biological determinism for a conceptualization of racial blood that performed much more associative social, political, and cultural work.

Indeed, making this post-Reconstruction pivot in the relationship between blood and black inferiority is one of the significant outcomes of *Plessy*'s infamously twisted and specious argumentation. To consider this point, recall *Plessy*'s reliance upon previous theories of natural racial aversion in order to support a Constitutional rationale for segregation despite the Fourteenth Amendment's guarantee of civic equality. To circumvent the Fourteenth Amendment's equal protection clause, American race law reached back to theories of natural race distinctions provided by the "American school" of ethnology from the 1830s to the 1850s. Scientific racialism, as legal historian Charles Lofgren has shown, "arguably supported the state's position in *Plessy*" by providing the "intellectual environment" for the series of legal decisions that chipped away at the protections of the Fourteenth Amendment (94). In a series of lower court cases, pro-segregationist judges gradually established what ultimately would become *Plessy*'s argument for the "reasonableness" of segregation as an issue of public peace and public good. Centering on transportation laws that delineated the rights and responsibilities of public carriers, these cases established a "doctrine of reasonableness" under which such carriers could discriminate against passengers but "must conduct their affairs in a reasonable manner, in the sense of promoting the welfare of their customers and of the public generally as well as advancing the interests of the proprietors" (Lofgren 118, 117). Scientific racism provided the court with a way to circumvent the Fourteenth Amendment by defining racial segregation within the scope of this reasonable concern for public good.[7] Public integration, it was argued, forced an unnatural and unwanted interracial mingling that threatened the peace.

It is here that the figure of blood served in the construction of a form of racialism engineered and required by *Plessy*. Although Homer Plessy's legal team strategized to confound segregation law by selecting a test case litigant who was considered legally black but exhibited no visible signs of his black ancestry, Louisiana's assistant district attorney Lionel Adams countered by defining Plessy's blackness for the court as a function of his blood rather than his skin color. Adams referred the court to a definition of "persons of color" that included "all persons descended wholly from African ancestors, but also those who have descended in part only form such ancestors, and have a distinct admixture of African blood" (*qtd. in* Lofgren 58). The definition would satisfy the Louisiana Criminal Court, the state Supreme Court, as well as Supreme Court Justice Henry Billings Brown. Plessy, the court concluded, was indeed black, and this blackness was a threat to the public peace in the space of an integrated train car. Consequently, Justice Brown's infamous majority opinion interceded the claims of racial science to block the granting of race-blind liberties and privileges that the Fourteenth Amendment had supposedly guaranteed. "Legislation is powerless to eradicate racial instincts or to abolish distinctions based upon physical differences, and the attempts to do so can only result in accentuating the difficulties of the present situation" (*qtd. in* Lofgren 178).[8] What the Fourteenth Amendment had not taken into account, Brown's decision implied, was that racial difference, as a matter of biology, was actually beyond if not above the reach of the law.

Plessy provides an instrumental moment for considering the work that blood performs in the American racial formation because the case served as an inflection point in the nation's racial logic and the function of blood within this logic. With respect to the arguments made in *Blood Work*, the significance of Albion Tourgée's (ultimately failed) objection to the illogic of America's racial blood distinctions as well as the significance of Justice Brown's response lies in the case's strategic transformation of the blood of racial science (the blood that supposedly made Homer Plessy black) to the blood of American legal discourse (the blood that would supposedly make his descendants black virtually in perpetuity). *Plessy* reveals the difference between how racial blood performs "scientifically" versus how racial blood performs legally. While the supposed presence of an imperceptible amount of black blood mixed with his white blood leaves Homer Plessy visibly white but legally black, the law strategically treats the presence of this blood, once discovered, as a mark that can no longer be diluted.

Significantly (and as I will discuss further in my reading of Twain's *Pudd'nhead Wilson*), the law therefore inherits the use of racial blood from scientific racialism but, in doing so, adapts this inherited blood for its own purposes. Unlike under the terms of American racial science, racial blood in American race law is not permitted to become diluted to the point of erasure. In *Plessy*, the court could thus dismiss such (otherwise reasonable) objections proffered by Tourgée as in the following from his brief:

> The Court will take notice of the fact that, in all parts of the country, race-intermixture has proceeded to such an extent that there are great numbers of citizens in whom the preponderance of the blood of one race or another, is impossible of ascertainment, except by careful scrutiny of the pedigree. As slavery did not permit the marriage of the slave, in a majority of cases even an approximate determination of this preponderance is an actual impossibility, with the most careful and deliberate weighing of evidence, much less by the casual scrutiny of a busy conductor. (Olsen 84)

What Tourgée fails to realize in his objection (or perhaps realizes but remains helpless to combat) is how *Plessy* capitalizes upon the opportunity for the federal government to fulfill its commitment to the American racial formation by codifying race, not as a stable scientific category possible of "ascertainment" by blood, but rather as a project infused with indeterminacy—or what Toni Morrison called the "thrill of discovery." "Will the court hold that a single drop of African blood is sufficient to color a whole ocean of Caucasian whiteness?" Tourgée asks, extending the logic of racial blood to its seemingly unnatural absurdity (Olsen 98). Here Tourgée suggests that a natural logic implied by the theory of racial blood itself makes the procedure of racial determination by blood hopeless. But the decision in *Plessy* could not be derailed by such an objection precisely because it was this tension between the terms of racial mixing and the terms of racial marking that the case sought to exploit.

In this sense, Tourgée's objections to the seeming illogic of racial blood are devastating but doomed. His appeal to the scientific logic of racial blood only underscores the manner in which *Plessy* culminates American race law's turn away from the blood of scientific racialism to the construction of a form of racial blood that could perform the duties required for legal racialism, a turn made necessary by the shift in the relationship between blackness and property brought about by emancipation. As we will see through a reading of Twain's *Pudd'nhead Wilson*, *Plessy* helped to satisfy American racialism's need for a legal, codifiable form of miscegenetic blood that behaved quite differently from miscegenetic blood in scientific racialism. "While miscegenation had increased property under slavery," observes Saidiya Hartman, "now it threatened to democratize or expropriate the exclusive property in whiteness, as had emancipation itself by making freedom a right enjoyed by all rather than a racial privilege" (Hartman 189). In the management of what Hartman calls the "revolution in property relations enacted by the Thirteenth Amendment," the American ideology of racial blood could no longer support miscegenation's reliance upon such a conception of racial mixture; instead, this ideology had to pivot in order to prevent it. And so despite the former commitment to a more natural logic suggested by the physical metaphor of blood mixture, by the turn of the twentieth century American racialism needed precisely what Tourgée perceived as a deeply problematic phenomenon, namely, a form of blood that did not perform naturally at all but that could perform the work of race required for the moment: fostering an imperative yet irresolvable tension between visible and invisible forms of blackness.

Moreover, as part of the insidiousness of *Plessy*, Justice Brown in his majority opinion mapped this tension onto the tension between federal and state power in a way guaranteed to energize sectionalism and southern racial discontent over the lost war. While Tourgée argued that the law could not segregate according to racial marks due to the problem of racial mixture—because the law cannot "see" what racial indicators lie beneath—Brown maintained that federal race law must segregate by color (by racial marks) precisely because it cannot overcome the power of (internal) natural aversions, and that it is the federal law's duty to determine and segregate by surfaces precisely because it has no power over the forces of racial aversion that lie beneath nor to decide who is black and who is white when these internal and external racial cues go out of alignment. This project, Brown insisted in his opinion, would be left to the states:

> It is true that the question of the proportion of colored blood necessary to constitute a colored person, as distinguished from a white person, is one upon which there is a difference of opinion in the different states, some holding that any visible admixture of black blood stamps the person as belonging to the colored race, others that it depends upon the preponderance of blood, and still others that the predominance of white blood must only be in proportion of three fourths. But these are questions to be determined under the laws of each State and are not properly put in issue in this case. (Olsen 167)

In a strategic abdication of the federal court's power, Brown claims the need for the federal government to withdraw its reach here due to its powerlessness over "natural" racial aversions and the local arrangements needed to manage their social consequences. Disavowing this power, *Plessy* implicitly authorizes acts of racial violence. By vacating itself and making the correspondence between the internals and externals of race beyond the reach of federal power, *Plessy* plays its part in conceding to the extralegal tyrannies of the lynching narrative.

In the process of codifying race in terms of blood, American race law is pressed to resolve a central conceptual tension inherent in the simultaneous application of what legal scholar Marvin Jones refers to as the "twin metaphors of blood and color," the two dominant systems for expressing race whose often contradictory implications constitute the "duality of the race conception" (451). In my reading of Twain's *Pudd'nhead Wilson*, I discuss the contradictory implications for race suggested by these metaphors as dramatized in Twain's novel. These "twin metaphors" alternatively construct a notion of race that marks the racial subject fixedly by color while also allowing for a form of racial character that can be altered by mixed blood. Twain's plot hinges around the tension in the narratives engendered by this dual conception of race, a tension that also provides a framework for understanding the bizarre inconsistencies of nineteenth-century American race law and the logic of the parody in Twain's plot. The logic of the law and the logic of Twain's plot both speak to the incongruous narratives engendered by these dual conceptualizations of race. The unashamed illogic of the laws of racial determination during this period may be taken, in one sense, as a testament to the invalidity of race as a biological category. But I argue that this illogic—this need to figure race through blood while asking blood to behave in ways that it obviously cannot—is actually characteristic of American racialism's deep investment in blood as the ultimate image of the nation's brand of racial identity. American racialism manifests through a form of race that always draws attention to its own uneasy figuration and its own defiance of natural logic, a form of race figured through natural images but one that behaves most unnaturally.

Through a reading of Faulkner's *Light in August* I will also demonstrate how the tension engendered by this dual conception of race, serves to stage racial violence. As it works to construct an invisible carrier for a form of identity reliant upon concepts of visible difference, the rhetoric of racial blood engenders real and fictional narratives of violence against the racialized body. Lynching, the preferred extralegal method for enforcing discriminatory race laws and attitudes of white supremacy during the late nineteenth and early twentieth century, stages violent racial spectacles in conjunction with American racialism's unnatural discourse of racial blood. Lynching provides the "real world" violent articulation of this racial blood discourse. Because the practice of lynching extends the dialectic of blood union discussed by Erkkila as stemming from the American Revolution, the bloody spectacle of lynching reinforces the terms of the nation's brand of racialism by materially revivifying the signifier of national sacrifice.

Lynching, as a practice that does violence to the racialized body and places bleeding bodies on display, provides the graphic articulation of American racialism's special imaginative regard for the substance that fills the interior of the racialized body. In *Racist Culture*, David Theo Goldberg explains that "racist exclusion finds whatever authority it has in a discourse of the body and that this 'body talk' (so to speak) forges an underlying, though abstract, unity for the discourse of race" (53–54). Keeping in mind that (as Goldberg explains) the body is "usually taken as the receptacle or 'container' of pleasures and pains, desires and needs," it becomes clear that the body's volume (its capacity as a container) is as critical for constructing such an underlying unity of racial discourse as are features on the body's surface (skin color, hair texture, etc.). The relationship between the rhetoric of racial blood and the practice of lynching becomes evident, then, when we consider the implications of this rhetoric's figuration of the racialized body in all of its three dimensions, a figuration that takes advantage of what Goldberg describes as the body's "unique paradigm: It is a symbol of a 'bounded system,' a system the boundaries of which are formed by skin at once porous but perceived as inviolable and impenetrable. Body parts and functions are accordingly related in a complex structure, their substance confined by boundaries and limits that are fragile, vulnerable, and threatened" (54). Goldberg reminds us that the racial imagination is as obsessed with what is inside the body as it is with what can be readily seen on its outside.

And so, more than making race seem biological by mere association, racial blood rhetoric works by appropriating the body as the site of race's underlying unity while simultaneously raising the tension between the body's inside and outside. As the visible indicator of the penetration of the porous boundary of the skin, blood feeds the American racial imagination's obsession with the interplay between the racialized body's inside and outside. Lynching is thus a form of racial violence that is also a form of racial discourse that speaks in terms of blood; its central role in American racial history tragically underscores the special grammar and diction of blood in the American racial imagination. If racialism's corporeal abstractions take advantage of the conceptualization of the body as a "receptacle" or "container," then American racialism's emphasis on blood as the sign of racial identity makes the breaking of this bounded system the telos of the narrative of racial determination.

Race, Blood, and the Problem of Paraphrase

Blood Work reads selected works of late nineteenth- and early twentieth-century American literature for the insights they provide into the function of blood as part of the American racial formation during this period. In particular, *Blood Work* examines the work that blood performs in the construction of race beyond suggestions of biological essentialism. One of the central tasks of this book is to broaden the consideration of what blood has meant in American racial discourse beyond determinism. *Blood Work* thus examines the meaningful connections between race and blood's associations with such concepts as sacrifice, sex, and violence. Race and blood are two of the most richly signifying terms in our vocabulary, and a key argument of *Blood Work* is that the meaning of blood in American racial rhetoric resists all efforts toward a simple, reductive paraphrase. That is, there is no single, stable approximation of what blood means in its metaphorical relationship to race. As one of the central metaphors at work in the American racial formation, blood, like race, is also performative and occasional, standing in for a constantly shifting array of presumptions about identity at work in the racial imagination. Rather than reproducing the same stable concept of racial identity each time it is utilized, blood enters the field of discursive play prepared to do the work that race requires at the moment.

Taken collectively, the readings in *Blood Work* thus argue against the notion that references to blood in American literary racial representations can always be paraphrased as, reduced to, or simply interpreted as references to biological essentialism. The tendency to reduce the meaning of racial blood in this fashion has perhaps been driven by accounts of racial construction provided by scholars of American race law. In accounts of how blood functions as a metaphor for race in the law, blood has been described as a convenient vehicle for tracking and dispensing racial rewards, particularly property. In these accounts, blood codifies ambiguous racial status through an image that can easily be conceived as traceable and inheritable. Moreover, because blood is itself a biological term, such accounts reason, speaking of race in terms of blood lends a biological meaning to race through the use of such expressions as "black blood" or "white blood." Legal scholar Eva Saks articulates such analysis in her influential study of nineteenth-century American antimiscegenation law. Saks contends that, as a response to the threat against white property rights posed by race mixing, American miscegenation law responded "on a rhetorical level, using the metaphor of blood to signify race. By choosing the internal, biological *res* of blood, miscegenation jurisprudence transformed race into an intrinsic, natural, and changeless entity: blood essentialized race" (48). Concerned with the construction of racial categories for the purpose of overseeing the inheritance of material property and race *as* property (perpetuating what George Lipsitz has called the "possessive investment in whiteness"), American legal discourse often employed blood to get race to do what the law needed race to do, to quantify and trace blackness through the genealogies of racially "mixed" American families. In this particular project of legal codification, blood does indeed work to essentialize race.[9]

But, as I hope to demonstrate in the literary readings that follow, we cannot always comfortably settle for such a biological paraphrase when images of blood are deployed in more literary contexts of racial representation. We should recognize that the tendency toward this understanding of blood in legal readings is after all motivated by an anxiety over ambiguity (one that is of considerably less concern in the interpretation of more explicitly literary texts). This anxiety is evident in the analysis provided by legal scholar Marvin D. Jones in his essay "Darkness Made Visible: Law, Metaphor, and the Racial Self." Following the claims of race's metaphoricity (provided by Gates, Appiah, and others), Jones concedes that "the problem of race is quintessentially a problem of language" (440, note 11). But Jones also explains how race as language poses a problem for the law's efforts to adjudicate it. The unfixed and contingent meanings of race as language must be contained and delimited lest they corrupt the logical operation of law, since, according to Jones, "as a construction, as a social product, and as a barrier to discourse, race lies beyond the ken of the conventional legal theory" (440). If race as language poses a problem for the law—how, after all, can the law legislate a metaphor that only poses as "something real, natural, and inevitable"—then decoding what race and its various metaphorical vehicles "really mean" becomes a necessary step if the law is to fix race into more manageable terms (Saks's "internal, biological *res*," for example). Jones makes his own effort to decode the meaning of blood in racial discourse when he writes, "The figure of blood imprisons 'black' identity within the confines of essentialist assumptions by metaphorically transforming assumptions about race as essence into received biological attributes. Blood in this narrative is the carrier of racial character, something deep within that determines one's social destiny" (453). While such paraphrasing does not help to rid the law of metaphorical language, translating blood as biology to explain what blood *means* when it means race at least helps the critical race scholar to tame the elusive metaphors threatening law's denotative efforts.

But these paraphrases proposed by Saks and Jones, while certainly central to the project of American racialism in terms of race law, are far from conveying the extent of what blood does for race in the larger American literary and cultural context. Jones provides only a partial analysis of blood's contribution to the "internal architecture of the idea of race" when he explains how the "blood metaphor" in racial discourse "creates a rule of differentiation" (455). While the inheritance of familial identity and thus property may be the function of blood in legal narratives, blood also performs myriad other functions for race as it draws from a host of cultural associations that are religious and secular, sacrificial and possessive, violent and peaceful, healthful and diseased, sacred and profane. To paraphrase blood as a rhetorical device that differentiates and essentializes is to provide only a partial account of the term's meaning, particularly when the meanings of the term are considered within the context of such thematically dense works of American race literature as Frances Harper's *Iola Leroy*, Pauline Hopkins's *Of One Blood*, or William Faulkner's *Light in August*.

We can see the problems that arise from a strictly biological paraphrase of blood in Anthony Appiah's critical reading of W.E.B. Du Bois's 1897 essay, "The Conservation of Races." In "The Uncompleted Argument: Du Bois and the Illusion of Race," Appiah charges Du Bois with falling short in his effort to pioneer a sociohistorical definition of race, partly due to Du Bois's reliance on the language of blood in his definition. Du Bois defined a race as "a vast family of human beings, generally of common blood and language, always common history, traditions and impulses, who are both voluntarily and involuntarily striving together for the accomplishment of certain more or less vividly conceived ideals of life" ("Conservation" 230). He also claimed the presence of "subtle forces" that "have silently but definitely separated men into groups" but that yet "transcend scientific definition" (230). In his reading of Du Bois's definition, Appiah's insistence upon paraphrasing Du Bois's references to blood as references to biological essentialism leads Appiah to regard Du Bois's references to blood as one of the "sources of tension in Du Bois's allegedly sociohistorical conception of race" (25). "The tension," Appiah explains, "is plain enough in his references to 'common blood'; for this, dressed up with fancy craniometry, a dose of melanin, and some measure for hair-curl, is what the scientific notion amounts to. If he has fully transcended the scientific notion, what is the role of this talk about 'blood'?" (25). Although Appiah's critique of Du Bois remains more persuasive in the systematic delineation of other seeming logical inconsistencies in Du Bois's cultural pluralist definition of race, his reluctance to view Du Bois's references to blood as anything other than the betrayal of Du Bois's commitment to a "scientific notion" of race is an example of the kind of reductive paraphrasing of racial blood rhetoric that the present study hopes to reconsider.[10] If Du Bois's definition falls short of a sociohistorical one, it is not because of his references to blood.

Contrary to the conclusions derived from Appiah's strict interpretation of the term, blood can indeed be used in a nonbiological redefinition of race without raising an argumentative contradiction, when blood itself is referenced for its nonbiological associations and meanings. The opening lines of "The Conservation of Races" situate Du Bois's own understanding of blood within a countervailing discourse not rooted in scientific racialism.

> The American Negro has always felt an intense personal interest in discussions as to the origins and destinies of races: primarily because back of most discussions of race with which he is familiar, have lurked certain assumptions as to his natural abilities, as to his political, intellectual and moral status, which he felt were wrong. He has, consequently, been led to deprecate and minimize race distinctions, to believe intensely that out of one blood God created all nations, and to speak of human brotherhood as though it were the possibility of an already dawning tomorrow. (229)

For Du Bois the biblical decree of "one blood" not only provides an inspirational message but the basis for an alternative ideology to refute assumptions about the "natural abilities" of African Americans, an alternative ideology of blood that is also a way to "deprecate and minimize race distinctions" rather than endorse them. As I will discuss further in the chapter on Pauline Hopkins's novel *Of One Blood*, only under the strictest paraphrase that limits blood to its biological meaning can we interpret this biblical decree as a concession to biological racialism. Read in their larger literary context, Du Bois's references to blood in the essay actually demonstrate his understanding that blood is as a term and concept not wholly defined by and through biological race thought. Near the end of the essay, for example, Du Bois proposes, as the first item in his creed for the American Negro Academy, a commitment to the belief that "the Negro people, as a race, have a contribution to make to civilization and humanity, which no other race can make" (183). In *The Souls of Black Folk*, Du Bois would rearticulate and expand upon this claim of black distinctiveness and the possession of a unique racial contribution to "civilization and humanity" in his famous description of double consciousness. There Du Bois insists that the individual "Negro" struggling with this form of duplicity would not choose to "bleach his Negro soul in a flood of white Americanism, for he knows that Negro blood has a message for the world" (*Souls* 11).

Lest the reader mistake Du Bois's reference here to "Negro blood" solely as a reference to racial biology, he explains in the final chapter of *Souls* that this gift and this message are not constituted biologically but rather culturally. In his chapter on "The Sorrow Songs," Du Bois reveals that "these weird old songs in which the soul of the black slave spoke to men" constitute "the articulate message of the slave to the world," although the message remains "naturally veiled and half articulate" (156, 159). If "Negro blood has a message for the world" (as Du Bois claims in "Conservation"), then this blood is by no means just a shared biological blood but rather a "common blood" comprised by the "true Negro folk-song [that] still lives in the hearts of those who have heard them truly sung and in the hearts of the Negro people" (156). It is this "common blood," in the form of culturally transmitted song, that runs through and unites Du Bois's "grandfather's grandmother . . . seized by an evil Dutch trader two centuries ago" to her child and "his children and . . . to their children's children . . . down to us" (157). Du Bois identifies this core material of the African American vernacular as among the strongest of the "subtle, delicate and elusive" differences described in "The Conservation of Races," "which have silently but definitely separated men into groups" although they have only "generally followed the natural cleavage of common blood" (177). While not reducible to biology, these cultural differences have nevertheless "divided human beings into races, which, while they perhaps transcend scientific definition, nevertheless are clearly defined to the eye of the Historian and Sociologist" (177). They are the essence of Du Bois's reenvisioning of the race concept and a critical element through which he seeks to conserve race as culture. Thus, according to Dickson Bruce, "for Du Bois the essence of a distinctive African consciousness was its spirituality, a spirituality based in Africa but revealed among African Americans in their folklore, their history of patient suffering, and their faith," and "this message, as he had been saying since at least 1888, was of a spiritual sense and a softening influence that black people could bring to a cold and calculating world" (301).[11]

Among other efforts made during the period to transcend biological racialism, Du Bois's discussions of racial blood in "The Conservation of Races" and *The Souls of Black Folk* demonstrate one of the central arguments of *Blood Work*, namely, how the presence of connotative and non-biological meanings of blood constitute a significant element of what the term means in American racialist thought. These connotative meanings allow blood to represent race without contradiction in texts nevertheless dedicated toward undermining race's biological meaning, including the major texts examined in the following chapters. The arguments and literary readings in *Blood Work* are thus not intended to suggest that references to racial blood carry no suggestions of biological race thinking (of course they do), but rather that references to racial blood carry many more suggestions that are critical for constituting race in non-biological ways as well.

Anthropologists have long documented the vast spectrum of signification carried by the image of blood, and *Blood Work* examines the ways in which this spectrum of associations has also contributed to what it means to talk about race in terms of blood. "Carnality and piety find in blood the congealing element to justify an ongoing exchange of pertinent symbols," writes anthropologist Piero Camporesi in his survey of blood's cultural meanings. "Vehicle of purity and impurity, of spurcitia and sanctitas alike, principle of putrefaction and at the same time of regeneration, of sacrifice as of rot and despicability, blood enters inexorably into the sacred and profane imagination, borne there by the idea of divine sacrifice, regeneration through wounds, torture, bloodletting" (102). While scientific knowledge has advanced our understanding of the actual physiological functions of blood, blood's cultural meanings remain extremely malleable. Walter Benn Michaels has written that "even if we acknowledge that the concept of black or white blood has no biological currency nowadays, we can still understand the appeal to blood as a metaphor for whatever thing there is in the body that does determine your race—your genes, for example" (129). But the presumption that blood serves the race concept primarily by imparting the suggestion of biological essentialism not only fails to capture the full range of meaning created by this metaphorical pairing but may also provide a dangerously reductive approximation that only serves to mask the true power and insidiousness of the system of metaphors that equate blood and race. As these readings in *Blood Work* will show, reducing blood to the notion of biological essentialism does not account for American racialism's deep investment in and creative deployment of the image, the seeming contradictions of blood in American racialist thought and jurisprudence, the interconnectedness of seemingly disparate references to blood imagery in racial discourse, or the interrelationships between the ways race is spoken about and practiced, often violently, in the American scene.

Interpreting figures of blood only as references to racial biology neglects much of the emotional content that the image of blood conveys to race and that energizes racial discourse with its cultural and psychological imperatives. To recuperate these often-neglected cultural and emotional meanings of blood is to recuperate much of the image's metaphorical power as it is used within racial discourse. Metaphor theorist Paul Henle writes of the "sense of shock about a metaphor . . . which results from the clash of juxtaposed literal sense. It has almost an epigrammatic quality and this must be lost in any paraphrase. Unquestionably it is part of the effect of the metaphor and, if all effects be counted as part of the meaning, then no paraphrase can be adequate" (102). *Blood Work* seeks to recuperate some of the meaningful "sense of shock" felt when blood appears in American racial discourse and to make us more aware of the "sacrifices [that] must be made in paraphrase" (Henle 102).

A strict paraphrase that reduces blood to a reference to biological essentialism does not fully convey the full range of connotations operating in such literary moments as when Frances Harper's character Iola Leroy defiantly claims that "The best blood in my veins is African blood, and I am not ashamed of it," or Du Bois's imagery of the "red stain of bastardy," or the horrors of Ida B. Wells's bloody *Red Record* of lynching, or James Weldon Johnson's "red summer" of 1919. The most memorable expressions of American racialism in terms of blood remain so impactful because they register the sexualized and violent texture of American racial history through their use of blood imagery. A more dynamic anatomy of this metaphor that recognizes the interplay between the concept of race and the images of blood through which it is figured in American racial blood discourse provides for a richer description of the cognitive as well as the practical or "real world" implications of speaking of race in terms of blood.

The literary readings of *Blood Work* are premised on the notion that the work blood performs through American racial discourse can be viewed most productively in the context of literary plots whose narrative and thematic logics reveal seams in the fabric of racial construction, plots that demonstrate the problematic logic inherent in the form of race that metaphors of blood seek to engender. Attending to the special circumstances of American racial formation made manifest through American literature, the literary analysis of racial blood metaphors given here provides insights into the use of racial blood metaphors that analysis of legal, anthropological, and social texts alone cannot. To move toward a fuller understanding of the work that blood performs in American racial rhetoric and in the American racial imagination, the meaning of blood must be considered within the broader contexts that frame these literary plots. Shaped by American science, religious history, racial history, and American "law and custom," they compose a dense network of discourse that makes any simple paraphrase of blood in American racial rhetoric virtually impossible. As these readings demonstrate, blood in American racial discourse is much more connotative than denotative. If one indication of the invalidity of the race concept is that, as Anthony Appiah has observed, "there is nothing in the world that can do all we ask 'race' to do for us," *Blood Work* analyzes selected plots of American literature whose contorted narrative and thematic logics reveal the limits of what race as blood can do for us (35).

In keeping with the view of race as metaphor, *Blood Work* refracts the meanings of blood in American racial discourse to provide a more detailed understanding of how race frames our understanding of everything that we see through its prism. Metaphor theorist Max Black, using his own vivid metaphor, describes the work of metaphor as a process of filtering and framing experience, like "look[ing] at the night sky through a piece of heavily smoked glass on which certain lines have been left clear" (41). *Blood Work* is a study of how blood filters and frames our perception of race, what we see when we look at race through the "heavily smoked glass" of blood's image. Analyzing the lines of thought and experience that have been obscured as well as those that have been "left clear," *Blood Work* describes this filtering work of racial blood metaphors. *Blood Work* closely reads individual instances of the use of these metaphors as functional and situational, each serving its unique cognitive and literary functions in its own given context. The study takes into account the varying functions of these metaphors within the works examined (as the meaning of blood changes according to individual narrative and dramatic situations) and also seeks an understanding of each literary work's larger poetics of racial blood—the overarching function of the rhetoric of blood for each literary plot—with the understanding that the function of blood in the plot of Twain's *Pudd'nhead Wilson*, for example, must be distinguished from that in Harper's *Iola Leroy* or Faulkner's *Light in August*.

Blood Work also shifts the standard focus of the analysis of racial blood discourse away from race and more toward the cultural and discursive meanings of blood. "Blood, with its diverse fields of meaning and discursive manifestations," writes Uli Linke, "consists of a dominant metaphor or gestalt, mapping fundamental cultural assumptions about gender, sex, and race" (vii). By taking a fuller range of blood's "diverse fields of meaning and discursive manifestations" into account, *Blood Work* enhances arguments made by previous examinations of race as blood relationship in legal and literary studies.

The analysis provided in this book seeks to demonstrate, for example, how "The great ancient blood myths seem to have been washed away by history, but blood itself still speaks of them" (Holtorf 30). This book argues that such ancient myths about blood "still speak" through the language and practice of race. In many ways, the race concept itself might be considered one of the most enduring vestiges of such ancient blood myths. Blood can perform so many functions for race because blood, as David Biale suggests in his study of blood covenants in the Jewish and Christian traditions, "inhabits the imagination as both substance and symbol" (1). Racial blood metaphors take advantage of blood's special ability to construct a concept of race that is itself a synthesis of the substantial and the symbolic. Through a synthesis of real and imagined properties, racial blood becomes a symbol that combines concepts of biological inheritance, mysticism, and animating force into one concept. If, as Mino Gabriele has suggested, "It is impossible not to reflect on the extent to which the power of metaphor influences the magic significance of blood," then it is also impossible not to reflect on how the magic significance of blood has influenced the power of the metaphor of race (39). In a process that metaphor theorist Donald Davidson describes as the "dreamwork" of metaphor, racial blood metaphors call upon the racial imagination to close the gap between the world as it is and the world the racialist wishes it to be, and in the very process, reducing any anxiety over the difference between the two (31).

Although *Blood Work* makes no effort toward a simple, single paraphrase of what blood means when it functions as a metaphor for race, the study does argue that blood metaphors construct race by raising images of a blood that performs most unnaturally. In American racial rhetoric, blood works and behaves very unlike the natural substance that it denotes, and this unnaturalness is central to the American racial imagination's interest in blood as an image and as a metaphor. What race draws from its figurative relationship with blood (what race "needs" from this relationship), even more perhaps than a sense of biological validity, is this connotation of the unnatural. Race is an unnatural concept in and of itself, and the image of blood in American racial discourse has helped to shore up this unnaturalness. Through readings of selected works of American literature, each chapter in *Blood Work* discusses an element of the cultural imagination about blood that American racial blood rhetoric contributes to the American racial formation. Each text examined places its own particular (and often odd) emphasis on blood as the critical term articulating the text's racial ideology, and in each case blood performs quite unnaturally.

In "Mark Twain and the Essence of Ink," I argue that the plot of Twain's *Pudd'nhead Wilson* (1894) hinges upon the conflation of two interrelated discourses of racial blood: a metaphorical discourse emphasizing blood's ability to mix for the purpose of representing pseudoscientific theories of unstable mulatto character, and a discourse imagining blood as a stigma or mark used for making legal racial determinations, particularly in the rhetoric of the so-called "one-drop rule." Much of the novel's tension over the viability of blood as a reliable indicator of racial character and identity derives from the tension between these two forms of racial blood ideology. The conflation of these ideologies is demonstrated in the frustrated motivations of two of the novel's leading characters, Judge Driscoll and Roxy. *Pudd'nhead*'s plot demonstrates the problem that racial blood metaphors pose for American race law as Roxy and Judge Driscoll both struggle to find the language to explain and the means to manipulate the character of the visibly white but legally black Tom Driscoll.

Tracing the tension over racial blood's determinant power to representations of mulattoes in nineteenth-century American racial science, I demonstrate the difference between the way racial blood behaves in scientific racial discourse from this period and the way blood is required to behave in American race law. This distinction, I argue, is critical to the plot of Twain's novel. The rhetoric of racial blood in nineteenth-century American racial science was designed to construct a degenerative notion of interracial blood mixture, but in order for the law to do its work of codifying race, the law must abandon the representation of a racial blood that mixes in favor of a racial blood that marks. Thus, the unnatural ability of racial blood to remain unmixed in American race law gives us the metaphorical catachresis felt in both the language and application of the "one-drop rule." Although the language of the one-drop rule derives from the premise of blood as a racial essence, the legal apparatus that the rule seeks to construct relies upon the paradox of a blood that does not dilute but rather remains suspended in perpetual stasis. The rule fabricates this suspension for the purpose of tracking blackness while supposedly maintaining white racial purity and supporting white social and economic privilege.

In Twain's novel, only the manifestation of literal blood in the form of an evidentiary bloody fingerprint can resolve the tension between the discourses of mixture and marking. As is well known, Twain drew his depiction of fingerprint science from the contemporary work of British biologist and statistician Francis Galton, later known as the "father of eugenics" for his fantasies of engineered racial breeding. Drawing from previous readings of *Pudd'nhead* by Michael Rogin, Susan Gillman, and others, I read the novel's appropriation of Galton's fingerprint science with attention to the blood that provides the material substance for the form of the novel's most critical fingerprint. Ultimately, my reading of Twain's novel demonstrates that the entire purpose of the one-drop rule is to make blood behave unnaturally.

"Frances Harper and the Blood of Sacrifice," a chapter on Harper's post-Reconstruction race melodrama *Iola Leroy* (1892), examines how the religious symbolism of blood in Harper's Christian imagery inflects her use of blood as a figure for race. I argue that the racial blood rhetoric used throughout Harper's novel is deeply informed by an iconography of Christian sacrifice drawn from the faith that motivated Harper's tireless political activism.

The plot of *Iola Leroy* is predicated on a series of self-sacrificial choices made by the novel's central characters, particularly Iola's own choices in marriage. For Harper, African American women's choices in marriage were fraught with profound political meaning during the Reconstruction and post-Reconstruction periods, and her views on the functions of African American marriage were deeply invested with the tenets of her Christianity. As a divinely sanctioned act of self-sacrifice in Harper's view, marriage was both an act of subsuming the individual will to social responsibility and an act that brought the participants in this act of self-abnegation closer to God. In *Iola Leroy*, Iola declines a marriage offer from Dr. Gresham, a white doctor for whom she has genuine desire, and chooses instead to dedicate herself to social acts of black uplift. The chapter examines Iola's decision in the context of the novel's other scenes of sacrificial choice and in the context of the religious, cultural, and racial significance of the principle of sacrifice as articulated in Harper's earlier speeches, poetry, and fiction.

More broadly, this chapter considers how the discourse of Christian symbolism works in tandem with a discourse of scientific racialism in the rhetoric of racial blood. Although many characters in *Iola Leroy* cast their expressions of racial solidarity in terms of blood, the language of blood in the novel derives less from biological scientific racism (exemplified in my reading by Frederick Hoffman's *Race Traits and Tendencies of the American Negro*) and more from the context of the sacrificial tenets of African American Christianity. A review of Harper's entire body of work, spanning more than three decades before the publication of *Iola Leroy*, demonstrates that she was among the century's most vocal and persistent champions of sacrifice as a personally edifying, socially progressive, and religiously devoted act that would also, in her own view, provide the characterological and political foundation for the black uplift movement. By refiguring the blood of scientific racialism as the sacrificial substance of her social, political, and racial philosophies, Harper invests in a blood that performs most unnaturally.

"Pauline Hopkins and the End of Incest" analyzes the sibling incest plot in African American author Pauline Hopkins's novel *Of One Blood* (1902–1903). By employing a biblical phrase used throughout American abolitionist discourse as an argument for racial unity ("of one blood") and investing that phrase with the double meaning of a nearly universal cultural taboo, Hopkins's sibling incest plot dramatizes the argument of my book as a whole, that the discourse of racial blood in American race discourse is inseparable from the long, complex cultural history of blood's associative meanings; and that whenever blood is used in the metaphorical language of race, this language connotes so much more than biological essentialism.

My reading of *Of One Blood* places the sibling incest plot at the center of the novel's dense thematic layers of race, gender, revisionist science, and pan-Africanism. Drawing from previous scholarly work on Hopkins's use of occult science, I argue that Hopkins performs a similar reconstruction of anthropological discourse on incest as a way of further eroding the logic of racial rhetoric. As a taboo rooted in cultural anxieties over relationships by blood, the incest prohibition operates in conjunction with miscegenation's rhetoric of deleterious mixtures of racial blood. I describe how Hopkins's incest plot undermines the scientific and cultural implications of the incest taboo as articulated in the work of such figures as Emile Durkheim, Edward Westermarck, and Claude Lévi-Strauss. Replacing the blood of nineteenth-century ethnological discourse with an occult substance that reenergizes and reempowers an African American genealogical line ravaged by rape and incest, Hopkins provides her characters with an alternative to the slave regime's "natal alienation" as she refigures the very meaning of "one blood." Thus I read the sibling incest plot in Hopkins's novel as a reconstruction of the metaphorical relationships between blood, race, and kinship. In my reading, Hopkins advances new conceptual and narrative contexts within which uncanny and even excessive sibling affinity can be considered redemptive rather than biologically and morally degenerative. Ultimately, her novel suggests a cultural and conceptual transvaluation that is tantamount to the end of incest as a cultural litmus test and as a concept more generally.

While chapters 1–3 discuss the anthropological, legal, and religious contexts of the meanings of blood in racial discourse, chapter 4 considers the significance of blood's literal physical and physiological properties for the construction of an aesthetics of racial visibility. "William Faulkner and the Color of Blood" argues that the color of blood really does matter, not, as the biological racialist would have it, because blood carries some essential "blackness" or "whiteness," but because the color of blood and the human emotional response to the sight of blood become elements of the aesthetics of race and the visible scrutiny of the racialized body.

The color of blood comes with its own cultural history that, while antecedent to the rhetoric of race, cannot be separated from the meaning of blood in this racial rhetoric. Racial blood rhetoric relies upon the cultural history of blood's visibility such that terms like "black blood" and "white blood" derive much of their meaning from cultural and psychological responses to the sight of literal blood itself. As I demonstrate through research into the cultural and scientific history of blood, the colors that blood takes on in its oxygenated and deoxygenated states have been taken as signs of the substance's association with the body's vital principles—the life of the body itself.

Although *Light in August*'s main character Joe Christmas is assumed to be of mixed racial background, his racial status ultimately remains indeterminate throughout the novel. The social obsession over the figurative color of Joe's blood is heightened by the contrast between the visible race cues of his "parchment"-colored skin and the social race cues of his community associations and behaviors. As the desire for knowledge about Joe's racial identity leads to his violent and bloody death, the figurative language of Joe's "black blood" becomes translated into a desire for the sight of his literal blood in a dramatic demonstration of what Linda Martin Alcoff describes as the "impervious visibility" of race ("Habits" 31).

The moment in which the color of Joe's blood matters most is not in any of the many figurative speculations about his "black" or "white blood," but rather the moment in which Joe's literal blood is released from his body into the visual register through an act of racially motivated violence. Faulkner critic Jay Watson reads this moment as the violent defiguration of the metaphor of "black blood." According to Watson, Faulkner "mobilizes the power of literal meaning and the natural world as a rejoinder to the discursive system that puts 'blood' in service of racial exploitation and violence" (69). Following Watson, I analyze the interpretive problems posed by Christmas's death scene in light of the real contrast between the pigmentation of arterial blood and the darker hue of deoxygenated venous blood. The literal blackness of Joe's blood may defigure the metaphor, but with respect to the physiological relationship between the function and color of blood, Joe Christmas's blood appears to be the wrong color. The narrator's description of this scene should not, of course, be taken as literal or realistic. But the discrepancy between the color and action of Christmas's blood constitutes part of the scene's metaphorical and symbolic meaning. The desire for racial violence motiving this moment stems from a practice of racial aesthetics based upon the juxtaposition between the color of skin and the color of blood—between the inside and the outside of the racialized body.

Faulkner's very visual novel reminds us that the modern practice of race developed in conjunction with a dedication to the epistemological value of the visible and that race remains a visual enterprise even when (or particularly when) racial "intermixture" shades skin tones toward complexions that challenge any easy effort to assign standard racial categories through the reading of visible criteria. Racial blood metaphors, I would argue, are as much invested in determining or reestablishing the terms of this racial visibility as they are in establishing race's biological essentialism. Through their references to color, the most prominent indicator of racial identity, racial blood metaphors carry their own significant meaning with respect to the construction of race's visibility as these metaphors conjure cultural responses to the sight of blood. Faulkner's novel is obsessed with both the rhetoric of racial blood and the operation of racial optics as well as the implications of the interrelationship between the two. I demonstrate how the sight of blood works its racializing effect by virtue of blood's own associations with cultural and psychological binaries; the sight of blood carries connotations of cultural dichotomies and political upheavals upon which racial difference becomes mapped and constructed. Race, we might say, needs the image of blood because the figure of blood provides a way for the race concept to force its way beneath the skin.

CHAPTER 1

Mark Twain and the Essence of Ink

When used as a metaphor for race, blood makes a difference. This is the "work" that blood performs as a metaphor for race, the work of altering the way race is conceived and practiced. This work can be observed when considering the conceptual differences between the rule of hypo-descent and the "one-drop rule." In *Patterns of Race in the Americas* (1964), anthropologist Marvin Harris identified the practice of giving determinative weight to an individual's racial ancestry from a socially subordinate group, using the term "hypo-descent" to describe this uniquely American system of racial accounting. As he described it, Harris marveled derisively at the "ingenious computation" and suspension of disbelief required by the rule. "This descent rule requires Americans to believe that anyone who is known to have had a Negro ancestor is a Negro. We admit nothing in between" (56). In terming the practice "hypo-descent," Harris sought to underscore the rule's ironic but strategic concession of determining power to the underprivileged racial category. "Hypo-descent means affiliation with the subordinate rather than the superordinate group in order to avoid the ambiguity of intermediate identity," he writes (56). Hypo-descent is the willful, ironic, and politically motivated denial of determining power to the genealogy of the "superordinate" race with the purpose of avoiding the anxiety of ambiguity in racial intermediacy.

By the time Harris gave hypo-descent this anthropological description and terminology, the rule had been practiced for three hundred years in America and, by the end of the nineteenth century, it had become more popularly known as the "one-drop rule." While Harris's description articulates the rule's social functions, it also brings into relief the differences between what are actually two related practices, one represented through the anthropological language of "hypo-descent" and another through the language of the "one-drop rule." Harris's hypo-descent has nothing to do with blood, although his use of the prefix "hypo" resonates vaguely with the one-drop rule's obsession with blood, a *hypodermic* substance. The "one-drop rule," the more popular term for the practice of hypo-descent in the American context—where the socially subordinate category of blackness dominates genealogically over the socially superordinate category of whiteness—overlays the American practice of hypo-descent with a myriad other "collective fantasies," some biological, others psychological and symbolic, drawn from the cultural discourse of blood. Consequently, while the rule of "hypo-descent" and the "one-drop rule" may seem to refer to the same social construction, they do not mean the same thing in practice. Indeed, it is through the many cultural connotations of "blood" that the one-drop rule enacts its particular ideological commitments in the practice of American racialism. The one-drop rule is more than the practice of hypo-descent, and blood makes all the difference.

Although the one-drop rule employs natural imagery, it conveys a sense of unnaturalness to the racial relationships it attempts to construct. The one-drop rule figures the disproportionate genealogical power it decrees through the unnatural logic imaged in one drop of blood that paradoxically *rules*. Like all metaphors, the one-drop rule draws meaning from the tension between the literal and figurative conditions it expresses. Here, the unnatural physics depicted in the metaphor instills a certain tension between the natural and the unnatural as part of its racial meaning. There is a sense of unnaturalness that is a critical part of the meaning of the one-drop rule, but that becomes lost in paraphrase when the rule is approximated as a rule of "hypo-descent." Through the unnatural image of one drop of blood performing in a way that it does not perform literally, the metaphorical premise of the one-drop rule conveys a sense of circumstances that are more subversive, insidious, and intolerable than those depicted by hypo-descent.

This sense of subversion conveyed through unnatural blood imagery has been one of the targets of the one-drop rule's various critiques. It is not the illogic of hypo-descent but rather the illogic of the one-drop rule, for example, that Homer Plessy's lead counsel, the activist and author Albion Tourgée, invokes during his brief before the U.S. Supreme Court in *Plessy* submitted in 1895 when he asks, "*Will the court hold that a single drop of African blood is sufficient to color a whole ocean of Caucasian whiteness?*" (Olsen 98). To do so, Tourgée suggests, beggars belief. Strategically extending the metaphor's own terms to their logical conclusion, Tourgée's objection argues that the application of the one-drop rule seems as unnatural and irrational—and as corruptive to the proper practice of the law—as the suggestion that one drop of any substance could dominate materially over the innumerable proportions in which this particular drop is rhetorically, if not literally, subsumed.

But, as I want to demonstrate through the following discussions of the one-drop rule and a reading of Mark Twain's *Pudd'nhead Wilson*, such critiques of the legal and social implications of the one-drop rule are ultimately ineffectual in that they only indicate the very work that the rule's metaphorical performance is designed to do. In particular, they indicate the one-drop rule's strategic conflation of two interrelated but different functions and forms of racial blood: a racial blood that allows for a mixability of racial character and a racial blood that materially marks identity. While both discourses employ the figure of blood, they do so by drawing from different metaphorical entailments of blood for different purposes. While the rhetoric of racial blood used in nineteenth-century American racial science was devoted to imagining gradations of racial character produced by the mixture of unseen essences, nineteenth-century American race law, for its own particular project of codifying race, adapted the figure of blood to mark, to print, and to make supposedly natural differences readable.

In order to accomplish these cooperating yet distinct missions, the scientific and legal discourse of American racialism employed the figure of blood divergently. While the rhetoric of racial blood as an expression of racial psychology and character entails the figure of blood with its property of mixture, the legal rhetoric of racial blood entails blood as a pigment or marker—a form of legal ink. Distinguishing between these connotations of blood becomes important for truly understanding the ideological, social, and psychological work performed by the language of racial construction that is the "one-drop rule," and seeing that the rule's aim is not (or at least not only) a pretense of biologism (only one suggestion conveyed by the image of blood). Indeed while the imagery of the "one-drop rule" may suggest a belief in a racial biologism determined by blood, its seeming paraphrase, "the rule of hypo-descent," Harris writes, is "an invention which we in the United States have made in order to keep biological facts from intruding into our collective racist fantasies" (56). And, as Tourgée and others have learned, attempts to point out the logical inconsistencies in the one-drop rule's biological imagery only serve to further obfuscate the strategies behind the rule of hypo-descent that the one-drop rule represents and supports. That is, while Tourgée objects that the rule makes no sense, on the contrary, the rule does exactly that; it makes sense for American racialism. Despite Tourgée's plea for a more natural logic for determining race, the unnaturalness of the rule that he derides presents no problem for the purposes of American race law. Because the law's very aim is to create an unnatural relationship between blackness and whiteness; indeed, the entire purpose of the one-drop rule is to make blood behave unnaturally.

As I argue here and in my reading of Twain's *Pudd'nhead Wilson* (1894), one of the particular problems resolved by American racialism's commitment to blood is precisely the need for both a rhetoric that allows for proportions of racial character and a more binary rhetoric for the purposes of marking and stigmatizing. The tension between mixable and codifiable forms of racial identity provides much of the energy behind the plot of *Pudd'nhead Wilson*. In Twain's novel, this tension is resolved through the device of a bloody fingerprint, a device that synthesizes the ability of blood to figure both characterological mixture and stigmatizing mark. The novel defamiliarizes the interrelated operation of these two discourses and presents a new form of forensic evidence by which the pseudoscientific and the legal discourses—mixture and marking—are fused into one image or sign.

Moreover, in Twain's plot, this new forensic technology provides a material sign that does the work of racial blood rhetoric even as it demonstrates the stakes of such rhetoric—what would have to happen in order for this rhetoric to signify what it claims to signify—what would have to happen for blood to indicate racial character, racial identity, and rights to property all at once. Addressing the need for a drop of blood that figures character while remaining undiluted for the purposes of marking the inheritors of property (the same conundrum that Albion Tourgée would present to the Supreme Court soon after the publication of *Pudd'nhead Wilson*), the bloody fingerprint that resolves the novel's plot racializes the subject (Tom) through one legally legible sign that also conveys character, meeting the seemingly illogical and incompatible demands of the one-drop rule.[1] This bloody fingerprint dramatizes the stakes involved in the law's appropriation of this metaphor by demonstrating the violence suggested in the rule's blood imagery, the violence truly necessary for the project of racial physiognomy, the evasive turning of the body inside out that takes place when the racial body's internal substances are mapped onto its external form.

In "Darkness Made Visible: Law, Metaphor, and the Racial Self," legal scholar D. Marvin Jones explains the problem American race law encounters as it becomes increasingly metaphorical, increasingly literary, in its efforts to legislate race. Arguing that "race lies beyond the ken of the conventional legal theory," Jones describes the deleterious effect of the race concept itself on the tissue of legal logic, tracing this breakdown to the *Dred Scott* decision of 1857: "It is here that law as a structure of reason begins to collapse into race, creating a structure of incoherent categories and meanings. This is why race construction is destabilizing to the law. . . . [Supreme Court Justice] Taney maintained power relationships in *Dred Scott*, but at the expense of jettisoning all pretense of stability in the very categories needed to create law in the slave regime" (440, 464–65). The project of racial construction destabilizes the law, Jones suggests, because it is much easier to imagine and figure racial difference than to practice it legally. Nineteenth-century American race law thus struggles to manage racial essences while preserving its dedication to rationality.

It has been suggested that, as a recourse to such instability, the figure of blood has been employed to impart notions of natural difference and thus predictability and determinability to the law's construction of race. As we have seen, legal accounts of how the metaphor of blood works to construct race in the American context have emphasized the use of blood for purposes of reification. By figuring race in terms of blood, it is argued, American racial rhetoric figures race as essential and natural difference; the image of blood serves to create the illusion of race's biological validity. Thus Eva Saks explains that, "By choosing the internal, biological *res* of blood, miscegenation jurisprudence transformed race into an intrinsic, natural, and changeless entity: blood essentialized race" (48). In practice, however, the use of this metaphor often requires the cooperation of a willful suspension of disbelief, even a kind of bad faith. Because in order for the law to translate pseudoscientific and popular notions of natural difference into legal rights, particularly property rights—in order for the law to get blood to do what it wants *race* to do—the law inevitably requires blood to perform so unnaturally as to shamelessly reveal, if not flaunt, its own status as mere metaphor. Racial blood rhetoric exhibits a metaphoricity that indicates its defiance of rather than its adherence to natural logic. References to black or white blood raise conceptual contradictions that undermine their own employment in the naturalization of race.

Race theorist Colette Guillaumin studies this defiance of natural logic as a central part of her critique of the race concept in "Race and Nature: The System of Marks" (in *Racism, Sexism, Power, and Ideology* (1988)). Identifying the critical contradictions raised by racial blood rhetoric's claim to the natural, Guillaumin decries the naturalness of race implied by this rhetoric as merely a pretense, an "adulterated naturalness" or "mask of naturalness" (137). For Guillaumin, this pretense becomes evident in "the American system" of hypo-descent, in which "even one ancestor out of sixteen makes you belong to a determined social group" (137).[2] Guillaumin's critique focuses on the illogical naturalism suggested by such a rule.

> For logically, if one takes the suggestions of natural realism literally (and not figuratively), having seven white great-grandparents certainly means being white. But this is not so! You are not white, you are 'black,'

> for it is the social system that decides. . . . Why then speak of pre-social, outside-of-society, 'scientific' classification—in a word, of 'natural' classification? It is this which makes us ask ourselves about this 'natural' that claims to be natural while being something else than what it claims to be . . . (137).

To take the one-drop rule's "suggestions of natural realism literally," Guillaumin argues, is to fall under the sway of a "naturalist false consciousness" as deep as that required of the South African system of apartheid, where "There are supposed to be two races, one white, the other black, each exhibiting its own characteristics and its own nature, *and* another race, completely different, without any relation to the preceding ones, a pure product in and of itself" (137).

But Guillaumin's particular objection to the American racial classification system can only quibble with its implications without attacking its core. For even the alternative Guillaumin imagines as a more natural application of the rule cannot escape the underlying illogic of racial proportionment, since it would retain the notion that blackness and whiteness are matters capable of being tallied into ratios. That is, if we were to do as Guillaumin proposes and "[take] the suggestions of natural realism" in this system "literally (and not figuratively)," of what proportion of "whiteness" would those supposedly whole-white "white" great-grandparents be? And, in the supposedly more "logical" conclusion that having these "seven white great-grandparents certainly means being white," what has happened to the one "black" great-grandparent if he or she has not been rendered as oddly and unnaturally irrelevant as the white great-grandparents are rendered under the terms of the logic that Guillaumin critiques? As Guillaumin herself explains, "All this rests on the clever finding that whites bear whites and blacks bear blacks . . ." and the "social idea of natural group rests on the ideological postulation that there is a closed unit, endo-determined [determined from within], hereditary and dissimilar to other social units" (136). Despite Guillaumin's well-intentioned comparison, then, between what happens to racial essences in the rhetoric of the American system and what *would* happen if the language were taken "literally," moving down an axis of figuration from metaphorical to literal provides no exit from the mystification of race.

For the truth is that there is no measure of whiteness or blackness that can be observed operating in any "literal" way from which the one-drop rule's metaphor of racial proportionment can be said to depart into mere figure. The unnaturalness of racial proportionment comes not only in speaking of a person with one black great-grandparent and seven white great-grandparents as black, but also in speaking of great-grandparents as essentially black or white in the first place (and then, in another formulation, speaking of them in terms of their essentializing blood). Even if this language of proportions *could* be taken literally, "having seven white great-grandparents" and one black great-grandparent would certainly not mean "being white." Rather, it would mean being exactly what the fraction denotes; it would mean being the mixture, seven-eighths white and one-eighth black.

Such efforts to undermine the implications of the one-drop rule, while well intentioned, rely upon a misunderstanding or underestimation of racialism's approach to using blood as a figure for racial identity. Such misnaming and misdescribing are what metaphors always do, and making race behave unnaturally is exactly what the rhetoric of race is always trying to do. So while blood may perform unnaturally in the rhetoric of race, this unnatural behavior is not so much a contradiction in the logic of racialism as it is one of the key functions that blood is called upon to perform. To charge the language of racial blood with being unnatural is not to undermine it but only to describe what it does. Put another way, to ask the figure of blood to "act naturally" in the rhetoric of race launches no critique of racialism *per se*; it is only to ask the discourse of race to be less metaphorical and ultimately less itself.

Nevertheless, the value of such critique (the same critique that is, as we shall see, implicit in Twain's novel) lies in its revelation of just how racial blood rhetoric indicates, through its very unnaturalness, its underlying purposes and ideological origins. Despite their ostensible denotative meaning, fractions of racial blood deliberately imagine an unnatural form of blood in stasis, a blood whose precise proportions can only be measured because it is a blood that, quite unnaturally, does not mix. The language of racial proportion is designed not to *express* a mixture of races but rather to prevent the races *from* mixing (cognitively and imaginatively, socially and legally). Despite the language of fractions that it deploys, the entire *aim* of the one-drop rule is to render the ratio of blackness to whiteness irrelevant, such that the proportion of blackness to whiteness does not *make* any difference; that is, such that the difference the proportions *should* make by the natural logic of the metaphor is actually unmade in reality. In this sense, the fractions expressing the one-drop rule signify precisely the opposite of what they denote, namely, that the larger denominator in the racial fraction matters less than the relatively miniscule proportion of blackness in the numerator.[3] Both graphically and psychologically, this vaguely mathematical language of racial fractions, what Werner Sollors has called the "calculus of color," isolates blackness from whiteness, achieving a kind of segregation. In this way, although they reference no real measurements whatsoever, these fractions of blood yet still do the work of race.

While these fractions of blood describe the genealogical strains of which the racial subject is supposedly composed, what they actually count and represent as a vulgar fraction are the "black" and "white" bodies of an imagined sexual history. In discussing the origins of racial blood rhetoric in American race law, Winthrop Jordan describes the psychological impulse for a typical white male colonist to invest in categorizing mulattoes as black as a reaction to his own inability to control his sexual drives directed toward his black slaves. Despite the social prohibition against such acts, the offspring of these unions testified to the male colonist's inability to refrain from such intercourse and "strikingly symbolized a union he wished to avoid. If he could not restrain his sexual nature, he could at least reject its fruits and thus solace himself that he had done no harm" (178). Thus the colonial statutes that categorized the offspring of these forbidden relationships as black by blood worked to undo the act that the colonist had done. "For the separation of slaves from free men depended on a clear demarcation of the races, and the presence of mulattoes blurred this essential distinction. Accordingly he made every effort to nullify the effects of racial intermixture. By classifying the mulatto as a Negro he was in effect denying that intermixture had occurred at all" (178). Saidiya Hartman argues similarly that the emphasis on blood in the American rhetoric of miscegenation speaks to the institution's particular "fixation on imagined sexual trespasses [that] revealed the degree to which the integrity and purity of whiteness depended upon black subjugation" (185).

Racial blood rhetoric thus retroactively polices against the supposed crime of miscegenation by returning to the moment of interracial intercourse entailed in the generative metaphor of blood, counting up the black and white bodies involved, and separating them out, thus undoing (at least imaginatively and rhetorically) the illicit acts of physical intermingling that led to the birth of the very racial subject they describe. By negating the determinative power of the white portion of blood (and by implication, the presence of the white bodies from which that generative blood supposedly issued), racial blood rhetoric effectively figures whiteness *out* of the mixed subject's genealogical inheritance and denies the past presence of the white interracial desire that led to this inheritance. Despite their dispassionate mathematical forms, these quantifying fractional expressions of race thus most certainly bespeak a racial imagination working *against* nature.[4]

It is in this denial of what is natural that the blood of legal race discourse often works at cross-purposes with the blood of scientific, biological racialism. While the legal discourse of race (including the one-drop rule) may derive from assumptions of race as a biological category, this legal discourse must depart from racialism's natural assumptions in order to fulfill its own purposes. The central claim made by the one-drop rule's appeal to blood is not the naturalness of race—that project, we might say, is the aim of scientific racialism—but rather the denaturalization of the form of race that scientific racialism has constructed. What the law requires after all is not a blood that acts like the race of scientific racialism, but a blood that acts like the race of legal racialism. Insofar as the one-drop rule provides the basis for legislating and ruling legally on matters of race, it does so in order to construct a notion of race (and of racial blood) that will perform legally, not scientifically—and certainly not naturally.

Before reading Twain's *Pudd'nhead Wilson*, I want to discuss how a more "natural" concept of mixture was necessary for the nineteenth-century scientific discourse of race but stripped as a property of racial blood in the legal discourse of race so that the law could do its codifying work. As I will argue, not only is the legal discourse of race wholly prepared to *abandon* racial blood's natural entailment of mixture as established by racial science; the abandonment of this entailment is much of what the legal construction of race consists of. This is more than to argue what is obvious, that the rhetoric of blood in the law is metaphorical, but to consider the critical differences between the blood of "mulattoes" in American racial science and the blood of "mulattoes" in American race law. For, if the logic of scientific racialism does not hold in the one-drop rule, it is because the blood of scientific racialism is not the same blood in American race law, a distinction that becomes operative in the narrative of Twain's *Pudd'nhead Wilson*.

American scientific racialism was committed to the possibility of racial blood mixture even though many racial scientists viewed such mixture as deleterious to individuals, races, and the societies and cultures that permitted it. Although viewed as abhorrent, the possibility of such mixture was a prerequisite for arguments against miscegenation. The scientific argument against miscegenation held that the blood of races could mix but that the result would be the mulatto's biological degeneration and psychological instability. Among the most notorious purveyors of this argument during the nineteenth century was the Alabama physician Josiah Nott, a member of the "American School of Ethnology" from the 1830s to the 1850s.[5] In his 1843 "The Mulatto a Hybrid—probable extermination of the two races if the Whites and Blacks are allowed to intermarry," a work of pioneering racism, Nott established the "certain facts connected with mulattoes": that they were a "degenerate, unnatural offspring, doomed by nature to work out its own destruction" (253, 255). In the context of ethnological debates over whether blacks constituted a variety or fixed type, Nott's essay reoriented such debates around the concept of mulatto hybridity, a term that in his view more clearly denoted what mulattoes actually were: "the offspring of two distinct species—as the mule from the horse and the ass" (254). Nott's body of work, perhaps more than that of any other single figure, popularized the notion of the negative effects of racial mixture.

Such pseudoscientific representations of interracial unions and their effects relied upon a notion of racial blood distinctly different from the figure employed to codify race through the one-drop rule. However rank in terms of its racist implications, Nott's theory of mulatto hybridity does not imagine black blood as an irreducible essence capable of eradicating whiteness from the mulatto's body and character altogether. For Nott, mulattoes were not unstable and threatening because their minute strain of blackness dominated over a plethora of whiteness; they were unstable precisely because their strain of blackness did *not* dominate over the force of their white blood. Nott's notion of mulatto hybridity entailed the possibility that mulattoes could even become white over the course of several generations of interbreeding. Providing anecdotal evidence from the West Indies and his own city of Mobile, Nott observes that, "Hybrids when bred together have a tendency to run out and change back to one of the parent stocks" (254). For Nott, mulattoes pointedly remained "whiter" both in physical features and character than their black counterparts, with what Nott considered the more positive traits inherited from white ancestry always remaining recognizable in the mulatto. "Every observer in the South will tell you that Mulattoes have more intelligence than the blacks" (256). Far from suggesting that small portions of blackness overrode whiteness in the mulatto, Nott argued quite the opposite: that the problem with mulattoes was that they *were not black*—and could never be.

With neither strain able to dominate over the other, the proportional contributions of whiteness and blackness within the mulatto created the potential for disaster. Thus Nott agreed with other southern commentators that mulattoes were "more liable to be diseased, and less capable of endurance than the whites or blacks of the same rank and condition" (256). The hybridity of mulattoes, not their blackness *per se*, created the problem for they "are intermediate in intelligence between the whites and blacks" (253). This intermediary state creates an unstable combination of white ambition with black inability, in Nott's view, leaving the mulatto incapable of repressing or even managing the freedom-loving agency inherited from white ancestry. White-black offspring were thus particularly problematic in the context of slavery, for the mulatto was a kind of Frankenstein's monster with an aspiring, white free will trapped within an enslaved black body. "The Mulattoes do not make good slaves, and are always leaders in insurrectionism," Nott warns (256).

This notion of proportional character, underwritten by the scientific theory of mulatto hybridity, resonates in mid-century representations of mulatto character based on a romantic racialism. In Harriet Beecher Stowe's *Uncle Tom's Cabin* (1852), St. Clare expresses his fear that racial intermixture will create an entire class of such insurrectionary hybrids.

> "[T]here is a pretty fair infusion of Anglo Saxon blood among our slaves now. . . . There are plenty among them who have only enough of the African to give a sort of tropical warmth and fervor to our calculating firmness and foresight. If ever the San Domingo hour comes, Anglo Saxon blood will lead on the day. Sons of white fathers, with all our haughty feelings burning in their veins, will not always be bought and sold and traded. They will rise, and raise with them their mother's race" (234).

With only enough blackness in them to impart a "tropical warmth" to their disposition rather than dominate the agency of their white inheritance, the mixed-race figures imagined by Stowe's St. Clare, like Nott's hybrids, are the victims of a tragically as well as dangerously mixed character.

Two decades after the publication of Nott's theories of mulatto hybridity, the term "miscegenation" entered the American lexicon when David Goodman Croly and George Wakeman drew from Nott's theories for their publication of *Miscegenation: The Theory of the Blending of the Races, Applied to the American White Man and Negro* (1864), a political hoax designed to derail Abraham Lincoln's reelection in 1864. The supposedly Republican voice and author of *Miscegenation* gives a vitriolic argument advocating racial mixture, designed to raise public anxiety over the party's antislavery stance. The text coined the term "miscegenation," complete with etymology: "*Miscegenation*—from the Latin *Miscere*, to mix, and Genus, race, is used to denote the abstract idea of the mixture of two or more races" (ii). As its title suggests (miscegenation as a theory of "blending"), the text's ironic advocacy for miscegenation relies upon belief in the possibility of racial mixture. The narrator thus implores the reader to concede the lessons of "Christianity, democracy, and science" which supposedly teach "that a people, to become great, must become composite" (1). The term "miscegenation" is invented to help the reader imagine such a blended utopia. Far from suggesting pure and rigid racial categories determined by single drops of one ancestry or another, the voice of *Miscegenation* imagines humankind achieving perfection through a gradual process of absorption only made possible by the natural balance of each race's contribution: "The ideal or type man of the future will blend in himself all that is passionate and emotional in the darker races, all that is imaginative and spiritual in the Asiatic races, and all that is intellectual and perceptive in the white races" (25). Nott's scientific views of mulatto instability fueled the creation of the very concept of miscegenation and the concomitant romantic racialism characterizing so many representations of mixed-race characters during the period.

The contrast between the behavior of blood in theories of racial hybridity that underlie miscegenation and the behavior of blood in the one-drop rule indicates the divergent ideological principles underlying scientific and legal racial blood discourse and the different narratives they engender. The discourse of mixed race character retains the notion of mixture entailed in mulatto hybridity, while black blood is not allowed to mix in the legal discourse of racial blood. The psychological discourse preserves the essences of both strains of blood rather than, as in the one-drop rule, wholly bracketing one. Black and white blood do battle in representations of the "tragic mulatto," conforming to what Werner Sollors has called the "warring blood melodrama," and Sterling Brown's description of the tragic mulatto of antislavery literature dramatizes Nott's description of mulatto hybridity: "The mulatto is a victim of a divided inheritance; from his white blood come his intellectual strivings, his unwillingness to be a slave; from his Negro blood come his baser emotional urges, his indolence, his savagery" (Brown 73). Whereas the one-drop rule proposes radically disproportional influences of blood's racial quantities, "This character [the tragic mulatto] works itself out with mathematical symmetry" (73).[6]

While duality is possible in the pseudoscientific imagination of racial blood mixture,there are no such properties of mixture, symmetry, balancing, or proportion in the legal discourse of racial blood rhetoric, particularly in the American legal context. In American race law, black blood does not mix but rather simply determines the race of the subject in a binary fashion; in the one-drop rule, black blood dominates while white blood is rendered radically impotent.[7] The legal discourse of race, unlike the "scientifically" based characterological discourse, derives from a different cultural history of blood: the cultural history of blood as a stigmatizing mark.

The stigmatizing or marking feature of American race law's figuration of racial blood becomes evident in the laws of colonial America, where the discursive and ideological turn to racial blood was made to address the problem of an invisible blackness. American race law turned to blood particularly on those occasions when phenotypical blackness had become less visible or even invisible. Encountering individuals with known black ancestry but complexion physically light enough to appear white, the law resorted to the rhetoric of racial blood to make blackness more visible. In *Shades of Freedom: Racial Politics and Presumptions of the American Legal Process* (1996), Leon Higginbotham traces the use of blood as a figure in American race law to a series of statutes enacted in Virginia between 1662 and 1723. Proceeding from what Higginbotham calls a "gospel of black inferiority," Virginia lawmakers codified "natural law" into formal divestments of the rights of black subjects. But, as Higginbotham explains, "In defining black inferiority in terms of the way African Americans looked and the way they led their lives, the colonists had painted themselves into a corner. African Americans may have 'looked black,' but when they began to enter into sexual relations with whites, their children eventually started to look less black and, thus, to use the logic of the colonists—less inferior" (31).

Virginia lawmakers escaped from this "corner" simply by defining a claimant's obligation to servitude in a manner that amounted to the construction of a rule of hypo-descent. Those who appealed to the court for freedom based on a claim to natural rights were met with rehearsals of their genealogy as grounds for their continued enslavement, such that black heritage became evidence antithetical to equality. "On a symbolic level, it meant that once one's skin displayed African heritage, one was marked with the taint of inferiority, which passed on to one's descendants forever" (36–37). Earlier statutes expressed the indelibility of black inferiority in broadly genealogical terms, but by 1785, Higginbotham explains, the Virginia legislature had "changed the legal definition of mulatto to those with 'one-fourth part or more of Negro blood'" with all subsequent changes in this legal definition "making a smaller proportion of black blood bar one from being considered white" such that by the early twentieth century, "*any* Negro blood at all meant that one was not legally white" (39). This legal movement, Higginbotham argues, constitutes the construction of a "precept of black inferiority": "To be black meant that somehow, somewhere, one had acquired some amount of black blood; it did not matter how much. At best, one might be called a mulatto if it strained the imagination to be called black. But no matter how many words were invented to classify the various hues that miscegenation had produced, with almost any amount of black blood, one remained basically black and, therefore, unalterably inferior" (41).

One drop of blackness endures in the law, in this rather unnatural fashion, so that blackness can be made legally visible when it is not literally visible. Unlike racial science or romanticized racial literature, the law takes no interest in the psychological dilemma of the white-black subject. The law thus has no reason to utilize a rhetoric of a blood that can be mixed or balanced, proportioned or diluted. In the legal discourse of race, the most important entailment of blood is not the concept of mixture but rather the entailment of blood as a marker (as a kind of ink or stigma). While the law relies upon an ideology of natural black inferiority to justify its unbalanced apportionment of civil rights, black blood enters legal discourse in an unnatural stasis for the purpose of legislating these unequal rights.

Ironically, and as Twain's parodic novel demonstrates, this unnatural behavior of racial blood is required for the law to preserve any hope of rationality. As Marvin Harris writes in his original anthropological description of the rule of hypo-descent, "That a half-white should be a Negro rather than a white cannot be explained by rational argument. The reason for this absurd bit of folk taxonomy is simply that the great blundering machinery of segregation cannot easily adjust itself to degrees of whiteness or darkness" (56). The idea that a "half-white should be a Negro" rather than a "half-white, half-black" also cannot be explained by rational argument (nor can the existence of "half-whites," "half-blacks," or, for that matter, "blacks" and "whites" in the first place), and the reason for the nonexistence of such racial halves in American race law is also attributable to the law's inability to deal with "degrees of whiteness or darkness." Racial blood does not mix in this legal discourse, and, as a result, there are in effect no mulattoes in American race law.[8]

As it codifies supposedly natural differences in blood by not allowing them to mix or dilute, the law recoups a readability of race lost in the chromatic confusions of miscegenation. The visible darkness of skin color becomes a figurative blackness codified in legal discourse as a blackness of blood—a blackness that cannot be seen but that nevertheless marks. Moreover, a certain emphasis on the materiality of blood as a sign itself in the legal text becomes imperative as the law attempts to make blood as visible as skin and thus as readable as the ink in which it is legally inscribed. Charles Chesnutt depicts this project of transubstantiating racializing blood into the ink in which it is inscripted in a scene from *The House Behind the Cedars* (1900). Judge Straight explains to young John Walden that although he is light enough to pass for white, he cannot become a lawyer in the state of North Carolina because of his legal blackness. "'You are black . . . and you are not free,'" the judge reminds him, and proceeds to list the legal prohibitions that make up the distinction between his rights and liberties and those of a white citizen. To substantiate his point, the judge refers John to the decision delivered by Justice Taney in *Dred Scott* "'that negroes are beings 'of an inferior order . . . so inferior that they have no rights which the white man is bound to respect, and that the negro may justly and lawfully be reduced to slavery for his benefit.' That is the law of this nation, and that is the reason why you cannot be a lawyer'" (379).

> "It may be true," replied the boy, "but it don't apply to me. It says, 'the negro.' A negro is black; I am white, and not black."
>
> "Black as ink, my lad," returned the lawyer, shaking his head. . . . Somewhere, sometime, you had a black ancestor. One drop of black blood makes the whole man black."
>
> "Why shouldn't it be the other way, if the white blood is so much superior?" inquired the lad.
>
> "Because it is more convenient as it is—and more profitable." (379)

Young John Walden's appeal to natural logic in the face of unnatural legal illogic (echoing Guillaumin and Tourgée) indicates to Judge Straight that he "'wouldn't make a good lawyer, in any event. Lawyers go by the laws—they abide by the accomplished fact; to them, whatever is, is right'" (379–80). As Judge Straight suggests, the law is perfectly willing to abandon natural logic for its own purposes of racial codification. In order to do so, the law appropriates just "one drop" of John's "black blood" to render him as "black as ink," as black as the ink in which the law is materially printed. The essence of black blood becomes, literally, the matter of the legal discourse, the readable, physical material composing the legal text itself.

The materializing of blood for the purposes of legal codification as a way to resolve the incompatibility between the logics of racial mixture and racial marking is one of the motivations behind the plot of Mark Twain's *Pudd'nhead Wilson*. The novel dramatizes the catachresis of "adulterated naturalness" in American race law through its depiction of Tom Driscoll, the legally black, visibly white changeling who has become the usurping heir to the Driscoll family fortune. Born to a black slave mother named Roxy and switched in infancy with her master's son, Tom is raised as white. Among the novel's central thematic questions is whether and how Tom's blood determines his character and racial identity.

Tom's slave mother Roxy and his biological uncle and adopted father Judge Driscoll employ various means to shape Tom's character in the context of their respective beliefs about his biological inheritance, and both confront the failure of blood to determine Tom's character in the ways that they believe it should. Caught between the influences of his biological mother and his legal "father," Tom becomes the character at the center of the novel's dramatization of the conflation of the scientific and legal rhetorics of racial blood. Roxy and Judge Driscoll are both stymied by the conflation of a natural discourse of racial blood mixture and a legal discourse of racial blood marking. In the novel's climactic trial scene, the problem of racial blood's "unnaturalness" is resolved through the device of a bloody fingerprint used as legal evidence of Tom's guilt and of his hidden racial identity, a device that synthesizes the characterological mixture of romantic racialism with the stigmatizing effect of legal marking.

The plot follows the divergent careers of two characters switched at birth, Tom and Chambers, both visibly white but one, Tom, born the son of a black slave woman named Roxy. To prevent her son from being sold away, Roxy switches her baby with the infant son of her master Percy Driscoll.[9] Although legally black, Tom Driscoll is raised as the visibly white "false heir" to the property and prestige of the "F.F.V." (the First Families of Virginia). Tom shirks the standards and responsibilities of the "ancient house of Driscoll" despite his uncle's best efforts to preserve them in his nephew: he drinks, gambles, lies, and steals. Nurtured into a corrupting sense of entitlement, Tom develops a character supposedly out of keeping with that bestowed by his Driscoll blood. He compensates his mother poorly for rescuing him from a life of enslavement, giving Roxy nothing but stress and heartbreak and developing for her an acute disdain. Even as a child, Tom thinks nothing of cruelly striking his mother and insulting her as a "'nigger wench'" (22). Desperate for relief, Roxy considers undoing her own exchange by revealing Tom's identity as an imposter, but then concedes to the fear of being sold down the river as a consequence. "'O, Lord,'" she laments,

"'I done so much for him—I lift' him away up to whar he is—en dis is what I git for it'" (22). As it turns out, by raising Tom as a white rich heir, she "had made him too strong" (22).

In what has become an infamous moment in the body of literary criticism on *Pudd'nhead*, Roxy struggles to understand the origin of her son's bad character and ultimately concludes that it derives not from his upbringing but from his ancestry. Dismayed by Tom's refusal to fight his rival Luigi Cappello in a duel, Roxy attributes Tom's cowardice to the small portion of blackness he has inherited through her. "'Thirty-one parts o' you is white, en on'y one part nigger, en dat po' little one part is yo' *soul*" (70). Roxy's proclamation is disturbing and jarring, especially considering that she is perhaps the character in the novel least expected to resort to such gross racial determinism given her own experience. If such a formulation of essential and inherited blackness is to be believed, then Roxy possesses the same blackness that Tom does, and in such a formulation, Tom would be considered black *because* of Roxy. Yet, her own act of switching Tom and Chambers in their cribs implies Roxy's disbelief in such racial determinants of character. After all, she switches her child with her masters' in order to avert her son's enslavement as determined by the law's adherence to the "one-drop rule," the law that renders him black and a piece of property. Thus many critics have read the scene as the novel's contradictory concession to biological racial essentialism and an especially egregious concession coming from one of Twain's most lauded characters.[10]

Along with the presumption of the inferiority bestowed by Tom's "nigger" blood, Roxy's error lies in the confusion of American racialism's divergent blood discourses of mixing and marking. She attempts to apply the logic of the rule that legally makes Tom black to a reading of his racial character, presuming that his character should be shown in the same proportion of his blackness and whiteness. She is flabbergasted when this logic does not hold. Roxy is not depicted here as staunchly devoted to a principle of racial determinism; she is rather left in the throes of a mental "storm," blindsided and confused by the illogic of her own assessment. "Roxana's storm went gradually down, but it died hard, and even when it seemed to be quite gone it would now and then break out in a distant rumble, so to speak, in the form of muttered ejaculations. One of these was, 'Ain't nigger enough in him to show in his finger-nails, en dat takes mighty little—yit dey's enough to paint his soul'" (70).

What "Roxana's storm" dramatizes is not her adherence to the rule of hypo-descent but rather her own difficulty in processing the irrationality of it. Here Roxy is as confused as John Warwick and Albion Tourgée by the problem of what Guillaumin called "adulterated naturalness." Particularly at issue in this moment is the incompatibility between a discourse of racial proportion in relation to Tom's character and the discourse of racial proportion that legally determines his blackness or whiteness. Roxy struggles in vain to apply the legal logic of the one-drop rule to explain Tom's character when, as her previous actions have demonstrated, she knows very well that the drop of determinant blood in him is merely a "fiction of law and custom." In her storm, Roxy fixates on the problem of disproportion: "What ever has 'come o' yo' Essex blood? Dat's what I can't understan'" (70). But the error that Roxy makes here is the same error made by Tourgée and Guillaumin, namely, that she has conflated two different discourses of racial blood while asking them to abide by the same natural logic. The minute proportion of Tom's African American ancestry does indeed mark him as legally black, but, as Roxy intuits but falls short of realizing, such legal marking is not concomitant with a wholesale "blackening" of his character.

If "Roxana's storm" dramatically delineates the conflicting logics of these two discourses, Judge Driscoll's response to Tom's character demonstrates how the law, in its construction of race and its appropriation of racial blood rhetoric, abandons the entailment of characterological mixture in order to construct race for the maintenance of property. Assuming the role of Tom's legal guardian after his father's death, Judge Driscoll takes his legal guardianship as a solemn responsibility, stewarding Tom into his role as the heir to the Driscoll estate and the family's long-held social prominence. An eminent member of the prestigious First Families of Virginia, Judge Driscoll invests heavily in an ideology of blood and character. "In Missouri a recognized superiority attached to any person who hailed from Old Virginia; and this superiority was exalted to supremacy when a person of such nativity could also prove descent from the First Families of that great commonwealth. The Howards and Driscolls were of this aristocracy" (58). The F.F.V. employ a proud rhetoric of blood to express the honor and longevity of their pedigree, as when Judge Driscoll boasts of "'the true old blood'" possessed by his nephew Tom that establishes him as "'the best blood of the Old Dominion" (59).

But as the novel also makes clear, F.F.V. blood is a poor determinant of character; instead, this character must be constantly performed, conditioned, and maintained. Like all F.F.V. gentlemen, Judge Driscoll understands that his "highest duty in life was to watch over that great inheritance and keep it unsmirched" (58). The "unwritten laws" of the F.F.V. code of honor dictate each member's lifetime course of action, and "if he swerved from it by so much as half a point of the compass it meant shipwreck to his honor; that is to say, degradation from his rank as a gentleman" (58). Thus, as a Virginia gentleman par excellence, Judge Driscoll is "respected, esteemed, and beloved by all the community," but this adoration and respect are contingent upon his continual devotion to practicing and performing the qualities recognized as elements of F.F.V. character. In actuality, one is not born an F.F.V. gentleman by blood, one is made an F.F.V. gentleman through constant upkeep of character and self-discipline. "He was very proud of his old Virginian ancestry . . . he kept up its traditions. . . . To be a gentleman—a gentleman without stain or blemish—was his only religion and to it he was always faithful" (6–7). Thus, unlike the permanent status of inferiority supposedly determined by the black blood of the slaves that they own, the upstanding character that is the legacy of the F.F.V. could be lost within the span of a generation (precisely the threat facing Judge Driscoll with his nephew's waywardness). Legally, black blood makes blacks slaves, but F.F.V. blood, much to Judge Driscoll's dismay, carries no such deterministic power with regard to white character. Judge Driscoll thus remains perpetually frustrated by the manner in which a "whole ocean" (to borrow Albion Tourgée's language) of Virginia's best white blood cannot seem to determine Tom's character and thus his claim to whiteness and property.

The F.F.V. participate in the construction of their own whiteness through social reputation rather than through biological determinism. As legal scholar Ariela Gross has demonstrated in her analysis of the types of evidence presented in mid-century court cases determining the disputed whiteness of claimants, "A white man's honor resided in the public sphere—in his statesmanlike behavior towards superiors and inferiors, his adherence to the gentlemen's code of conduct, his mastery of slaves, and his exercise of citizenship. For a man, performing whiteness meant the performance of rights and privileges" (157). The F.F.V.'s adherence to a sacred set of "unwritten laws" to underwrite their property in elite whiteness constitutes a strategy for averting the kind of biological essentialism that supposedly defines their social subordinates (black slaves).

But the inscription of such white entitlement in texts that cannot be read also renders the claim to such whiteness ambiguous because it requires proof. In the context of a one-drop rule that determines blackness, the process of proving one's whiteness, Gross explains, becomes fraught with the problem of proving a negative—proving that one does not have any black blood lurking in one's genealogy. Thus trials of racial determination "required a confrontation between everyday ways of understanding race and definitions that fit into the 'official,' well-articulated racial ideology that supported the maintenance of slavery and postwar racial hierarchy. That is, legal rules based on 'blood' had to be translated into practical action 'on the ground,' where people were more likely to describe someone's race in terms of how they looked and behaved than in terms of their fractional ancestry" (119). While the one-drop rule depended upon a rhetoric of hidden blackness, the provability of this drop becomes as (if not more) problematic for the legal determination of whiteness. Ironically, the insistence by such racial supremacist groups as the F.F.V. that whiteness remain above the level of primitive determinism figured by black blood creates the possibility for the very phenomenon of passing that blurs the color line. Visibly white but legally black individuals are taken as possessing white blood but gain the opportunity to pass precisely because white blood has such little determining power.

Unlike Judge Driscoll, Tom remains undedicated to the maintenance of his F.F.V. character, and his waywardness creates a contentious struggle between himself and his uncle, paralleling Tom's relationship with his mother. Judge Driscoll and Roxy both assume responsibility for Tom's character, but because F.F.V. character is not a function of blood—a lack of claiming power figured through Driscoll's relationship to Tom as uncle and legal guardian rather than biological father—Driscoll can only wish for the kind of biological determinism of Tom's character assumed to govern Tom's blackness. "'He is worthless and unworthy, but it is largely my fault,'" Driscoll laments. "'He was entrusted to me by my brother on his dying bed, and I have indulged him to his hurt, instead of training him up severely and making a man of him'" (67). The judge's lament that his nephew's poor character is his own fault due to his negligence of Tom's proper training parallels Roxy's lament of Tom's poor character as the effect of the "nigger" blood she has supposedly passed to him. But whereas Roxy must contend with the apparent failure of the dominant proportion of white blood she has supposedly passed on to Tom, Judge Driscoll must contend with the failure of F.F.V. blood to effectively carry character. The seemingly unnatural power of black blood that Tom's biological mother Roxy finds so illogical is precisely the kind of determinism by white blood that Judge Driscoll, as a figure of the law, can only dream of. The question of Tom's character highlights a tension in the power of blood as he becomes the object of dispute between his biological mother's desire for a more "natural" mixture of racial character and his legal father's desire for an extralegal biological determinism.

Driscoll is perpetually frustrated by the impotency of racial blood to perform its unwritten, extralegal function of shaping Tom's character, which is particularly galling since the F.F.V. code supposedly transcends the law. "It had its unwritten laws, and they were as clearly defined and as strict as any that could be found among the printed statutes of the land" (58). Thus, when Driscoll learns that Tom has evaded the duel that would have settled a personal dispute, he does not blame Tom's misbehavior on a subversive and unnaturally powerful portion of Tom's blood (as Roxy does), but rather he laments the implication that Tom's blood has been usurped by legal procedure: "'Do you mean to tell me that blood of my race has suffered a blow and crawled to the court of law about it?'" (60). Driscoll objects to Tom's stooping to the lowness of legal appeal to settle a dispute, a mockery of F.F.V. honorable conduct. He takes his nephew's appeal to written legal codes as an affront to the supremacy of the "unwritten laws" that should influence and determine the motivations and character of an F.F.V. gentleman.

With Tom undedicated to the maintenance of his own character and his F.F.V. blood unable to determine it, Judge Driscoll finds himself forced into a legal procedure to square Tom's failure to maintain his character with his inheritance of wealth, an action that, for the judge, serves as a poor substitute for biological determinism. When Tom admits his fear to duel his adversary, the judge is rocked from his senses. Maddened and calling his nephew a coward, Driscoll "tottered to his secretary in the corner" in search of his will, repeating the lament of Tom's cowardice "again and again in heart-breaking tones" (60). He destroys his own will as Tom watches. Tearing up the will may be the only response the judge can muster, but the act places him in a bind, as the very act of destroying the will deprives Tom of his inheritance while forcing the judge to repudiate the unwritten power of the F.F.V. code.

Destroying the will admits the true relationship between Tom's character and the legalized inheritance of property inscripted in the legal document. The act also serves as a bitter reminder of the surrogate role that the law plays in the shaping of Tom's character and that Tom, or any member of the F.F.V, can be written in or written out of what Judge Driscoll would prefer as an unwritten and natural right. "'Once more,'" exclaims Judge Driscoll, "'you have forced me to disinherit you, you base son of a most noble father!'" (60). Through this act of legal disinheritance, Driscoll is "forced" to admit the law's role in the construction of Tom's character and to admit the role of the law, as the method of transmitting property, not blood, as the true conduit of F.F.V. social and economic prominence. Forced to take legal action where blood should suffice, Driscoll is also forced to concede legal print, not blood, as the true carrier of F.F.V. character, and property as the essence of the F.F.V.

Realizing the precariousness of the family fortune should he die without leaving Tom any of the Driscoll estate, Driscoll reverses his decision to disinherit Tom. "'I have violated my trust, and I must not add the sin of desertion to that. I have forgiven him once, already, and would subject him to a long trial before forgiving him again, if I could live; but I must not run that risk. No, I must restore the will. . . . and I will not tell him until he reforms and I see that his reformation is going to be permanent'" (67). Desperate, he secures the financial power of the F.F.V. in a hidden will—"'I will hide it away and he will not know'"—effectively constructing Tom's hidden whiteness, carried not in blood but in legal print (67). Overhearing his uncle's decision to reconstitute the will, Tom commits himself to a project of personal reform or at least the appearance of it. "'I've got the fortune again, but I'll not let on that I know about it. And this time I'm going to hang on to it. . . . I'll gamble no more, I'll drink no more, because—well, because I'll not go where there is any of that sort of thing going on, again'" (68).

But desperately needing money to pay his gambling debts and to purchase his own mother (whom he has sold down the river with her own cooperation to cover his debts), Tom soon finds himself in dire financial straits and resolves to rob his own uncle. Donning blackface, he commits the burglary and then murders Judge Driscoll when the judge confronts him. While fleeing the crime scene, Tom leaves incriminating evidence in the form of a bloody fingerprint—the blood of his dead uncle—on the knife used in the murder. Tom's rival Luigi Cappello is accused of the crime and put on trial. In the novel's courtroom finale, a local lawyer named David "Pudd'nhead" Wilson uses the bloody fingerprint found at the crime scene to clear Luigi and identify Tom as the murderer. Wilson has been collecting fingerprints from members of the Dawson's Landing community for several years and, during a routine examination of his collection, discovers that Tom is not Tom but rather Chambers, and not white but black. The same fingerprint evidence used to identify Tom as the murderer also reveals Tom's blackness, and he is consequently remanded to slavery and sold down the river.

As is known, Twain derived the fingerprinting science depicted in the novel from his reading of Francis Galton's book *Finger Prints* (1892).

This, according to Twain, provided the final inspiration he needed to complete the manuscript of *Pudd'nhead*, with which he had been struggling for some time.[11] As scholars reading *Pudd'nhead* have discussed, the use of Galton's science in the novel complicates the work's stance on racial determination, particularly considering Galton's own notorious contributions to the most heinous forms of scientific racialism. Known as the "father of eugenics," Francis Galton developed his system for classifying fingerprints in conjunction with his search for measurable determinants of race and character, hoping that fingerprints "might be the elusive visible markers of heredity for which he had long been searching" (Cole 74). To his disappointment, Galton could discover no reliable racial indicators in the patterns and shapes of the fingerprints he studied. "I thought that any hereditary peculiarities would almost of necessity vary in different races, and that so fundamental and enduring a feature as the finger markings must in some way be correlated with temperament" (17). Finding that this earlier hope of correlating fingerprints with racial ability had been based on "some accidental observations," Galton admits that, "There is no particular pattern that is special to any one [race], which when met with enables us to assert, or even to suspect, the nationality of the person on whom it appeared" (193). Although he holds out the possibility that some future ethnologist might discover what he has missed, Galton concludes that, "No indications of temperament, character, or ability are to be found in finger marks, so far as I have been able to discover" (197).

Although the science of fingerprinting had been developed since the late 1880s, Twain's knowledge of fingerprinting science seems to have been limited to his reading of Galton, so it is unclear how much the author may have known about previous uses of fingerprinting (in the administration of colonial India, for example) or the relationship between Galton's work on fingerprints and his larger body of eugenic science.[12] Nevertheless, Twain's representation of fingerprinting demonstrates his own philosophical and literary interest in individual and racial indicators of character, and the implications of Twain's use of Galton's science for the themes of racial determination in *Pudd'nhead* have been considered extensively in the novel's body of criticism.[13] As

Susan Gillman suggests, "The problem of identity and imposture—that is, of a unitary, responsible self—led Twain to become interested in potential solutions embodied in the processes of identification and legitimation, primarily legal and scientific, that were available in the world around him" (3).

But we should also recognize how the fusion of racial science and the practice of printing in Galton's science speaks to the interrelationship between racial blood's ability to mix and to mark and provides the device for *Pudd'nhead*'s resolution of these discourses in the sign of a bloody fingerprint. Galton's main contributions to fingerprinting came in his system for identifying, naming, classifying, and physically recording the loops, whorls, and arches seen in the ornate patterns of the papillary ridges on the balls of human fingers ("little worlds in themselves" as Galton described them) (2). But as Galton makes clear in the language and tone of *Finger Prints*, he regarded himself as perfecting the science as a kind of racialist print artwork. For Galton, fingerprints were printed images of art that transcribed natural forms through the medium of ink. Thus, the term that Galton gave to this work, *Finger Prints* (now commonly contracted as "fingerprints"), promoted his own view of the print artistry and skill required for the proper practice of this form of anthropometry, and the book conveys Galton's view of himself as the science's original craftsman. (Galton produces his own fingerprints on the cover of the work).

Fingerprinting relies upon a relationship that Galton clearly enjoyed, a relationship between racial determination and the art of printing. Amid explanations of his theories of heritable racial traits, Galton devotes the book's third chapter, "Methods of Printing," to explaining "how to make really good and permanent impressions of the fingers. It is very easy to do when the principles of the art are understood and practiced" (30). Here Galton lavishes the fingerprinting process with care and demonstrates his appreciation of the evocative meanings arising from the divination of nature's mysterious signs carved on the body's surfaces. "It is no violent misuse of metaphor to compare the ridges to the crests of mountain ranges, and the depth of the blackening that they ought to receive, to that of the newly-fallen snow upon the mountaintops in early autumn, when it powders them from above downwards to a sharply-defined level" (32–33). Often effusive in its romantic descriptions of the art involved in this racial science, the chapter details the process for taking prints composed in ink and even suggests the particular kinds of ink to be used. "The ink used may be either printer's ink or water colour, but for producing the best work, rapidly and on a large scale, the method of printer's ink seems in every respect preferable" (32). On occasion, Galton suggests passing the fingers through the hair to oil them as a substitute (a technique that Twain employs in the plot of *Pudd'nhead*), but for the most part, Galton works in ink, and the book is full of images of inky prints carefully applied to paper. Blending science, art, and print culture, Galton viewed fingerprinting as a way to transcribe naturally made racial indicators in ink, thus making race legible. In *Pudd'nhead Wilson*, Tom makes fun of the finger-mark "scientifics" practiced by David Wilson (the novel's figure of Galton) by deriding his science as a kind of palmistry or "'rank sorcery'" (49, 50). "Why, he'll read your wrinkles as easy as a book, and not only tell you fifty or sixty things that's going to happen to you, but fifty or sixty thousand that ain't'" (49).

The level of artistry in Galton's practice underscores the significance that the substance of each fingerprint brings to its forensic and racial meaning. Galton emphasized the choice of ink for proper printing because of his view of the art's precision as essential to the scientific practice. He painstakingly describes the precise methods for obtaining the most clear and distinct fingerprints from the soft, malleable ridges of flesh. A precise printing process was required because Galton sought to compare an individual's fingerprints against those of individuals with "known" racial types. Here the care that Galton takes in printing becomes paramount for the purposes of matching the minute and detailed loops, whorls, and arches.

But, of course, in the forensic science that would come to employ Galton's innovation (depicted in its nascent application in Twain's novel), criminal investigators, judges, and juries would be asked to compare the well-formed prints from a fingerprint database (like David Wilson's collection) with the much less distinct (and usually partial) prints taken from a crime scene. Fingerprint impressions "are often blurred, smudged, overlaid upon one another, and distorted by foreign matter. The detective must match this distorted crime scene print to an inked print, taken under pristine 'laboratory' conditions, to the exclusion of all other fingerprints in the world" (Cole 89). Thus, while Galton depicted his science as an art based on pristinely made prints, the prints that most often matter for the purposes of forensic identification are hardly ever made in legible black ink on white paper but rather in other substances and on other surfaces much less likely to provide such clarity of distinction: sweaty prints found on a gun handle or window ledge, prints left nearly invisibly in dust, bloody prints found on a knife. Fingerprint analysis is thus almost always a process comparing ornate shapes printed in ink against their ill-formed counterparts made in substances of various viscosity and legibility—whatever substance in which the crime-scene fingerprint is made.

We are reminded then that the full signification of a fingerprint as a forensic artifact derives not only from the shape of the print but also from the substance of which the print is composed, that while the shape of the print speaks to the presence of a particular individual's body (or at least their finger), it is the substance of the print (as well as the substance upon which it is found) that signifies the crucial narrative surrounding the body in question and the individual's potential involvement in the crime under investigation. The print's identification is meaningless without such contextual information, which places the individual in an indicting narrative involving his or her physical location, often (but not necessarily) at the crime scene itself. The shape of the fingerprint indicates who, but the location and substance of the print speaks to the individual's legal guilt or innocence and, by extension, their character.

The substance composing a fingerprint is thus constitutive of the print's meaning, conveying crucial information about the narrative of the crime being reconstructed and the body of the accused person's involvement in this narrative. Fingerprints left in blood constitute a special case in this regard. While all fingerprints can place an individual's body at the scene of a murder, fingerprints in blood indicate more than that the individual was at the location at some unspecified time but that he or she was there when blood was spilled. Here the individual can hardly deny literally having blood on their hands. Prints composed in virtually any other substance other than the blood of the victim provide no sure indication of the individual's actual participation in such an act of violence. Formed by the shapes of the papillary ridges on the tips of the individual's finger and composed in the victim's blood, the bloody fingerprint fuses victim and assailant into one symbol or sign and speaks to the assailant's presence at the moment of the victim's suffering of bodily violence. Moreover, their composition in such a culturally symbolic substance cannot help but signify in ways that transcend their denotative forensic meaning. Because "blood inhabits the imagination as both substance and symbol," the evidentiary power of a bloody fingerprint becomes conflated with, if not overwhelmed by, its irrepressible cultural symbolism (Biale 1). If blood always oversignifies in the context of forensic science, it carries particular resonance in the context of late nineteenth-century legal racial discourse, especially when a bloody fingerprint provides, as it does in *Pudd'nhead's* plot, evidence of racial identity.

It is here that the plot of Twain's *Pudd'nhead Wilson* expands upon the implications of Galton's science as it provides a device for resolving the tension between the mixing and marking projects of scientific and legal racial blood discourse. Blood, the material in which the operative fingerprint in the novel is composed, changes the meaning of the print, both in terms of *how* and *what* the print signifies, and it does so within the context of the interrelated discourses of characterological mixture and legal marking. The crucial fingerprint in Twain's novel is composed of Judge Driscoll's literal blood, the figurative "white" blood of the First Families of Virginia, the blood that the judge vowed to preserve "unsmirched." Taking full advantage of the dramatic courtroom moment, Wilson pauses during his presentation of fingerprint evidence and holds the murder weapon up before the jury and the town's community in attendance "where all could see the sinister spots upon its ivory handle" (109). "'Upon this haft stands the assassin's natal autograph," he exclaims, "written in the blood of that helpless and unoffending old man who loved you and whom you all loved" (109).

Wilson's dramatic proclamation before the courtroom filled with Judge Driscoll's admirers articulates the violence that must have taken place in order for blood to compose the fingerprint evidence and for the murderer to sign his name to the crime. Driscoll's blood is no longer performing its proper, literal, and physiological function of maintaining the judge's life. Instead, it has been reduced to printing matter and made complicit in a metaphor of the assailant's signature. That the judge's own blood has been used by the murderer in this way ("the *assassin's* natal autograph") somehow deepens the crime against him. Wilson's phrasing suggests that the murderer has left his signature, perhaps even intentionally, as a deliberate mock, as a gesture suggesting his dominance over the judge, and as a self-aggrandizing use of the judge's bodily remnant.

In addition, Wilson's reference to the blood that would otherwise maintain the life of the "old man" adds the testimony of Judge Driscoll's character to the body of evidence. The judge, Wilson suggests, did not deserve such treatment and such a fate. He was an "unoffending old man who loved you and whom you all loved" (109). This is supposedly the very substance of F.F.V. blood, sanctified by Judge Driscoll's "assassination," a form of death that only deepens the community's attachment to him. Judge Driscoll's blood has been spilled in a way that his nephew's blood, because of Tom's cowardice, had not been spilled in the duel against Luigi (the judge took Tom's place in the duel, with Howard Pembroke as his second). Even as the blood speaks to the character of the murderer who would perpetrate such an act, it also testifies to the judge's character in signifying his own self-sacrifice. It is thus evidence of the unwritten code of Driscoll's character made through a textual inscription written in his own blood.

Yet even as it speaks to his character, Driscoll's blood also serves as a marking agent, an ink as it were, as it takes the shape of the loops, whorls, and arches on the ends of *Tom's* fingers. Tom's fingerprint is an uncanny amalgam of internal and external, content and form, black and white. It is literally *made up* by two subjects: the shape of the print is provided by the external and "natal" physical form of the immutable "'arches, circles, long curves, whorls'" of ("black") Tom's finger, and the actual material of the print is composed of ("white") Judge Driscoll's blood. Indeed, this fingerprint is an actual portion of Judge Driscoll; it is a *fraction* of him, but the exact proportion one can hardly say. This fingerprint is, indeed, literally composed of one *drop* of Judge Driscoll's blood. In the process of solving the murder using Tom's print, Wilson also discovers that Tom has been switched at birth with the true white heir. So in yet another of the novel's proliferating and nested ironies, it is the one drop of "white" Driscoll blood which "makes" Tom black. In what is perhaps one of the greatest ironies in a novel full of them, it is this literal drop of blood from Tom's white, legally surrogate father that accomplishes what the figurative drop of blood from his black biological mother could not: it blackens Tom.

The one-drop rule aimed to make blackness visible while, in his pioneering of fingerprints, Francis Galton hoped to provide a technology by which the law could mark racial identity as clearly as it was marked through skin color. But it is only Twain's image of the bloody fingerprint that carries the conglomerate character of the socially eminent white Judge Driscoll and the supposedly degenerate "black" Tom while also providing the legal evidence that legally marks Tom. The fingerprint thus literalizes the one-drop rule as it writes hypo-descent's unnatural persistence of blackness in blood.

Although the essence of white blood is subordinate to that of black blood in the legal discourse of "one drop," Twain's bloody fingerprint nevertheless interjects the weight of Judge Driscoll's social reputation and his property in whiteness into evidence in a legal proceeding that will solve his own murder and determine Tom's black racial identity. The evidentiary value of the bloody fingerprint restores the essence to Judge Driscoll's white blood. This is perhaps the only way, as contrived as it may be, that the essence of white blood can dominate over blackness in the legal discourse of race. A portion of the judge's vital substance—a substance that is *essential* to Judge Driscoll because it is a substance that he literally cannot live without—is there on the murder weapon, where its presence signifies the violent release of that essence from his body that caused his death. Driscoll's blood also serves as his presence in the courtroom—a literal part of him is there, and so it—he—testifies and bears witness to his own murder. When the bloody fingerprint is used to convict Tom and reveal his blackness, Judge Driscoll has finally determined Tom's fate in a way he could not manage through legal means during his life. Judge Driscoll can only determine Tom's future, it turns out, by giving up his essence.

Thus the bloody fingerprint provides the novel's ultimate symbol of the synthesis (or mutual constitution) of the characterological and legal discourses of racial blood in American race law. As it fuses the legal and racial scientific contexts of fingerprint science through its narrative, Twain's novel speaks to the manner in which the law's treatment of fingerprints as a kind of printed signature fuses with racial science's interest in fingerprints as a substitute for blood. Twain's bloody fingerprint thus resolves the tension between the characterological and legal discourses of blood, allowing blood to act as both the proportional carrier of character and the binary indicator of racial identity. Helpless to affect Tom's character through legal means, Judge Driscoll finally does so by leaving his intentions written not in the ink of a legal document but "written in the blood" on the weapon used in his own murder. And so, it is through this sign of a bloody fingerprint left in a desperate act of physical violence that the novel represents the law's negotiation of the dual discourses entailed in its appropriation of the pseudoscientific idiom of blood and race—a sign that registers the metaphorical violence required and the literal violence authorized by the law's codification of the figure of "blood" as the essence of ink.

CHAPTER 2

Frances Harper and the Blood of Sacrifice

Early in the story of Iola Leroy, a martyr dies holding her hand. The death of Tom Anderson, the rebellious former slave who gives his life to save a company of black soldiers in the Union army, establishes the moral framework of sacrifice and martyrdom that refigures the meaning of the rhetoric of racial blood in Frances Harper's 1892 novel *Iola Leroy*. Unable to fight due to his own "physical defects," Tom volunteers to row a band of Union enlistees across a river and shares in their misfortune when the company is ambushed by rebel forces (Harper 40). Injured, Tom is carried to a Union field hospital with "blood streaming from his wounds" (52). His friend Robert, also a former slave, listens anxiously as an eyewitness relates the circumstances of Tom's mortal injury. The boat carrying the company had become stuck in a mud bank when Tom, "a man of herculean strength and remarkable courage," willfully laid down his life to save the others. "'Some one must die to get us out of this,'" Tom reportedly said. "'I mought's well be him as any. You are soldiers and can fight. If they kill me, it is nuthin'" (53). With "a look of recognition and rapture" upon his face, Tom dies under the care of the novel's titular heroine, Iola Leroy. As Frances Smith Foster notes in her collection of Harper's work, *A Brighter Coming Day*, Tom Anderson's fictional death repeats nearly verbatim a true story of black Civil War heroism that Harper related seven years earlier in her speech "A Factor in Human Progress" (270). Harper used the incident as a parable of heroic sacrifice, offering the unnamed Civil War hero as a model for her post-Reconstruction audience to emulate. "Who shall say that the race out of which such men could spring from under the dark shadow of slavery has not within it elements out of which a great people may yet be produced?" (*Brighter Coming Day* 280).

Such a spirit of sacrifice would be the defining factor in black progress during the post-Reconstruction period, Harper argues in her essay, and the future remained bright for those willing to sacrifice their own blood as this unnamed man had sacrificed his.

As Harper resurrects this black and unknown martyr as a character in her most popular work of fiction and places him to die in the care of her most enduring heroine, Tom's self-sacrificial death inspires Iola's own humanitarian work and establishes the ethical and moral tone of the novel. "Iola, with tearful eyes and aching heart, clasped the cold hands over the still breast, closed the waxen lid over the eye . . . and then went back, after the burial, to her daily round of duties, feeling the sad missing of something from her life" (55). If, as many critics have suggested, Iola Leroy is a version of Frances Harper, then such a scene of motivational martyrdom draws one of the most significant parallels between character and author. Throughout her own life, Harper was motivated and inspired by martyrdom, and she drew martyrs throughout her fiction, poetry, essays, and speeches with a compelling fascination. Her deep interest in martyrdom is undoubtedly rooted in Harper's own devout Christianity, a faith grounded in sacrificial death, and exercised by her vivid and intimate experience with John Brown, one of the most influential martyrs of nineteenth-century America. Through her literary work, Harper meditated on the meaning of martyrdom and on how images of the blood that Christ, John Brown, and other martyrs sacrificed for others had become ideologically mingled with the blood of racial affiliation in the rhetoric of her black feminist Christian politics and the graphic imagery of her literary art.

As I will argue in the following reading of Harper's *Iola Leroy*, this spirit of sacrificial death provides the context for the novel's entire rhetoric of blood and Frances Harper's ethics and aesthetics of individual, political, and social sacrifice. "'The best blood in my veins is African blood, and I am not ashamed of it,'" Iola famously declares (208). The rhetoric of blood employed by Iola in this defining expression of race pride, a rhetoric so often associated with an adherence to deterministic racialism, is, in Harper's symbology, informed by the sacrificial deaths of figures like John Brown and Tom Anderson. Indeed, Iola's devotion to her "African blood" emerges from her response to epic loss. As ironic as it is inspiring, Iola's adamant declaration of blood fealty belies the capriciousness and volatility of her own racial experience. Raised as the white daughter of a slave owner, she only learns about her African American ancestry during her adolescence when her white father Eugene Leroy dies and the legal ties between her father and her legally manumitted slave mother Marie are dissolved, casting Iola and her two siblings back into slavery with their mother. With a racial consciousness that she herself describes as a synthesis of both of the racial identities she has inhabited, Iola seems an unlikely source for such expressions of racial chauvinism. And yet it is precisely this pride in black ancestry that Iola regards among what she will later describe to Dr. Gresham as the life-altering "'[t]houghts and purposes [that] have come to me in the shadow I should never have learned in the sunshine'" (114).

Iola's devotion to her "African blood" is forged within the context of a discourse of sacrifice as both a religious and political principle, and it is only within this context that the nonbiological meanings of her use of "blood" as a racial metaphor can ultimately be reconciled. By interweaving imagery of sacrificial blood with the standard late nineteenth-century rhetoric of racial blood throughout *Iola Leroy*, Harper demonstrates Iola's race pride as less a function of her belief in the essentialism of a biological notion of blood than her belief in a Christian ideology through which Iola's blood becomes sanctified—like Christ's, like Brown's, and like Tom's—through her own agency. "'I am constantly rousing myself up to suffer and be strong,'" she tells Dr. Gresham. Her prideful possession of "blood" is galvanized by the memory of everything she has given up for it, and because her racial identity has been shaped by loss and the reparation of that loss through her own deliberate acts of self-denial, Iola's blood, like the blood of all martyrs, connotes this selfless sacrifice.

Harper was by no means the only prominent figure from her era to employ racial blood metaphors in such oblique critique of deterministic racial thinking, and one aim of this argument will be to situate Harper's work within ongoing reassessments of African American literary engagements with the terms and conditions of nineteenth-century scientific racialism. Several African American writers from the Reconstruction and post-Reconstruction periods have been credited with providing incisive critiques of the deterministic relationship between blood and race long before similar arguments would be made by anthropologists and geneticists during the early part of the twentieth century. For example, scholars have examined Pauline Hopkins's refiguring of racial science through the application of new psychology derived from her reading of William James in her novel *Of One Blood*. Eric Sundquist and others have considered how Charles Chesnutt deconstructs the logic of nineteenth-century racial blood discourse in his fiction and in essays such as "The Future American" (1900) and "What is a White Man?" (1889). Writing during the same period, W.E.B. Du Bois has been credited for his efforts to pioneer a nonbiological definition of race by recontextualizing his rhetoric of blood within a sociohistorical discourse of race. And Geoffrey Sanborn's own reading of the racial aesthetics of the "flush" *in Iola Leroy* provides an original and insightful way of approaching Harper's subtle critiques of the function of blood in the construction of race in Harper.[1]

But as I will argue, Harper's rebuttal against scientific determinism originates from a source unlike any of these others, the perhaps unlikely source of her Christian faith. The Christian theology and piety at the root of Harper's characteristic didacticism and middle-class gentility (which have drawn criticism of Harper's politics and literary style) is also at the root of her unique critique of scientific racialism and her refiguring of the meaning of racial blood rhetoric. Harper's language of blood is motivated and infused by her lifelong valorization of the Christian principle of sacrifice and the role that the image of blood plays in the theological rhetoric and iconography of that principle. Sacrifice became the very core of Harper's literary vision and her political and social ethos, the most integral concept framing her views on African American education, black uplift economics, a black nationalist imperative toward moral reform—in short, Harper's entire vision of post-Reconstruction black uplift. Because of her valorization of Christian sacrifice, even in the context of racial blood rhetoric, Harper's use of blood imagery throughout her work remains informed by the meanings of the image of blood in Christian iconography and symbolism.

Sacrifice was Harper's most predominant literary theme and blood one of her most prevalent images. The image of blood was so important for Harper primarily because of its status in her theological worldview as the substance that Christ had shed to save mankind, but the iconography of a dying Christ would also provide the imagery from which the substance and meaning of Harper's racial blood rhetoric could flow. Blood confers identity in Harper's work, but not in the mechanistic fashion of racial determinism. By virtue of its function in a sacrificial act by which, in Harper's faith, a man who was also a God forged a leveling covenant between Himself and mankind, blood defined the relationship between man and man, between man and God. Such unnatural sacrifice made blood sacred; it made blood *blood.*

Nineteenth-century racial discourse provided a particularly problematic rhetorical climate for racial reformers like Harper to comfortably employ racial blood rhetoric in their work. By this period, the appeal to blood in racial argument had become strongly identified with a biological discourse of race positing a deterministic relationship between blood and racial identity. One of the most racist tracts of the 1890s supportive of such claims was published only four years after *Iola Leroy*, when the Prudential Life Insurance Company statistician Frederick L. Hoffman encapsulated a century's work of scientific racism in his influential article "Race Traits and Tendencies of the American Negro," in the *Publications of the American Economic Association*. Faced with a backlash from white customers over the interracial pooling and disbursement of insurance policies, Prudential commissioned "Race Traits" as a statistical study of African American mortality rates that would justify racially segregated rate increases or the elimination of insurance policies for African Americans altogether. Hoffman's article was "a compilation of statistics, eugenic theory, observation, and speculation," all "intended to prove—with statistical reliability—that the American negro was uninsurable" due to inherent and irreversible inferiority (Wolff 84). Hoffman viewed his study as providing the scientific data necessary for answering the most pressing sociological and legal race questions of the post-Reconstruction era.[2]

In this work, Hoffman relies heavily on deterministic theories of blood mixture (quoting extensively from the work of other scientists) to support his most racist arguments. Throughout "Race Traits and Tendencies," Hoffman argues for the deleterious effects of race mixture, providing tables of scientific "evidence" demonstrating, in his view, "the physiological changes that have taken place in the mixed races as a consequence of the infusion of white blood" (185). Hoffman argues that a natural black inferiority could be deduced from the effects of such interracial mixture, as "mulattoes" exhibited healthier compositions than "pure blacks." His data purportedly show "an increase in brain weight with an increase in the proportion of white blood. . . . We have, therefore, the contrast of the mulatto being physically and possibly morally the inferior of the pure blooded negro, while intellectually he is superior" (186). Increasing the population of such unstable mulattoes—who are so often, Hoffman argues, the products of black prostitution, "concubinage," or other such illicit relations between individuals of the lowest character from both races—would be detrimental to both races, and thus "the physiological consequences alone demand race purity and a stern reprobation of any infusion of white blood. Whatever the [black] race may have gained in an intellectual way, which is a matter of speculation, it has been losing its greatest resources in the struggle for life, a sound physical organism and power of rapid reproduction" (206–7). Although Hoffman's conclusions and statistical methods were sharply criticized by W.E.B. Du Bois and Kelly Miller among others, his work would be praised by leading figures in sociology for years to come (Wolff 85).

As "a key text in one of the central social preoccupations of the turn of the century: the supposed Negro Problem," Hoffman's article provides a context for considering Harper's efforts to revise the relationship between blood and racial identity during this period (Wolff 84). Such racist discourse steeped in images of black and white blood provided the backdrop of racial ideology against which Harper wrote *Iola Leroy*. But while Hoffman's racial views clearly oppose Harper's, Harper employs similar references to blood in her representations of racial identity. When Harper's Iola learns that her brother Harry intends to marry Miss Delaney, a woman whose "'hair nor complexion show the least hint of blood admixture,'" Iola expresses her own approval of her brother's marital choice in terms that suggest her own belief in the effects of blood admixture on Miss Delaney's physical and intellectual makeup (199). "'Every person of unmixed blood who succeeds in any department of literature, art, or science is a living argument for the capability which is in the race'" (199). Iola extols the political benefits of such race purity, although her belief in the social value of the accomplishments of those with "unmixed blood" comes, of course, as a rebuttal to the kind of arguments posed by Hoffman.

Iola's indirect endorsement of the race-as-blood premise, however, brings her uncomfortably close to Hoffman's antimiscegenation stance. Hoffman denounces racial intermixture , deeming it "contrary to the interest of the colored race, [and] a positive hindrance to its social, mental and moral development" (206). While Hoffman's motivations against racial intermixture are very different from Iola's—"the physiological consequences alone demand race purity and a stern reprobation of any infusion of white blood," Hoffman wrote—both seem to adhere to a principle of race purity based on a racial blood calculus as a viable starting point for addressing racial conflict (206). Harper's blood imagery thus comes within the contemporary discursive context of such language supporting theories of race essentialism, a context that cannot be ignored when assessing the significance of her literary references to racial blood and assessing whether and how they make a difference with respect to the racial discourse of her era.

In the context of such racial theories purporting to show the detrimental effects following from disadvantageous mixtures of black and white blood, alternatively minded advocates of race equality would seem inclined to forgo the use of racial blood rhetoric entirely, lest such language be taken as an implicit endorsement of racial determinism. Yet, as any reader of post-Reconstruction-era African American literature can attest, the most prominent authors of the period—Pauline Hopkins, Charles Chesnutt, and W.E.B. Du Bois among them—employed racial blood rhetoric liberally, with little ostensible concern for ideological conflict.

Consequently, scholarly scrutiny of this rhetoric and its ideological implications for the development of African American thought during the period has become an identifiable subset of late nineteenth-century African American literary criticism. The work of nearly every major African American literary figure of the period has been examined for its investments in racial blood rhetoric. Cynthia Schrager, Thomas Otten, and Hazel Carby have analyzed such rhetoric in the work of Pauline Hopkins; Geoffrey Sanborn has analyzed the politics of the blush and the "circulation of blood" in *Iola Leroy*; and philosophers Anthony Appiah and Lucius Outlaw have engaged in rigorous and extended debate over W.E.B. Du Bois's references to blood in his effort to pioneer a nonbiological definition of race at the turn of the twentieth century.[3] The historian of science Nancy Stepan has discussed the difficult bind faced by progressive turn-of-the-century scientific professionals and commentators devoted to refuting the work of racist professionals such as Hoffman. Stepan explains that, while theological arguments based on biblical decrees of universal humanity "had the disadvantage of seeming illegitimate or 'unscientific' when measured by the canons of mainstream science," the high barriers placed against minority access to the channels of professional science "limited the nature of the [scientific] response" (82, 85). When they met scientific rhetoric on its own terms, these authors negotiated a compromise in which, although their "form of writing moved the resisting author further away from total acceptance or accommodation to the dominant discourse of difference, the terms of the dominant discourse were very far from being transcended" (92).

In the defense of these authors' continued use of "blood" as a metaphor for race, the prevailing scholarly strategy has been to suggest that post-Reconstruction black writers adeptly recontextualized racial blood rhetoric in ways that undermined its deterministic implications. In marshaling this defense, it is often argued that the use of blood as a racial metaphor by these authors comes in response to the terms of scientific racialism, and that nineteenth-century black authors countered scientific racism by, as Stepan suggests, "appropriating the idioms of science." In this line of argument, black writers received terms from racial science and then put them into practice in order to gain critical access to professional scientific dialogue. From this position, they could then proceed to critique scientific racialism "from within."

The problem with such an argument is that it locates the image of blood in the provenance of science, disregarding other discourses of blood that had already emerged from within the circle of African American rhetoric. Long before nineteenth-century black writers made their claims against scientific racialism, African American culture and rhetoric had already been integrally shaped by the substance and symbol of blood by virtue of the substance's function in African American Christianity. Through this avenue of ideological articulation, blood emerged as an image deeply endemic to African American political rhetoric and thought long before it had become the vehicle of racial determinism in scientific rhetoric. Thus, any analysis of the African American appropriation of blood as an idiom of racial science must also take into consideration the interrelated appropriation of this idiom taking place in relation to African American Christianity.

And indeed the Christianity that Frances Harper promoted through so much of her literary work—the religion that generations of African Americans adopted, synthesized, and modified into a core of African American culture—prompted its adherents toward a lifelong meditation on blood as part of the centuries-old faith from which it derived. As Miri Rubin details in "Blood: Sacrifice and Redemption in Christian Iconography," Christian iconography speaks to the centrality of blood as an image from the earliest representations of Christ's crucifixion, which encouraged and facilitated Christian meditation on the substance and meaning of blood. Beginning with the earliest graphic depictions of biblical imagery in the Middle Ages, Rubin explains, "The devout were encouraged to turn their thoughts to Christ's sacrifice and to imagine his suffering. A world of empathy was developing around the image of a suffering body . . . [while] the most affective engagement seems to have been brought about by the representation of Christ's red, mediating blood. This precious liquid, which was spilled at the Crucifixion, was cherished and reproduced at every Mass" (89–90). Rubin's work focuses particularly on such imagery produced in Europe during the Middle Ages, but this sacrificial blood has been represented, imagined, and reimagined throughout the history of Christian art as "Christian belief and practice . . . came to place growing value and enhanced meaning on the blood of sacrifice, the blood of salvation" (89). This iconography of blood in Christian art graphically depicts an imperative of blood at the core of the religion itself. Theologically and psychologically, Christ's death and resurrection must not only be believed by Christians, but also internalized and identified with. As demonstrated through ritual graphic representations of Christ's trial, suffering, and death during Easter Week passion plays, the violent manner of Christ's death contributes to its sacred remembrance. As the foundational moment of the faith, Christ's violent and bloody death installed blood—second perhaps only to the image of the cross itself—as the most significant symbol in Christianity.

When one considers the politics of blood rhetoric within African American literary and political discourse, then, the theological practice at the root of this discourse must be taken into account. African American Christianity developed within the larger context of a Christian theology that regarded blood as sacred and, nearly simultaneously, within the crucible of a race-based system of slavery that from its very outset sought to define blacks out of natural history by attributing to them an irredeemably corrupt form of blood. Thus, during the same period in which African Americans were adopting a religion that promised them salvation through one form of blood, they were being systematically denied their legal and social rights in terms of another form of the same substance. This ideological tension between the blood of a saving faith and the blood of a damning legal and scientific discourse developed African American racial blood rhetoric into one of most fraught and complex currents of nineteenth-century black thought. On one hand, the religion that so many slaves and freed men and women regarded as an inexhaustible source of hope sustaining them through the otherwise unbearable experience of slavery, decreed that "the blood is the life." Yet a nineteenth-century scientific discourse of blood insisted that "black blood" was by no means a lifegiver. A high-stakes negotiation between scientific and sacred blood became a distinct feature of African American rhetoric and thought during the nineteenth century, as the appeal to blood by African American rhetoricians required a unique negotiation between salvific blood and the deterministic implications of blood as constructed through racial science. If the "life of the flesh is in the blood" and "it is the blood that maketh an atonement for the soul," as it is proclaimed in Leviticus, then African American Christians would find such scriptures to be problematic interpretive moments given the similarly deterministic slogans emerging from scientific racialism.

It should come as little surprise, then, that although African American political rhetoric relies heavily upon analogous readings of the Old Testament narrative of the Israelites' delivery from Egypt related in Exodus, African American redemptive blood rhetoric exhibits a decidedly New Testament derivation. If in the Old Testament blood demarcates the population of the chosen through the terms of the blood covenant between God and the Israelites and outlines the strict terms of the very practice of the faith through the injunctions of Leviticus, then the blood of the New Testament redeems and does so all-inclusively. Thus, while the ideology of scientific racialism flowed naturally from the delimiting blood of the Old Testament, the most prevalent biblical verse employed in abolitionist and antidiscrimination rhetoric throughout the eighteenth and nineteenth centuries comes from the New Testament book of Acts 17:26: "And he hath made of one blood all of the nations of the earth."

African American Christianity continued to hold blood sacred as a matter of faith, and if anything, because African Americans were considered as biologically inferior by virtue of their blood, the saving power of Christ's blood meant all the more to them as a political and rhetorical touchstone. Indeed black Christians may have been more devoted to the principle of blood's salvation than any other religious group in nineteenth-century America, because blood was not only the substance of their salvation as part of Christ's saving of all of mankind, but because they believed in this blood as the substance of a salvation to become manifested in the present moment in the form of the deliverance from slavery. Since the image of blood is so critical to the belief in and practice of Christianity, and because the rhetoric of blood has been so critical for the limitation and delimitation of African Americans, an African American rhetoric of blood emerges almost necessarily as a negotiation between these two lines of thought, such that, ultimately, if there is a uniquely African American Christianity (of course, there is), then there is also a uniquely African American rhetoric of racial blood.

During the nineteenth century, Frances Harper was among the champions of an African American rhetoric of racial blood. As we will see, her arguments for African American uplift were rooted in an awareness of the power of blood to shape character and identity. But the function of blood in her racial and political philosophy cannot be described in terms of an appropriation of the idioms of science limited to the refutation of scientific racism, as Nancy Stepan suggests in her reading of other African American writers from the period. Harper certainly welcomed the opportunity to combat scientific notions of black inferiority, and she stayed abreast of the contemporary discourse of racial science produced during her era. In her 1875 speech "The Great Problem to be Solved," for example, Harper observes that "Ethnologists may differ about the origin of the human race. [Thomas Henry] Huxley may search for it in protoplasms, and Darwin send for the missing links, but there is one thing of which we may rest assured—that we all come from the living God and that He is the common Father" (*BCD* 220). But unlike her contemporary Pauline Hopkins (an advocate of the "one blood" mantra and principle), Harper held no aspirations toward ethnological study.

Instead, as debates over the question of human origins were raging in the late 1850s, Harper was publishing her essay "Christianity" (1857), in which she declares Christianity a "system so uniform, exalted and pure, that the loftiest intellects have acknowledged its influence, and acquiesced in the justness of its claims" (*BCD* 96–97). Published amidst the height of the ethnological debates on human origins—squarely between the publication of Nott and Gliddon's polygenist manifesto *Types of Mankind* (1854) and the publication of Darwin's *On the Origin of Species* (1859)—Harper's essay on "Christianity" indirectly commented upon such debates and effectively dismissed the combatants from the field, claiming that the knowledge provided by faith trumped all other modes of human inquiry, including natural philosophy and the biological sciences traditionally devoted to resolving questions of race. "Philosophy and science have paused amid their speculative researches and wondrous revelations, to gain wisdom from [Christianity's] teachings and knowledge from her precepts" (97).

Harper was raised within and led a life dedicated to the nineteenth-century African Methodist Episcopal Church. While little is known of the religious affiliation of her parents, her close friend and first biographer William Still records that the young Frances Watkins (born free in Baltimore in 1825) spent her formative early years within the social and educational structure of the A.M.E. Orphaned at the age of three, Frances was raised first by an aunt and then by her uncle the Reverend William Watkins, a pillar of Baltimore's African American Methodist community and a teacher in a school for free blacks. She was educated and trained in the A.M.E.-affiliated school founded by her uncle, The William Watkins Academy for Negro Youth, "well known for its emphasis on biblical studies" and its emphasis on "high academic standards and Christian service." Here "the Bible was read daily, Greek and Latin were a major part of the curriculum, and discipline was strict" (*BCD* 7). Frances studied at the Watkins School until 1839 and, around 1850, left the South for Ohio, where she would continue to serve within the A.M.E. Church as the first female teacher at Union Seminary, which had been established in 1844 by the Ohio Conference of the A.M.E. (later to become Wilberforce University). In 1852, Frances moved again to fulfill a teaching position in Little York, Pennsylvania where she first became involved with the abolition movement. Later in the 1870s, Still would recall the woman he had met two decades earlier. "Her mind being of a strictly religious caste," he recalled, "the effusions from her pen all savor of a highly moral and elevating tone" (Still 756).

Given Harper's deep and lifelong engagement with African American church life and theology, the influence of religious experience should be considered a key frame of reference for interpreting the contours of her literary work, including her frequent references to blood, one of the central images of the Christianity she practiced daily. The literary and political use of blood imagery and racial blood rhetoric in her work can only be fully explicated within the context of blood as a symbol in the African American Methodism she practiced and tirelessly promoted. We cannot parse the racial implications of Harper's blood rhetoric without considering the extent to which her understanding of the relationships between blood and identity, blood and character, and blood and morality were less likely informed by racialist scientific theories and more by her own understanding of the image and symbol of blood in Christian iconography and theology. Committed as she was to the interdevelopment of racial theory with black feminist and Christian politics, Harper would synthesize her rhetoric of their advocacy through the image of a sacrificial blood that would become perhaps the most prevalently image recurring through four decades of her poetry, fiction, speeches, and letters.

Like the broader denomination of American Methodism from which it separated during the late eighteenth century, the African Methodist Episcopal faith that Harper practiced placed its own due emphasis upon the sacred nature of blood. Harper's articulation of her political philosophy of reform through images of blood and acts of sacrifice can be viewed within the context of Methodism's departure from the Calvinistic doctrine of predestination. According to the historian of religion Sydney Ahlstrom, John Wesley's "most original contribution to Protestant theology" was a "doctrine of Christian perfection" that allowed for agency in one's own salvation through a synthesis of grace and the "second blessing" of an attained sanctification (326). Although African American Methodism had separated from the Methodist establishment due to racism within the church, the A.M.E. Church retained many of the tenets of Wesleyan Methodist theology, inspired by a faith that provided an avenue for the redemption of all sinners regardless of race, class, creed, or color, and a theological basis for social reform. African American Methodist reformers such as Harper could easily view their reform efforts as working in tandem with their faith, since "Through a dynamic interaction of divine grace and human will the Christian could and should respond to the scriptural bidding, 'Let us go on to perfection'" (Ahlstrom 326).

Christ's blood served as the symbol of this attainable perfection, and within this context Harper drew often from the imagery of sacrificial blood for her literary art and political rhetoric. "To man, guilty, fallen and degraded man, [Christianity] shows a fountain drawn from the Redeemer's veins; there she bids him wash and be clean," she writes in "Christianity" (*BCD* 97). References to Christ's blood appear not only throughout Harper's explicitly religious statements but also her articulations of social theory and political argument. The "word of God" was as much the cure now, in the late nineteenth century, as it ever had been for "this material world" (98). Harper's political ethos, an ethos of individual and social sacrifice, was motivated by her vision of a post-Lapsarian world in which her emblematic Christian continued to find all of mankind "stained by transgression and defiled with guilt, and directs him to the 'blood that cleanseth from all unrighteousness and sin.' It finds him athirst and faint, pining amid the deserts of life, and shows him the wells of salvation and the rivers of life" (98). In Harper's view, a renewed meditation on Christ's sacrificial blood was sorely needed in the face of the driving materialism promoted by a rising capitalism, which, in her view, threatened to overtake the socially minded interest cultivated within the African American community.

As Harper takes every opportunity to remind her readers of the principle of sacrifice underwriting her social reform, the Christ that appears so often in her writing is most often depicted amidst the "pathos from the agony of Gethsemane and the sufferings of Calvary," forever placed in the geography of his final hours (*BCD* 97). Images of a crucified and bleeding Christ, always numerous in Harper's work, become more frequent in her poetry from the 1890s, during which Harper offered the power of Christ's blood as a force from which to draw energy in the battle for civil rights retracted after Reconstruction. "In these days of doubt and error," she writes in her poem "The Resurrection of Jesus" (1893), "In the conflict for the right, / May our hearts be ever strengthened / By the resurrection's might" (*BCD* 332–33). Here Harper finds parallels in Christ's suffering upon the cross and the plight of post-Reconstruction-era African Americans. By the early 1890s, African Americans could see the coming onslaught against their civil rights, if not their very existence, and very well might have identified with the pitiable figure in Harper's "Christ's Entry into Jerusalem" (1893). They too could see the "storms of hatred" breaking around them as Christ had as he was led to the cross, but Harper's poem encourages them to view their burden as Christ did, the "cross of shame transfigured / To a throne of love and light" (*BCD* 330). Like the Christ depicted in the poem, African Americans should experience the "Joy to know his soul's deep travail / Should not be a thing in vain, / And that joy and peace should blossom / From his agonizing pain" (330).

As she repeatedly placed Christ's bleeding body on display for her readers' contemplation, Harper urged them to enact as best they could what she refers to in "A Factor in Human Progress" as the "spirit of self-surrender" in their daily lives by performing individual acts of sacrifice and self-denial that were, in her view, the engine of social change (*BCD* 279). If Christ's blood served as the symbol of such sacrifice, then martyrs—those willing to give their lives for others—embodied this spirit of self-surrender through acts of self-abnegation. Christ's divine act could, of course, not be emulated, but other biblical and historical acts of martyrdom demonstrated the lengths to which individual sinners could go in their own devotion to the principle underlying Christ's purposeful suffering. Harper thus populates her poetry and fiction with biblical, historical, and fictional martyrs, not to encourage her readers toward their own literal acts of martyrdom but rather to provide models for social reform based on sacrifice. She valorizes martyrs in her fiction as those willing to bleed—sometimes literally, sometimes only figuratively—and ultimately to die in order to inspire others toward progressive change.

Harper's martyrdom poems—an identifiable subset of the many poems she would write about death—analyze the psychological construction, impact, political value, and existential nature of the decision to die for a cause. She dramatizes the making of martyrs in such poems as "A Mother's Heroism" (1854), a historical poem exploring the political and psychological narrative of martyrdom through the consciousness of Elizabeth Pattee Lovejoy. Elizabeth was the mother of the Illinois abolitionist Elijah Parish Lovejoy, editor of the *Alton Observer*, who was notoriously murdered in 1837 for criticizing a judge's lenient ruling in a case against a mob of whites accused of burning a black man alive (Franklin and Moss 198). (Lovejoy's death became an abolitionist cause celebre with the publication of a popular account of his life and death written by brothers Joseph and Owen in 1838.) Beyond memorializing Elijah Lovejoy, Harper depicts the consciousness of Elizabeth Lovejoy as she comes to terms with the meaning of her son's death.

Containing virtually no dramatic action, the poem is concerned less with the tragic events of Elijah's murder than with the process through which Elizabeth embraces his death in response to unidentified voices framing his death in a martyrdom narrative. "They told her how he'd spent his breath / In pleading for the dumb, / And how the glorious martyr wreath / Her child had nobly won" (*BCD* 71). The poem's psychological climax comes in the moment that Elizabeth accepts her son's death. "''T is well! 't is well!' the mother said, / That thus my child should die'" (72). Elizabeth's act of heroism lies in her transcendent acceptance of and participation in the construction of a martyrdom narrative to frame and redefine Elijah's death, taking command of her son's legacy and preventing him from being remembered as yet another victim of proslavery violence. Instead, she renders her son an agent of his own death, effectively returning the agency deprived him by the slaying mob, choosing to imagine her son not as a murdered man whose life has been brutally and unfairly taken, but instead as one who had deliberately "yielded up his life" (71). In this retelling, Elijah chooses death and "had nerved himself to die, / In battling for the right" (71). This martyrdom narrative functions as Elizabeth's own psychological comfort, as it is only through the belief that her son has died for a cause that Elizabeth can achieve a state of contentment. As the poem's title suggests, while the death and its rationale (resistance to injustice) belong to the dead son, the heroism is shared by Elizabeth Lovejoy through her act of accepting his death as an act of martyrdom.

The epigraph prefacing Harper's martyrdom poem "The Tennessee Hero" (1857)—"He had heard his comrades plotting to obtain their liberty, and rather than betray them he received 750 lashes and died"—emphasizes the act of deliberate choice at the core of martyrdom acts, as the poem reflects on the effect of a martyr's death on the cause for which he or she ostensibly dies (*BCD* 79). "The Tennessee Hero" dramatizes the final moments of an unnamed figure cornered by a "savage throng" and asked to divulge the identities of "his comrades plotting to obtain their liberty" (79). The hero's captors make his choice clear for him and for the reader: name the coconspirators and "life thy gain shall be!" but his response comes with equal clarity, "'death and torture I defy, / Ere I betray that band'" (80). Providing little further dramatic context, the poem isolates the hero's final choice to reveal the grammar underlying martyrdom's implicit argument. "Yes, rather than betray his trust, / He'd meet a death of pain; / 'T was sweeter far to meet it thus / Than wear a treason stain!" (80). As the poem dramatizes, acts of martyrdom work through a transference of meaning akin to that enacted through the use of metaphor, bringing death and the principle for which the martyr dies into a cognitive relationship with each other for the benefit of the martyr's survivors. The meanings of the martyr's death and the import of the cause itself for which the martyr sacrifices life mutually construct each other. Through this grammar, every act of martyrdom makes an implicit argument, intensely dramatic and poetic in its finality: the balance of human life against a principle signifies the denial of that principle as akin to death.

The psychological and political energies of acts of martyrdom explored in these poems would come to characterize and define the activist edge of Harper's own brand of sentimentalism. Although known for her own investments in this literary mode, Harper increasingly came to regard sentimentalism as a relatively passive strategy of persuasion and turned to representations of martyrdom to solicit feeling while also provoking her readers toward action. Harper's martyrdom poems thus emphasize the effect that self-sacrificial acts have in mobilizing others toward acts of social change. Such depictions of death distinguish Harper's sentimentalism from that of such figures as Harriet

Beecher Stowe, a figure Harper nonetheless greatly admired, whose political ethics and literary style have often been compared with Harper's. Although Harper would publish several poems in the 1850s praising Stowe and her novel *Uncle Tom's Cabin* ("To Mrs. Harriet Beecher Stowe," "Eliza Harris," and "Eva's Farewell" all appeared in *Poems* in 1854), she would soon begin to articulate her own preference for a literary activism set against the solicitation of emotion. In "Be Active" (published in *Frederick Douglass's Paper* in 1856 and *Weekly Anglo-African* in 1859), Harper eschews bare emotional response in favor of political action. When encountering victims of oppression the "sons of freedom" should "Sit not down with idle pity / Gazing on [the victim's] mighty wrong; Hurl the bloated tyrant from him— / Say my brother, oh, be strong" and "Set to work the moral forces / That are yours of church and state" (*BCD* 76–77). Harper viewed martyrdom narratives in particular as ideal inspirations toward such action beyond feeling, as the martyr's death was not only an event to be lamented but also an expression of the worthiness of the martyr's cause for the attention and active devotion of the martyr's surviving supporters.

Harper's representations of acts of martyrdom as transformative calls to action were informed by her own experiences with life-altering, motivating deaths. In her speeches, essays, and correspondence, Harper would describe several of her own experiences with death as formative moments of personal development. At the age of three, she was orphaned after losing her mother, the emotional impact of which she conveyed years later in a letter to friend William Still. "'Have I yearned for a mother's love? The grave was my robber. Before three years had scattered their blight around my path, death had won my mother from me. Would the strong arm of a brother have been welcome? I was my mother's only child'" (Still 755). In this autobiographical act related through a private letter, Harper's lament serves as the author's claim to a certain authority by virtue of experience. Unlike Stowe, Harper would be fortunate enough never to experience the death of a young child (a considerably common loss for many nineteenth-century women), and thus could not draw from a mother's personal experience for the dramatizations of maternal loss in her sentimental poetry and fiction.[4] But the loss of her mother provided Harper with experience from which to dramatize maternal loss from the perspective of the child survivor.

Although she never lost a young child to death, Harper experienced the severing of her own maternal bond when she was separated from her stepchildren following the death of her husband Fenton in 1864. As Frances Watkins, she had not married until the relatively late age of thirty-five (likely due in part to the demands of her intense work schedule) and had only been married for four years when Fenton passed away, devastating her emotionally and financially. In her 1866 speech "We Are All Bound Up Together," Harper makes "heuristic use of her own disenfranchisement," recalling this period as one in which "great sorrow had fallen upon my life" and also as a moment of great awakening and a rise in self-consciousness that sharpened her analysis of the identity politics of her era (Stancliff 55; *BCD* 217). Upon her husband's death, the house and small farm the couple shared in Ohio were interned, and Harper was left financially destitute and in charge of four small children: her own daughter Mary and three others from Fenton's previous marriage (Boyd 54; *BCD* 217). Harper was forced to leave Ohio and return to Pennsylvania with only one of her children, her biological daughter Mary. "I tried to keep my children together. But my husband died in debt, and before he had been in his grave three months, the administration had swept the very milk-crocks and wash tubs from my hands" (*BCD* 217).

In recounting this difficult period, Harper aims for more than the evocation of sympathy. Delivering this speech before the Eleventh Women's Rights Convention at the height of the debate over the ratification of the Fifteenth Amendment, Harper relates her husband's death and its impact on the structure of her family and the trajectory of her life as an experience that convinced her (despite the racial divide becoming increasingly apparent in the feminist movement) that the issues and experiences of black and white women were (as the title of the speech suggests) "Bound Up Together." The impact of her husband's death provides a personal example of Harper's awakening to what would later come to be recognized as the "intersectionality" of race, class, and gender. "Born of a race whose inheritance has been outrage and wrong, most of my life has been spent in battling against those wrongs. But I did not feel as keenly as others, that I had these rights, in common with other women, which are now demanded" (*BCD* 217). The insecurity of her class status becomes apparent upon her husband's death as Harper finds herself determined by the social restrictions placed upon her as an African American woman. "I was a farmer's wife and had made butter for the Columbus market; but what could I do, when they had swept all away? . . . Had I died instead of my husband, how different would have been the result! By this time he would have another wife . . . and no administrator would have gone into his house, broken up his home, and sold his bed, and taken away his means of support" (217). Although she had been born a free black woman, her husband's death starkly reveals the tenuousness of her class status and its dependency upon her legal connection with him while simultaneously awakening her to the relative security guaranteed by racial bonds.

Although her marital connection could not protect her against a double standard in terms of financial independence, the bond of race served as a safety net in this time of need. Harper thus gained simultaneous firsthand experience of the tenuousness of mortality as well as the dramatic change in circumstances resulting from her husband's death, a particularly life-altering event for nineteenth-century African American women whose economic statuses were so often dependent upon their husbands. Harper turned the psychological and political implications of such personal tragedy into literary art by incorporating the raising of consciousness through death into the plots of her best-known works, particularly "The Two Offers" (1859) and *Iola Leroy* (1892).

By Harper's own account, the death of a slave she never met would change her life yet again and motivate her toward her career as an avid social reformer. Although born free to a financially secure northeastern black family, Harper chose to sacrifice the comforts of her life for the rigors of the abolitionist cause after learning of the plight of a slave who died in his own attempt to escape. In the years immediately following the loss of her husband, Harper found work as a teacher in Little York, Pennsylvania but was left pondering, in William Still's words, "how she could best promote the welfare of her race" (Still 757). Entering the teaching profession seemed admirable and desirable (Harper would spend much of her life as a teacher and wrote extensively on the subject of African American education), but as Still relates, upon learning of the 1853 death of a fugitive slave, Harper was "moved to enter the Anti-Slavery field as a lecturer" (Still 757). Soon after Maryland passed a law banning free blacks from entering the state, Harper became aware of a free black Maryland man sold to Georgia who died during his attempt to escape. The episode provided another death whose significance for Harper again altered the trajectory of her life and career. As she reportedly wrote to a friend: "'Upon that grave I pledged myself to the Anti-Slavery cause'" (Still 758).

Taken from Still's 1872 biographical sketch in *The Underground Railroad* (still the primary source for details of Harper's biography), this somewhat novelistic autobiographical episode—reminiscent of so many scenes of slave traders turned devoted abolitionists as depicted in antislavery literature—has become part of the lore of Frances Harper, appearing as a frequent set piece in biographical accounts as the moment that "made" Frances Harper. In Still's own narrative, the moment provides the turning point from which the "little known . . . young and homeless maiden" becomes transformed into "one of the most liberal contributors, as well as one of the ablest advocates of the Underground Rail Road and of the slave" (Still 758, 755). Harper soon moved to Philadelphia, where "She visited the Anti-Slavery Office and read Anti-Slavery documents with great avidity; in the mean time making her home at the station of the Underground Rail Road, where she frequently saw passengers and heard their melting tales of suffering and wrong, which intensely increased her sympathy in their behalf" (Still 758). The autobiographical truth of such a dramatic professional conversion narrative remains difficult to assess, but whether influenced by her own life-altering experiences with death or by virtue of her personal commitment to the practice of her faith, Harper dramatized death's power to transform the living as a dominant theme in her work. She drew from these personal experiences to construct martyrdom narratives in verse and prose that modeled responses to a loved one's death as a way for turning loss into gain.

But it would be the life and death of nineteenth-century America's famous martyr, the antislavery crusader John Brown, that would galvanize Harper's representations of martyrdom and shape her reflections on the philosophy of self-denial which she would develop in *Iola Leroy*. Harper knew John Brown personally and tended to his family while Brown awaited execution for his raid on Union Army munitions at Harper's Ferry, Virginia in 1859. William Still recalls how Harper "passed two weeks with Mrs. Brown at [Still's] house . . . while she was awaiting the execution of her husband, and sympathized with her most deeply" (Still 762). Harper, now a veteran antislavery lecturer, found renewed passion for her primary cause and rededicated herself anew. "Scarcely was it possible," wrote Still, "for a living soul to be more deeply affected than this female advocate. Nor did her sympathies end in mere words. She tendered material aid as well as heartfelt commiseration" (762). During her experience at Brown's side, Harper (like the Elizabeth Lovejoy of her poem) participated in the construction of Brown's martyrdom legacy. With Brown's execution pending, Harper wrote a series of letters to Brown's wife, his coconspirators, and Brown himself. These letters articulate Harper's developing theory on the political function of martyrdom, and they give insight into Harper's process of synthesizing her own political activism with the terms of her Christian faith as she reconciles Brown's cause, the violence with which he pursued it, and the potential impact of his fate on interracial politics.

Harper's letter to Mary Brown, whom she calls "the noble wife of the hero of the nineteenth century," articulates the author's vision of martyrdom as a synthesis of activism and what Jane Tompkins has called "sentimental power."[5] In the letter, Harper says little to assure Mary of the righteousness, ethics, or bravery of her husband's raid, choosing instead to construct meaning from Brown's imminent death. For Harper, Brown's martyrdom becomes an event demonstrating the limits of sympathy. "In an hour like this," she acknowledges in opening, "the common words of sympathy may seem like idle words . . ." (*BCD* 48). Any effort to identify with Mary's pain may seem hollow, but Harper seeks to console Mary by drawing her attention to the possible benefit of her husband's death, a benefit that will come not in the extension of "sympathy" or "idle words" but rather in the change effected by his death through the actions taken by others in its aftermath. "Our heart may grow more hopeful for humanity when it sees the sublime sacrifice it is about to receive from his hands. Not in vain has your dear husband periled all, if the martyrdom of one hero is worth more than the life of a million cowards" (48). Harper accepts the practical failure of Brown's raid but suggests this failure is ultimately inconsequential in light of the revolution that will be sparked by his execution. Brown's death will serve as a call to arms, engendering a newly dedicated army of antislavery foot soldiers of which Harper views herself as a willing member. In losing her husband, Brown's wife has made her own sacrifice, and Harper resolves to repay that debt in any way she can by dedicating herself to Mary. "If there is one thing on earth I can do for you or yours," Harper writes in closing, "let me be apprized. I am at your service" (49).

Harper thus immediately recognized the unique symbolic possibilities of Brown's death and its potential for elaboration through her own brand of Christian abolitionist philosophy and rhetoric. As she wrote in her letter to Brown himself, Harper hoped "that from your sad fate great good may arise to the cause of freedom" (*BCD* 49). Despite the comparisons that Harper often made between the soul-saving effect of Christ's death and the politically mobilizing effect of Brown's, she was far too devout to conflate Brown's violence with Christ's submission. Yet as a galvanizing event, Brown's death fell squarely in line with Harper's own Christian antislavery ethos. "We may earnestly hope that your fate will not be a vain lesson," she writes, "that it will intensify our hatred of Slavery and love of freedom, and that your martyr grave will be a sacred altar upon which men will record their vows of undying hatred to that system which tramples on man and bids defiance to God" (49–50). Although Brown expressly denied the incitement of slave insurrection as the intent of his raid, his death nevertheless did reenergize the abolitionist movement in the late 1850s.[6] Moreover, in the moral logic of the martyrdom narrative that Harper participated in constructing, Brown's death endorsed the violence by which he had died. Like other martyrs before him, including Christ, Brown had sanctified the means of his death with his own blood. "The hemlock is distilled with victory when it is pressed to the lips of Socrates. The Cross becomes a glorious ensign when Calvary's page-browed sufferer yields up his life upon it. And, if Universal Freedom is ever to be the dominant power of the land, your bodies may be only her first stepping stones to dominion," Harper writes (49).

Brown's death not only provided an inspirational act of martyrdom for political purpose but also a dramatic narrative through which Harper would forge an ethos of interracial unity. Like Brown himself, Harper realized the critical function which Brown's race played in the legacy of martyrdom that quickly obscured Brown the historical man behind an impenetrable mythology. Regardless of Brown's actual motives or the true historical reach and impact of his actions on the material lives of African Americans, Brown's martyrdom would be heralded as a historic act of interracial sympathy. Brown himself underscored this aspect of his actions when commenting on his punishment during his famous court speech. Here Brown suggested that it was not the violence for which he was being put to death but rather the interracial sympathy motivating his act: "[H]ad I so interfered in behalf of the rich, the powerful, the intelligent, the so-called great, or in behalf of any of their friends—either father, mother, brother, sister, wife, or children, or any of that class—and suffered and sacrificed what I have in this interference, it would have been all right; and every man in this court would have deemed it an act worthy of reward rather than punishment" (Ruchames 126). The interracial dimension of the event, the spectacle of a white man putting his life on the line for black slaves, would become a central theme of later reflections upon Brown's legacy. Frederick Douglass would describe Brown's willingness to die for black slaves as the "true glory of John Brown's mission" and "the key to the whole life and career of the man" (Douglass 61). "It was not Caucasian for Caucasian—," Douglass claimed, "white man for white man; not rich man for rich man, but Caucasian for Ethiopian—white man for black man—rich man for poor man—the man admitted and respected, for the man despised and rejected" (61). This spirit of interracial sympathy underwriting Brown's sacrifice would be mentioned with deeply appreciative solemnity in many remembrances of Brown by African

American commentators throughout the nineteenth and twentieth centuries as Brown's seeming identification with the African American community became part and parcel of the meaning of his death. Such memorials often suggested that, in dying for blacks, Brown had somehow become closer to them—one with them, if not actually one of them. Echoing the sentiments of such notable black nationalist thinkers influenced by Brown's legacy as W.E.B. Du Bois, H. Rap Brown, Eldridge Cleaver, and Malcolm X, the African American historian Lerone Bennett would articulate, in his own seemingly hyperbolic assessment, the profound level of interracial identification Brown was believed by many to have achieved. "There was in John Brown a complete identification with the oppressed. . . . It was not happening to Negroes; it was happening to him. . . . John Brown *was* a Negro, and it was in this aspect that he suffered" (*qtd. in* Reynolds 504).

During her own experience with Brown, Harper would express a similar appreciation for this interracial sympathy in her letter to Brown's wife. Identifying herself as among the class of people for whom Brown had effectively given his life, Harper seems genuinely humbled by the actions committed by one of those who took on the suffering of the oppressed class to which she belonged. "Belonging to the race your dear husband reached forth his hand to assist, I need not tell you that my sympathies are with you" (*BCD* 48). In a similar vein, Harper would write in her letter to Brown, "In the name of the young girl sold from the warm clasp of a mother's arms . . . in the name of the slave mother . . . I thank you, that you have been brave enough to reach out your hands to the crushed and blighted of my race" (49). When she refers to Brown's act of antislavery violence as the "first stepping stones" in the "dominion" of "Universal Freedom," Harper does not mean to suggest that Brown's blow against slavery had truly been the first (Harper was of course well aware of the long history of black antislavery activism). As a radical act of antislavery aggression in the context of Nat Turner and other pre–Civil War slave rebellions, Brown's raid was not unique. But in the eyes of many slaves and free blacks, Brown's had been the first act to vividly demonstrate a true commitment to ending slavery on the part of white America. The interracial sympathy that his raid symbolized is the core of Brown's legacy—indeed, it is his legacy. Brown biographer David Reynolds goes so far as to suggest that "Brown's violent actions seem aberrant and insane if torn from their racial referents. Without the racial factor, Pottawatomie seems like heartless butchery and Harper's Ferry appears inane and quixotic. With the racial factor, both make sense" (505).

Brown's sacrifice was considered all the more extraordinary because it was made in behalf of a race of people to which he not only did not belong but, by virtue of his own guaranteed property in whiteness, from whose enslavement he had actually benefited (whether he was at peace with the enjoyment of those benefits or not). In this respect, Brown was not only viewed as dying for others, he was viewed as dying for *others*. "'Heroes of other days died for their own rights,'" the abolitionist Wendell Phillips would declare after Brown's death. "'John Brown died for a race in whose blood he had no share'" (*qtd. in* Nudelman 23). But as an expression of "white" rage against an institution that denigrated blacks, Brown's death carried him to the limits of interracial sympathy. In Brown's own view, his violent action and certain death authorized and sanctified his own sympathy for black slaves and their plight. He would earn an otherwise inconceivable interracial identification with his own blood. But by becoming a martyr for this cause, Brown had ironically revealed the impenetrability of what Harper's character Iola Leroy would call the "insurmountable barriers" between the races. Brown had effectively demonstrated the difficulty of achieving such interracial identification by virtue of the lengths to which he had to go, self-immolating himself in the name of achieving this interracial sympathy. Even if Brown had effectively crossed the color line (as some commentators suggested), this interracial identification could be achieved only through his own death, only through his own willful self-elimination. Despite the suggestions of later commentators that Brown had become some kind of honorary member of the African American community, no act of, course—not even martyrdom—could make Brown black.

But as Frances Harper considered the implications of Brown's legacy of interracial sympathy, his self-abnegating death provided her with a complex new model for approaching the representation of racial intermixture and racial passing. Brown's act of martyrdom had been based in a racial sympathy consecrated by his own blood spilled through violence; his death expressed a political argument in which an interracial bond could be formed through the spilling of blood between others, for others. Brown had insisted at his trial, "if it is deemed necessary that I should forfeit my life for the furtherance of the ends of justice, and mingle my blood further with the blood of my children and with the blood of millions in this slave country whose rights are disregarded by wicked, cruel, and unjust enactments—I submit; so let it be done!" (Ruchames 126). As Franny Nudelman reads these words in her perceptive cultural study of Brown: "Brown used the figure of blood to ally his extraordinary fate with the routine of abused slaves. . . . Combining his lifeblood with the 'blood of millions,' Brown participates in, and radicalizes, a tradition of abolitionist sympathy that dramatizes slave suffering in an effort to mobilize readers" (18). But in a reversal of the detrimental effects to be feared through interracial mixture in the scientific statements of figures such as Frederick Hoffman, Brown's language of mingling his blood with the blood of others also suggested a kind of symbolic miscegenation.

Whether or not Harper fixated on these particular words of Brown's, the interracial dimension of his martyrdom could not help but make an impression on the development of Harper's radical Christian abolitionism, interrelated as it was with her theories of race and interracial mixture. Moreover, Brown's death would prompt Harper toward a more abstract consideration of the relationship between the martyr's renunciation of life and identity for the sake of others, and the cultivation of sympathy between the martyr and those for whom the martyr gave his or her life. With its suggestions of self-denial, Christian martyrdom, and miscegenation, Brown's act provided a conceptual matrix for Harper's ethic and aesthetics of racial sacrifice and a theory of martyrdom that she could use as a political ethos underlying her interracial plots. The martyrdom narratives circulating around Brown made his antislavery violence echo with images of Christ's sacrifice of blood, but in the context of the nation's interracial divide, Brown's sacrifice dramatized the racial and political implications of the deep self-denial required by such acts of sacrifice.

Harper drew political lessons from Brown's suicidal endeavor and translated the martyrdom narrative into the form of a didactic parable that she would repeat as the primary vehicle of her pedagogical literary style. She regarded Brown's death as an inspiring act to be remembered, but it was of course not an act that could reasonably be promoted for mass emulation. Harper did not go so far as to advocate for her readers the violent actions of self-immolation for a cause. Instead, she extracted the conceptual core of Brown's choice for her reader's consideration and installed the logic of this choice as the engine of her instructive literary plots. The racial politics of Brown's death provided a compelling approach to synthesizing the politics of racial passing with the narrative and ethos of sacrifice central to Harper's own Christian faith. While the violence of Brown's act certainly complicated the interpretation of Brown as a Christ figure, its interracial dimension within the context of a nineteenth-century racial discourse that posited the mutual exclusivity of races, provided a compelling historical application for the principle of Christian sacrifice. By giving up the legally and socially granted privileges of his own race —by abdicating the privilege in whiteness guaranteed to him by law and social custom—Brown had chosen, in the context of the period's racial binary, to stop being the social person who he was.

In Brown's willingness to relinquish the constructed fortune of his property in whiteness, Harper found a theme she could explore in her fictions of interracial romance as she interpreted such sacrifice as a transcendence of self with racial implications. By focusing on the severe choice of martyrdom—a self-*severing* rather than a self-*serving* choice—that Brown had made, Harper developed her own distinct ethos of self-sacrifice as a practical and politically active metaphor for martyrdom, a substitution for martyrdom in which agents of change could give up their lives for a cause and yet live on. Harper thus promoted self-sacrifice as martyrdom in a minor key—the end of one identity and the assumption of another—a martyrdom without death. Harper's self-sacrificing characters view themselves as martyrs, not giving up their physical life but rather all attachment to and performance of their former selves. Harper thus crafted her most laudable characters, culminating in her ultimate heroine, Iola Leroy, as those who effectively chose to kill themselves off—to kill the *self* off—by committing a suicide of identity in the name of advancing a social or racial cause.

"A Factor in Human Progress," published in the *African Methodist Episcopal Church Review* in 1886, is Harper's manifesto of self-sacrifice, the culmination of thoughts she had been developing and exploring through her fiction and poetry at least since the 1859 publication of "The Two Offers." Writing in response to a previous *Review* article imperatively advocating the advance of black education, Harper implores her audience to consider that such efforts will ultimately be worthless (and possibly even dangerous) without an accompanying moral education. "The culture of the moral and spiritual faculties is destined to play the most important part in our future development," Harper argues (*BCD* 275). In support of this claim, she traces the principle of sacrifice through the lives and teachings of the world's most influential religious and spiritual leaders, emphasizing their shared willingness to embrace adversity, public scorn, destitution, and poverty for larger social good. "On this subject of self-surrender for the sake of others, there has been a symphony of thought under different forms of religion and various phases of civilization" (278). Harper thus praises Buddha for exchanging "his princely station for a mendicant's position in his search for knowledge" and dedicating himself to spreading his teachings of the path toward enlightenment "although conscious that his teaching would bring opposition, neglect and scorn" (278). She extols the Roman figure of Curtius, who abdicated his "manhood" to leap into a chasm that threatened the city "by the surrender of his life" (278). And as always, Harper reserves her strongest reverence for Moses for "entreating God to forgive the sins of his people, or blot his name out of the book he had written. Was ever human love more tender and devoted than that which could forego God's remembrance for the sake of a people who could smite his ears with cruel murmurs, and be almost ready to stone him in their disappointed wrath?" (278). As she reflects upon this series of religious and historical figures embodying sacrifice, Harper deems this principle as the most necessary for African Americans during the post-Reconstruction moment; as the essay's title suggests, sacrifice is a most significant factor in black social progress because it has been such a factor in all of human progress.

By the latter part of the nineteenth century, Harper's devotion to the principle of sacrifice had come to full fruition, as she promoted sacrifice as the chief necessity for former slaves and the first generation of freed men and women to unify in preparation for the onslaught against racial equality marshaled especially by state and local governments during the post-Reconstruction era. The principle of sacrifice served as the civilizationist element of Harper's brand of black nationalism. "However low down a people may be in the scale of character and condition," she would write in "A Factor in Human Progress," "absorbed in providing for their physical wants, or steeped in sensuous gratifications, the moment their admiration is awakened and their aspirations kindled by the recital, or the example of deeds of high and holy worth, and the spirit of self-sacrifice and self-surrender for some good cause is awakened and developed, there comes in that race a dividing line between the sensuous and material, and the spiritual and progressive" (*BCD* 278). For Harper, this "dividing line between the sensuous and material, and the spiritual and progressive" was as much a racial dividing line as it was a moral one. Harper reminds her audience of the magnanimous acts of sacrifice committed with regularity by members of previous generations, and suggests these acts are a part of their own racial legacy. "During the days of slavery we read of a man who knew the plan of some of his fellow slaves to obtain their freedom, but rather than betray them, he received seven hundred and fifty lashes, and died" (279). Here Harper relates the true story of sacrifice that she would later adapt for the aforementioned scene in *Iola Leroy*. "Among the annals of the civil war is the story of a colored man who was in a boat which became stranded, and there was a lack of strength to shove her from the sand, unless some one would expose himself to the fire of rebel bullets" (279–80). Facing "danger and death" to save his comrades, the man "received a number of bullets, and died" (280). These stories of sacrifice during slavery were designed to assure the current generation of African Americans that a propensity for sacrifice resided within them—that this propensity for sacrifice was part of their racial inheritance. "Nor has this spirit of self-devotion been only confirmed to the strongest races of the earth," Harper wrote, but it could and must be cultivated by the current generations of the disenfranchised (279). "Who shall say that the race out of which such men could spring from under the dark shadow of slavery has not within it the elements out of which a great people may yet be produced?" (280).

Harper's ideology of Christian sacrifice emerges as a critical element of her own distinctive negotiation between reformist ideology and the terms of nineteenth-century hereditary science. Like her contemporary Mark Twain, Harper was fascinated with the problem of individual character reform in the context of the increasing influence of hereditary science. Harper accepted Darwinism intellectually but, as a committed social reformer, sought ways to balance the force of inheritance with her own belief in the possibility for the individual cultivation of character. In her 1885 vision of an "Enlightened Motherhood," Harper describes her model of the enlightened female caregiver of the nation's youngest and most impressionable as a mother knowledgeable of the limits and possibilities of characterological conditioning. As those traditionally charged with raising society's children, Harper argues, mothers should make a special effort to stay abreast of the current science concerning the relative effects of heredity and environment. After all, she writes, "God has trusted her with a child, and it is her privilege to help that child develop the most precious thing a man or woman can possess on earth, and that is a good character" (*BCD* 287). Harper briefs mothers on contemporary scientific debates in preparation for their influential role. "Among the things I would present for the enlightenment of mothers are attention to the laws of heredity and environment" (289). Her message to mothers is a sober warning. Conditioning and training provided within the home may be employed to rectify flaws in character developed after birth, but Harper believes there exists only a narrow window for overcoming the "fearful legacy" of poor inheritance. "For stolen money and slandered character we may make reparation, but the opportunity of putting the right stamp on an antenatal life, if once gone, is gone forever; and there never was an angel of God, however bright, terrible, or strong he may be, who was ever strong enough to roll away the stone from the grave of a dead opportunity" (289). Instead of simply conceding the battle for character to the deterministic forces of nature, Harper proposes that mothers, as reform leaders, inquire into the problem of what they can do given these limitations. "Would it not be well for us women to introduce into all of our literary circles, for the purpose of gaining knowledge, topics on this subject of heredity and the influence of good and bad conditions upon the home life of the race, and study this subject in the light of science for our own and the benefit of others?" (290). Far from suggesting the strength of environmental forces over inheritance, Harper advocates strongly for the reform of character because in heredity she claims to have understood what mothers were up against.

Sacrifice provided Harper with a concept by which to negotiate her acceptance of Darwinian science with her steadfast belief in the possibilities of individual and social reform. For although she was committed to such programs of reform (as evidenced by her lifelong involvements in abolitionism, the women's movement, and the temperance campaign), Harper never considered dispensing with the notion of hereditary character, even though this concept was central to the deterministic ideologies of race she opposed. Indeed, Harper's own brand of African American exceptionalism relied upon a notion of hereditary character. "We are living in the midst of a people who have in their veins the blood of some of the strongest nations on earth . . ." she wrote in "A Factor in Human Progress" (*BCD* 276). Like Du Bois, Harper sought to conserve the notion of race even as she explored ways of thinking about racial bonds that transcended definitions based merely on family lineages or physical morphology. Harper employed the concept of sacrifice to synthesize Darwinian science with her own faith and to conserve African American racial distinctiveness without gross determinism. "Men may boast of the aristocracy of blood; they may glory in the aristocracy of talent, and be proud of the aristocracy of wealth, but there is an aristocracy which must ever outrank them all, and that is an aristocracy of character" (292). As we shall see, Harper's political ethos develops through a kind of Christian existentialism, dramatized in her work by scenes in which characters make formative decisions shaping and revealing their moral development. In such quintessential moments of Harper's work, characters offered the opportunity for lives of ease and comfort instead choose suffering. Here it should be recognized that the biblical model for such moments is Moses, "a key figure in Harper's personal mythology," the figure whom Harper regarded as the paragon of self-denial and socially minded self-sacrifice, and "continually called for more women and men to emulate" throughout her literary career (*BCD* 135). While Moses had long symbolized the promise of deliverance from bondage in abolitionist rhetoric by virtue of his role in the Exodus narrative, Harper's valorization of Moses is based more on his propensity for sacrifice. As Frances Smith Foster notes, between the 1856 publication of "The Burial of Moses" and the 1869 publication of *Moses: A Story of the Nile*, Harper rediscovered Moses's value; Foster suggests that "the ambivalence of the Reconstruction Era during which the second work was created may have influenced Harper's increased emphasis upon individual sacrifice and personal commitment to a common human cause" (37).

Within this context, the Moses that Harper depicts is less the great emancipator and more the Moses that turns away a life of privilege to embrace a life of struggle and hardship with his people. "I like the character of Moses," Harper wrote in "Our Greatest Want" (1859). "He is the first disunionist we read of in the Jewish scriptures. The magnificence of Pharaoh's throne loomed up before his vision, its oriental splendors glittered before his eyes; but he turned from them all and chose rather to suffer with the enslaved, than rejoice with the free" (*BCD* 103). Harper's epic verse biography *Moses: A Story of the Nile* (1869) thus unfolds as a fictional manifesto of self-sacrifice. Moses leaves behind the Egyptian princess who adopted him as an orphan as he seeks to cast his lot with his own downtrodden people. "I go to join / The fortunes of my race, and to put aside / All other bright advantages, save / The approval of my conscience and the meed / Of rightly doing" (139). More than making the choice to rejoin his own people, Moses's deliberate choice to suffer (to "put aside / All other bright advantages") indicates his divergent communal purpose as distinct from that of the Egyptian family that has adopted him. While the princess has heard of ambitious men risking everything for a "throne" or some other "imagined good," she cannot fathom how Moses could willingly choose to abdicate fortune, much less out of the mere sense of allegiance to his people. "I / Never heard of men resigning ease for toil," she says. "The splendor of a palace for the squalor / Of a hut, and casting down a diadem / To wear a service badge" (144). Moses's choice is not only indicative of his character, it constitutes the action that separates him from his adopted family and binds him to his own. As the princess frankly admits, "I cannot comprehend thy choice" (144). Harper uses the story of Moses to help her readers comprehend this choice, the value of choosing suffering.

Years later, in "A Factor in Human Progress," Harper would reference Moses as the model for her post-Reconstruction audience to follow in the difficult decisions they faced as they collectively charted a path up from slavery. "Had Moses preferred the luxury of an Egyptian palace to the endurance of hardships with his people, would the Jews have been the race to whom we owe the most, not perhaps for science and art, but for the grandest of all sciences, the science of true life of joy and trust in God, of God-like forgiveness and divine self-surrender?" (*BCD* 279). Engaging in her own form of romantic racialism here, Harper praises Moses as an example for her late nineteenth-century African American audience of a figure who earns his racial citizenship through his "endurance of hardships with his people."

With Moses as a model, Harper stylized the narrative of his sacrifice into the device that characterizes her literary style. Repeatedly depicting characters who, in their daily lives, choose destitution over fortune in the name of a higher principle, Harper's pedagogical fiction urges her readers to employ self-sacrifice as a litmus test. All of life's major choices, including marital and occupational choices, should be considered as opportunities to deny the self or to regulate the desires of ego.

In "The Two Offers," Harper depicts marriage as a sacrificial choice that can only reach its ideal as "divine sacrament for the soul's development and human progression" when both parties deny their own individual urges toward self-indulgence and relinquish aspects of their own identities to forge a bond dedicated to Christian living and social progress (*BCD* 508). The deepest character flaw in Laura Lagrange's husband is not his intemperance but rather his unwillingness to do what character reform requires, practice self-denial, and rid himself of the addiction to drink so obviously destroying his marriage. He repeatedly fails to choose "home influences" over "unhealthy and unhallowed excitements" because the "pleasures of a well-regulated home, were enjoyments too tame for one who had vitiated his tastes by the pleasures of sin" (110). He cannot love because he cannot sacrifice. Such an abdication of self, the story suggests, is the very definition of love and why "intense love is often akin to intense suffering . . ." (109). The institution of marriage becomes the divinely sanctioned compact designed for the practice of self-denial as bonding one's self to another requires each individual to give up a portion of their own individuality for the advancement of a larger, socially beneficial good. Thus Janette's unmarried life becomes more satisfying than her cousin's married life because through Janette's dedication to the many social causes she adopts, including the antislavery movement, she finds avenues for practicing selflessness and had thus "learned one of life's most precious lessons, that true happiness consists not so much in the fruition of our wishes as in the regulation of desires and the full development and right culture of our whole natures" (114). Marriage for Harper was essentially a ritualized version of Christological sacrifice in which individuals transcend self through sacrifice.

Harper refigures the rhetoric of racial blood by applying the principle of sacrifice to the choice of passing, appropriating the standard passing narrative for the construction of pedagogical parables of self-denial. As Michael Borgstrom argues in his reading of *Iola Leroy*, Harper's narratives of post–Civil War black subjects choosing not to pass dramatized her call for more emphatic gestures of black unity. "To contend with the dominant culture's newly-stoked hostility toward blacks, cultural survival comes to depend less on covert alliances and more on open displays of racial unity. . . . After the war, whites routinely pathologized (black) cultural difference; in response, Harper's novel suggests that during Reconstruction blacks created community not by masking their political concerns but rather by publicly asserting their loyalties to race" (781). By mapping the narrative of sacrificial choice onto her narratives of interracial romance, Harper created her own distinct brand of passing narrative and redefined the underlying terms of the passer's choice between black and white "blood." In the context of the late nineteenth century, the color line offered the most effective field of reference for articulating Harper's belief in the progressive benefits of such self-denial. Framing the choice between blackness and whiteness as a choice between self-sacrifice and self-indulgence, Harper redefined racial passing into a vehicle for her brand of Christian existentialism. In this context, the races between which the passing character chooses are rendered less biological categories or social constructions than opportunities for self-determination.

Harper valorized acts of self-sacrifice as personal acts of identity martyrdom and as one of the centripetal forces of racial affiliation. As they choose between blackness and whiteness, Harper's characters consecrate the value of their own racial blood by choosing the hardships socially associated with "black blood" over the gains to be secured by choosing whiteness. The blackness that Harper's characters choose becomes defined through their very act of choosing that blackness as a path of suffering and self-denial. The martyrdom logic by which blackness becomes self-immolation in her novels is prefigured in Harper's letter to John Brown. "The hemlock is distilled with victory when it is pressed to the lips of Socrates. The Cross becomes a glorious ensign when Calvary's page-browed sufferer yields up his life upon it" (*BCD* 49). Like the hemlock chosen by Socrates and like the cross that becomes transmogrified into symbol through Christ's choice, the "blood" of race becomes consecrated through the choice of deliberate self-sacrifice as Harper's characters choose to affiliate themselves with the experience of the socially despised race.

As I will argue in the following reading of the novel, *Iola Leroy* is Harper's fictional martyrdom manifesto, her epic depiction of the rewards to be reaped through willful acts of self-destruction. The deliberate choices that Harper's characters make to turn down lives of fortune and ease become acts of self-immolation—minor acts of martyrdom—

that redefine the character of the supposedly "servile" race. Synthesizing a sentimental ethics of death with elements of the passing narrative, Harper creates plots in which the choice not to pass rings with the finality of death. When Harper's characters choose to live as black rather than as white, they effectively martyr themselves, killing off one identity for another in liberating fashion. Characters in *Iola Leroy* choose this little version of death so that they and others can finally live.

Iola Leroy (1892) dramatizes the application of Harper's black uplift and black feminist ideologies through acts of self-sacrifice, linking African American social progress to the achievement of individual acts of identity martyrdom. If, as Michael Stancliff has argued, the novel's "assertion of progress resulting from exceptional character serves as a political heuristic," then this exceptional character is defined by the novel as one devoted to sacrifice as the individual's own assertion of progress (142). The novel's plot revolves around stark and critical choices made by its main characters in moments that exemplify Harper's ethics and aesthetics of the martyrdom of identity. The novel unfolds through a series of scenes in which characters are confronted with ethical choices that poise them between the gains to be reaped through expediency and self-indulgence and the hardships surely to be endured if these boons are laid aside: Uncle Ben choosing whether to escape with his fellow slaves or remain on the plantation in an act of loyalty to his master; Marie Leroy (Iola's mother) deciding whether she should marry Eugene Leroy; Harry Leroy (Iola's brother) choosing between a white or black regiment during the Civil War; Iola's own decision whether to accept Dr. Gresham's marriage proposal. These moments are designed pedagogically to instruct Harper's audience in the value of sacrificing the self.

In this sense, the dramatization of these choices, their rationales, and their consequences throughout the novel shapes *Iola Leroy* as a fictional manual of self-denial. Early in the narrative, Thomas Anderson's act of martyrdom sets the tone for this series of self-sacrificial decisions, and although these other characters are not asked to give up their lives to save others as Tom has done, the decisions they make are presented as nonetheless tantamount to Tom's more literal martyrdom. These acts of sacrifice and self-denial are versions of Thomas Anderson's martyrdom, versions of John Brown's martyrdom, and ultimately, versions of Christ's martyrdom. In each case, Harper encourages her characters (and by extension her readers) to give so completely of themselves as to give themselves up, to break with their pasts and with their potential futures in such a distinct, radical, and self-negating manner that it constitutes a kind of self-destruction. Each major ethical choice provides the opportunity for Harper's characters to effectively immolate their selves in the name of a cause.

The critical choice made by Harry Leroy demonstrates Harper's ethics of choice. Raised as white, Harry learns of his African American lineage only during his early manhood in a moment that effectively disrupts the continuity of his racial identity. "It seems as if the past were suddenly blotted out of his memory" (123). Almost immediately after receiving a letter from his sister divulging the details of his racial past, Harry must make a decision that will shape his life's trajectory. Mr. Bascom, the principal of the northern boys' school in which Harry has been educated, suggests that Harry may move south and join the Confederates. The idea strikes Harry as a choice worse than death. "'I would rather die than do it! I should despise myself forever if I did'" (125). Mr. Bascom presents Harry with the choice between enlisting with a black or white regiment, a choice that prompts Harry toward an existential rumination:

> He felt the reality of his situation as he had not done before. It was as if two paths had suddenly opened before him, and he was forced to choose between them. On one side were strength, courage, enterprise, power of achievement, and memories of a wonderful past. On the other side were weakness, ignorance, poverty, and the proud world's social scorn. He knew nothing of colored people except as slaves, and his whole soul shrank from equalizing himself with them. . . . He sat, thoughtful and undecided, as if a great struggle were going on in his mind. (125–26)

Despite the narrator's dichotomous language here, the choice that Harry must make is not one between whiteness and blackness, and certainly not a choice between being and nothingness. Harry and Mr. Bascom may understand Harry's choice as that between whiteness and blackness, but this moment in which Harry is confronted with the "bizarre option to *choose* racial affiliation" only undermines the most essential premises of the race concept (Stancliff 158). Race, in standard definition, is not something that can be chosen, and the very idea that Harry has a choice to make undermines the fixity and determinacy of racial identity. If Harry's race is biologically determined, then no choice he makes can alter it; meanwhile, if his race is merely a construction, then he has no fixed race to alter through his choice. Instead, the moment dramatizes Harper's philosophy of the character-constructing effects produced by making ethical choices even as it undermines the notion of racial essentialism.

Although Harry's choice cannot make a difference in terms of his race, this moment of becoming does nevertheless change him. The weight of the choice now open before him is described as a construction of Harry's own associations: blackness with "weakness, ignorance, poverty, and the proud world's social scorn" and whiteness with "strength, enterprise, power of achievement, and memories of a wonderful past" (125). Harry regards these associations "as if two paths had suddenly opened before him," but the true difference between them lies only in his own attitudes, although undoubtedly supported through legal codification, scientific discourse, and social custom. Yet, this is a difference that makes all the difference from Harper's perspective, as the ethical heroism Harry displays in choosing the colored regiment—and by extension, life on the black side of the color line—derives, ironically, from his own prejudice. Harry's lifelong prejudice against the race from which his "whole soul shrank from equalizing himself," the race that he now learns to be his own mother's race, provides the circumstances under which he is forced to align himself with everything that he abhors, loathes, and fears. This aversion for blackness becomes the most important aspect of his choice's meaning, as it is the attitudinal axis upon which Harry may pivot toward the sacrificial act.

To fulfill the novel's themes of racial chauvinism, Harry must choose the black regiment, but to fulfill Harper's self-sacrificial philosophy, he must choose that which he least desires. Harper constructs Harry's choice of blackness as a sacrificial choice by balancing the reunification of his family against the whiteness that he clearly prefers; by joining the black regiment, Harry will enjoy (as Mr. Bascom describes) "'better facilities'" for finding his mother and sister. By aligning self-indulgence with whiteness and self-denial and self-sacrifice with blackness, Harper provides Harry with the opportunity to make a seemingly racial decision while simultaneously remaking and reforming himself. In the wake of this "racial" choice, Harry will truly be a different person, not because of the race he chooses—not because his choice effects a true transition from whiteness to blackness—but because he has willingly abnegated these riches, including "memories of a wonderful past."

A similar dynamic governs the novel's signal choice, Iola Leroy's response to Dr. Gresham's proposal of marriage. When Iola rejects the offer that would require living the rest of her life as a white woman, she rejects the life of security, economic possibility, and love that she sorely desires. Because this moment must be one of suffering, Iola's strong feelings for Dr. Gresham are integral to the moment's dramatization of Harper's ethos of self-sacrifice (as Harry's antipathy for blackness had been in his decision). "In Dr. Gresham she saw the ideal of her soul exemplified" (110). Not only is Iola "not indifferent to Dr. Gresham" (as the narrator puts it more circumspectly), she holds true and strong feelings of attachment for him. "His kindness to her had been a new experience. His companionship was an unexpected pleasure. She had learned to enjoy his presence and to miss him when absent, and when she began to question her heart she found that unconsciously it was entwining around him" (110, 111). These statements of Iola's affection toward Gresham serve more than the heightening of the novel's melodrama; they establish the terms of the self-denial Iola will enact through her declination of the proposal. Indeed, the difficulty of turning away from that which Iola strongly desires is, formally, the very function of this proposal in the novel. Gresham serves Iola by providing such an opportunity for selflessness. While accepting Gresham's proposal would entail hiding her blackness and thus living out the duplicity proscribed by a racial ideology that casts her identity in terms of bifurcation, Iola understands that, ironically, it is only by putting aside the fulfillment of her own desires through the act of serving others that she can be herself.

In a similar vein, later in the novel, as Gresham persists in asking for Iola's hand in marriage, she will express her consistent gratitude for suffering when she reflects on the opportunity provided by the lowly social condition of her own race: "'It was . . . through their unrequited toil that I was educated, while they were compelled to live in ignorance. I am indebted to them for the power I have to serve them" (235). In both instances, we are reminded of how Janette, the moral heroine of "The Two Offers," "learned one of life's most precious lessons, that true happiness consists not so much in the fruition of our wishes as in the regulation of desires" (*BCD* 114). Gresham's marriage proposal provides such an opportunity for Iola to actively regulate her own desire by relinquishing the life she desires most. "I do like him," she admits in her private reflections, "but I can never marry him" (111). In choosing to reject Dr. Gresham, Iola must deliberately choose that which will make her least happy yet most fulfilled. "I could not consent to choose the happiest lot on earth without first finding my poor heart-stricken and desolate mother" (111). So, in this moment of struggle, Iola "fought with her own heart and repressed its rising love" (111). She resolves to reject Gresham and "at whatever cost of pain it might be to herself, to explain to Dr. Gresham what she meant by the insurmountable barrier. Iola, after a continuous strain upon her nervous system for months, began to suffer from general debility and nervous depression" (112). Iola thus feels unbearable pangs of self-denial—the pain of denying her *self*—while rejecting Gresham for a life devoted to the welfare of others. "I am constantly rousing myself up to suffer and be strong. I intend, when this conflict is over, to cast my lot with the free people as a helper, teacher, and friend. I have passed through a fiery ordeal, but this ministry of suffering will not be in vain" (114). Harper renders Gresham's marriage proposal (perhaps ironically in the context of representations of marriage in nineteenth-century racial melodrama) as a moment that Iola must suffer through, as it is this suffering that makes Iola the novel's moral heroine.

Iola's rejection of Gresham culminates a process of suffering that also serves as her own self-immolation, the martyrdom of her very identity. As she explains the decision to Gresham by way of backstory, the magnanimous character of Tom Anderson—the servant whose martyrdom affects her so deeply in the novel's opening chapters—compelled her own process of self-actualization, which Gresham's proposal now helps her to analyze. "Instead of coming into this hospital a self-sacrificing woman, laying her every gift and advantage upon the altar of her country, I came as a rescued slave, glad to find a refuge from a fate more cruel than death; a fate from which I was rescued by the intervention of my dear friend, Thomas Anderson" (113). Iola regards herself no longer as the woman she used to be. In this, her own autobiographical conversion narrative, she has transformed from "a rescued slave" to a "self-sacrificing woman" and interrelates her own transformation with her experience of Tom Anderson's own purposeful death, his own selfless act of martyrdom. The same spirit of selflessness that prompted Tom to lay down his life has prompted Iola to deny herself.

Figuring Tom's literal death in turn, Iola's rejection of Gresham is a breakthrough, so radically altering as to be tantamount to a kind of personal death and resurrection—the death of one identity and the emergence of another. Iola's decision is so completely self-abnegating, that in the process of making and explaining it, she no longer recognizes herself. "'I feel that my mind has matured beyond my years. I am a wonder to myself'" (114). In the process of rejecting her own happiness, Iola articulates her achievement of a place of perspective from which to survey herself in totality. This position is only achieved through the gradual process by which she has left her former self behind. "'Thoughts and purposes have come to me in the shadow I should never have learned in the sunshine'" (114). Only by severing all ties to her previous self—by cutting and killing her self off completely—can Iola advance toward living completely for others and prepare for her life as a post-Reconstruction leader of racial and humanitarian reform. To marry Gresham would have been to continue upon the life trajectory of the "rescued slave" seeking "refuge from a fate more cruel than death," but to reject Gresham is to accept that fate as a death of its own sort and to choose that death willingly in order to subsume her self to the collective cause of black uplift. As the final act of divestment from this trajectory, Iola's rejection of Gresham becomes the finest moment in the life of the novel's heroine because it is the moment in which Iola finally brings her self to an end.

As a painful yet liberating crossroads of experience, Iola's rejection of Gresham suggests the nature of the original suffering that inspired Iola's author to create her. Dr. Gresham (perhaps along with some readers) mistakes Iola's decision as one based in the same kind of desire for race purity that motivates his own stance against miscegenation. "'Iola,' he exclaimed, passionately, 'if you love your race, as you call it, work for it, live for it, suffer for it, and, if need be, die for it; but don't marry for it. Your education has unfitted you for social life among them'" (*BCD* 235). Iola does indeed marry for race, although not for "blood" in the biological sense of the term. The very fact that Iola spends her early life ignorant of her own genealogical blackness suggests the inability for "blood" to determine her racial consciousness. Iola's blackness is neither inherited nor chosen but rather consecrated through her act of self-sacrifice, and her seemingly racially motivated act of self-denial gives meaning to the blood she proudly claims. In this sense, Iola's life becomes a minor version of the sacrificial acts enacted by Christ and by Harper's historical example of sacrifice in John Brown. Iola's denial of self sanctifies the instrument of her "death," her own "blood." More than three decades earlier, Harper had assured John Brown as he awaited his execution that, like so many martyrs before him, the sacrificial acts he had made would forever alter the meaning of the instrument of his death. "The hemlock is distilled with victory when it is pressed to the lips of Socrates, she wrote," and "The Cross becomes a glorious ensign when Calvary's page-browed sufferer yields up his life upon it" (49). As a fictional distillation of Harper's valorization of such sacrifices, the sacrifices Iola makes for her blackness sanctify her "African blood" as well. By giving up her property in whiteness, Iola forfeits a life of privilege and chooses instead to accept the burdens that life as an African American woman living in the late nineteenth century will place upon her. When Iola claims the "best blood" in her veins as "African blood," she does so in the context of the sacrifices she herself has made, sacrificing the civil rights, economic security, the life of relative pleasure and ease—her property in whiteness—everything that would surely come to her if she were to choose life as a white woman. The best blood in her veins is her black blood, not because it bestows blackness upon her but rather because it is what she has given up her whiteness for.

Iola Leroy synthesizes the principles of sacrifice, martyrdom, and race pride that had come to form the ideological core of Frances Harper's political and racial ethos. As Michael Stancliff writes (in the context of his analysis of Harper's rhetorical pedagogy), "Any approach to a general account of Harper's work requires coming to terms not simply with her *ethos*, but with her *ethical theory*, the system of recurring characterological precepts she taught as a matter of lived principle and committed linguistic practice" (13). Here I have argued that martyrdom constitutes a central plank in Harper's ethics of sacrifice and her political and social views with respect to "black uplift." As she viewed martyrdom as the foundation of her religious faith and recalled John Brown's martyrdom as the crystallization of her political faith, the martyr's spilled blood came to forge one of the most critical links between Harper's spiritual and political practice. Harper was dedicated to a rhetorical practice of blood, rooted in her Christianity and her consistent political vision. As David Biale has observed, "Blood is a matter not only of belief but also of practice. In rituals such as sacrifice, circumcision, and the Eucharist, the most physical of objects—blood or wine—come to symbolize the most mysterious, indeed spiritual, of entities, whether the covenant of the Jews or the mystical blood of Christ" (4). As one of the most effective and popular practitioners of the tradition of African American secular sermon, Frances Harper practiced the development of her political thought and her political rhetoric with as much dedication as she practiced her faith. Iola's ability to develop such pride in her "African blood" after years of denigrating blackness reminds us that race too is "a matter not only of belief but also of practice," a reminder that this practice can be changed. Iola Leroy stands as Harper's finest creation among a long series of "heroines at interpretive crossroads, inventing self-definition in relation to the signs of cultural power in the nineteenth-century United States" (Stancliff 50). Iola Leroy invents self-definition in relation to "blood" as one of the most powerful signs of cultural power in nineteenth-century America. Infused as it is with a form of blood that Harper believed in more deeply than the blood of biological determinism, her rhetoric of racial blood invents a definition of self rooted in the form of blood that she believed should replace biological blood as the sign of cultural power in the United States, a form of blood inextricably mingled with the blood of sacrifice.

CHAPTER 3

Pauline Hopkins and the End of Incest

The fundamental problem in Pauline Hopkins's novel *Of One Blood* (1902–1903) is the problem of incest. Incest is so critical to the novel's themes, structure, and political purposes that *Of One Blood* stands as a singularly notable if not pioneering treatment of the subject in the African American literary tradition, a tradition in which the theme of incest has been considered, as Trudier Harris once observed, "especially taboo" (495).[1] The restrictions of literary decorum during the period of her most active literary production (1900–1905) prevented Hopkins from engaging in the explicit depiction of incest's physical and psychological traumas, yet there remains no other text in the African American tradition more concerned with the manner in which "[i]ncest represents the mysterious, vexing, sometimes ungovernable but always undeniable power of kinship ties and their widespread ramifications for individuals and society at large" (Barnes 1). The treatment of incest in *Of One Blood* demonstrates Hopkins's concern with the cultural presumptions of an ideology of racial blood that devalued African American kinship ties during the post-Reconstruction era, a period in which the social value and power of such ties had become particularly important.

As an example of the popular late nineteenth-century "American race melodrama," *Of One Blood* speaks to the continuing post-Reconstruction anxieties over slavery's impact on African American genealogical knowledge and, more broadly, on narratives of American kinship. As Susan Gillman demonstrates, the narratives of tangled interracial genealogy so often depicted in this genre provide "a means of negotiating the social tensions surrounding the formation of racial, national, and sexual identity in the post-Reconstruction years. The basic plot . . . centers on the reconstitution of the black family separated under slavery, culminating in the revelation of secret identities, or hidden race mixture, and finally of separated and reunited parents and children" ("Mulatto" 222). *Of One Blood* raises the stakes for the American race melodrama's plot of improbable, dramatic family reunions by adding a sensational twist: the possibility that separated descendants of an American slaveholding aristocracy and a disrupted slave family would cross paths later in life and, without recognizing each other, become involved in marital or sexual relationships.

Of One Blood forces a reconsideration of the cultural, political, anthropological, and ideological bases for the absolute value of incestuous desire in its critique of American racial blood discourse. Revising the scientific and metaphorical meanings of "one blood," the novel's plot daringly allows for a sympathetic embrace of sibling affinity and the consummation of incestuous desire. Ranging inexorably and uncomfortably toward a form of kinship considered most unnatural, the plot of *Of One Blood* exposes the cultural politics by which the presumptions of a relationship between blood, family, race, and identity construct the incest taboo's prohibitions against an unnatural relationship of blood. In the process, the novel's risky resolution of its own incest plot provides Hopkins's most radical and incisive critique of the supposed naturalization of race and gender differences achieved through the American rhetoric of kinship by blood.

My focus on the novel's sibling incest narrative in this respect extends the critical discussion of Hopkins's engagements with scientific rhetoric in readings by Cynthia Schrager, Thomas Otten, and Susan Gillman, where Hopkins's revision of racialist discourse and particularly the figure of blood through occult science has developed into one of the most provocative and influential lines of argument regarding *Of One Blood*. Gillman's explication is exemplary of this line in the body of criticism:

> Hopkins transforms "blood" from a biologized term, the staple of nineteenth-century scientific racism, into a multivalent figure of speech capable of generating new meanings—including some drawn directly from, rather than countering, contemporary scientific discourses. Hop-

> kins not only draws on existing meanings of "blood," she also invents some of her own. If Hopkins's "blood" refers . . . to the literal passing down of inheritance theorized by the biological sciences, as well as to the biblical inheritance of spirit or culture, it also refers, in the novel's occult context, to hereditarian theories of a psychic identity that endures over time and space. No simple transvaluation of scientific terms, Hopkins's strategy placed her in the more ambiguous position of challenging the claims of science from within, of being, that is, occupied by such terms and yet occupying them herself. ("Hopkins and the Occult" 76)

Taking the scientific and political implications of the novel's sibling incest narrative into account, the problem of incest in *Of One Blood* becomes inseparable from this revision of blood's meanings and the host of deterministic and differential concepts that this figure insinuates into scientific and legal discourses of race and gender.

Deeply cognizant of the power of blood as a figure in the lexicons of the scientific and political discourses of race in her era, Hopkins was more than a casual student of contemporary anthropological and ethnological debates. She published two extended ethnological treatises, both of which argue for the single-origin theory of human genealogy, known in nineteenth-century ethnological debates as the theory of monogenesis. Hopkins often articulated her monogenism through references to the apostle Paul's "one blood" decree (Acts 17:26), and she maintained arguments for the decree's scientific implications.[2] In her ethnological series, "The Dark Races of the Twentieth Century" (1905), Hopkins writes, "In this study of the dark races actually living today upon the globe, the reader or student is deeply impressed with the infinite variety of mixture in these races. This very mingling of races proves the theory of 'one blood.' Indeed, the principle that the human species is one cannot be disputed, and all men that inhabit the earth are but varieties of this one species" (191). From this ethnological perspective, Hopkins's outlook on the genealogical implications of "one blood" remains considerably more optimistic in comparison with the profoundly ambivalent explication of the scientific, cultural, and political meanings of "one blood" suggested in her final work of fiction, where the meaning of "one blood" as a metaphor for monogenesis becomes conflated with its meaning as a metaphor for destructive incest.

But, at the beginning of *Of One Blood*, the problem of universal brotherhood remains far from the mind of the protagonist Reuel Briggs, a brilliant but despondent Harvard student whose "desolateness" and "loneliness" lead him toward thoughts of suicide. These feelings of isolation are compounded by the gnawing secret of his racial passing. Reuel tries to alleviate this torment by poring over his research in occult phenomena, through which he hopes to unlock the hidden metaphysical mysteries of transpsychic connections. Against his protests of being unconcerned with the pressing "Negro problem," Reuel is dragged away from his work by his white friend Aubrey Livingston to attend a concert by the traveling Fisk Jubilee Singers. There Reuel becomes captivated with the group's lead soprano, Dianthe Lusk. By the end of the novel, the reader will discover that this trio of main characters—Reuel Briggs, Dianthe Lusk, and Aubrey Livingston—are not only "of one blood" with respect to their racial identities, but also "of one blood" with respect to their siblinghood. While Aubrey Livingston has been raised as the white heir to his family's wealth, all three are actually the legally black offspring of Aubrey Livingston Sr., a Maryland plantation owner, and his slave, Mira.

The romantic attraction that both Reuel and Aubrey soon feel for Dianthe and that they both believe to be miscegenous is actually an incestuous desire for their own sister. More than a sensational and dramatic turn in the plot, this revelation is the return of repressed interracial slaveholding and slave family legacy, revisited upon the descendants of the Livingston family as the irreducible threat of incest. The corruption of "one blood"—from monogenetic slogan to incestuous warning—becomes the present dilemma for such characters in post-Reconstruction-era fiction, where the drama of unwitting incest besets the descendants of intertwined, interracial families dispersed by slavery, segregated by Jim Crow law, and left without certain knowledge of their kinship relations across the color line.

While dramatizing the consequences of slavery's genealogical disruptions, the incest plot also acknowledges a broader conceptual problem entailed in the advocacy of monogenesis as a viable alternative to nineteenth-century deterministic racialism and a reconciliation of the post-Reconstruction racial divide. Marc Shell explains that while the "rhetoric of the universalist position—'All human beings are siblings'—is beguiling," a position that embraces monogenesis but ignores the problem of incest is inconsistent, for "even in the entire world, the hypothesis of human monogenesis—the belief that all men and women are descended in common from a single couple (Adam and Eve, say)—might mean that any and all sexual liaisons would be potentially incestuous and hence, teleologically speaking, also actually incestuous" (Shell 625, 641). The problem of Hopkins's novel—the problem of *one blood*—is precisely this problem of incest as the seemingly unavoidable end of monogenesis. Or as Gillman suggests, "'One blood' refers textually both to a horror and a promise: to the horror of the incestuous, sibling relations among the three protagonists, exposed as literal blood brothers and sisters . . . and to the biblical promises of racial unity . . ." (Gillman, "Hopkins and the Occult" 63).

The radical resolution to the problem of incest comes in the novel's ironic drive *toward* sibling affinity rather than away from it, a movement that culminates in a dramatic finale in which sibling affinity is considered redemptive rather than culturally degenerative and morally abhorrent. This is not to suggest that the novel advocates incest, but rather that it refuses the premises and implications of the universal application of the incest taboo, particularly those premises that naturalize the symbolic properties and cultural anxieties associated with the figure of blood. Hopkins's plot, in which the apparent choice of miscegenous romantic relationships turns out to be the accident of incest, dramatizes the cultural and discursive rather than natural or biological difference between exogamy and endogamy. Altering the scientific, conceptual, and political terms of sibling affinity, the narrative depicts the new moral valuations and narrative possibilities allowed by a radically different conception of what it means to be "of one blood." Moreover, this reconceptualization of sibling affinity is no mere incidental by-product of Hopkins's rejection of scientific racialism, but rather the *strategy* for that rejection. In conjunction with the representation of the occult through which Hopkins achieves what Susan Gillman describes as a "radical recontextualizing" of "blood" as a metaphor for race, *Of One Blood* also reconceptualizes the incestuous implications of the "one blood" decree as a way to "make blood thus speak out of school . . . to underscore its excessive meanings" (*Blood Talk* 69). By replacing the "blood" of incest and miscegenation rhetoric with the occult "blood" of the "hidden self," the novel undoes the logic of the genealogical narrative that leads (as Shell puts it) "teleologically" from monogenesis to the universal violation of the incest taboo.

Blood, after all, is the operative term in the conflation of monogenesis and incest, and Shell's suggestion of a "teleological" movement from monogenesis to universal incest overlooks the important role that the figure of blood plays in their discursive conflation. In a truly monogenetic human population, "sexual liaisons" between members of the same family become the unavoidable rule, however remote the relations between the family members may be. While there are no exceptions here to intrafamilial relations, this is not to say that all such relationships should be considered incestuous or even endogamous. A completely monogenetic world may preclude the possibility of relationships outside of a grand family, but it does not necessitate even the observance of endogamy, much less the violation of its tabooed form, incest. Endogamy and incest are not necessary ends of the genealogical narrative beginning with a single origin but rather culturally defined prohibitions against certain degrees of kinship.

The critical difference between monogenesis and incest is made apparent by the etymological roots of "incest": from the Latin *incestus* (*in-* + *castus*), incestuous relationships are *impure*. Monogenesis, however, indicates a unitary genealogy wholly resistant to the *incestuous* notion of being outside of caste. While certain relations under monogenesis may be deemed impure and thus prohibited by custom, there is no formal "teleology" from monogenesis to incest. That is, there is no genealogical narrative alone by which the purity of monogenesis leads inevitably to the impurity of incest. The impurity of incest does not refer to the endogamous or intrafamilial relationships themselves but rather to the pretextual impure circumstances that are understood to occur when family members become intimately related. The original source of this impurity and the disseminations into kinship discourse of its cultural associations are the underlying subjects of Hopkins's novel. In anthropological theories of the incest taboo, the origins of incestuous impurity are traced back to the (seemingly universal) grounding of cultural concepts of inter- and intragroup difference in the perceived properties of literal blood. Ultimately, endogamy is *incestuous* because certain forms of blood are *impure*.

The cultural stigma associated with incest, based on the presumption of an unnatural biological relationship, is not a necessary element of any paraphrase for the language describing relationships that take place between members of a monogenetic, genealogically pure family, although this stigma and its anxieties become greatly enhanced by virtue of incest's associations with blood itself. "Blood," writes Emile Durkheim, "it has often been said, has a horror of blood. But such an explanation is a refusal of explanation. To invoke the instinct to account for a belief or a practice, without accounting for the instinct that one invokes, is to pose the question, not to resolve it. It is to say that man condemns incest because it appears condemnable to him" (68). In his anthropological analysis of the origins of the incest taboo, Durkheim reminds his reader that what is truly "universal" about the operation of taboo is not the aversion for any specifically prohibited behavior (incest for example) but rather the culturally universal effort to categorize and to regulate, distribute, and maintain power between social categories. "[T]aboo, a word borrowed from a Polynesian tongue . . . is the name given to the collection of ritualistic prohibitions which have as their objective to avert the dangerous effects of a magical contagion by preventing all contact between a thing or a category of things, in which a supernatural principle is believed to reside, and others who do not have this same characteristic, or do not have it to the same degree. The first are said to be tabooed in relationship to the second" (70).

As a taboo deeply associated with the substance of blood, the incest taboo carries particularly strong emotional valence in its enforcement of social order due to blood's associations with the body, gender norms, life and death, and public and private contagion, all of which the image of blood imparts to the rhetoric and ideology of monogenesis, including the "one blood" decree. Incest and monogenesis actually have nothing to do with each other; blood—by imbuing the discourse of genealogy with cultural concepts of contagion and impurity—makes it seem as if they do. In a process of conceptual contagion that takes place through the mobilization of associations entailed in the use of blood as a metaphor for kinship, the cultural and symbolic terms associated with the figure of blood spoil monogenesis into incest. This symbolic, rhetorical, and ultimately political spoilage of the phrase "of one blood" is the central problem of Hopkins's novel, and, as we will see, the novel's sibling *affinity* plot redeems genealogical monism from incest by divorcing monogenesis from the scientific premises and moral condemnations of incest, condemnations that follow only from the narrow selection and application of the cultural concepts associated with the substance and figure of blood.

The crucial players in this redemption are the novel's major female characters—Aunt Hannah, Mira, and Dianthe—who comprise the matrilineal line of the slave family owned by the white Livingston family. All of these women—along with the ancient African matriarch Queen Candace, who ultimately achieves the radical refiguring of incest in the novel's finale—demonstrate the power to overcome vast generational, geographical, and psychic distances to repair the destruction that rape and incest have wrought upon their family legacy. In "Passing Shadows," Dana Luciano argues persuasively for the "maternal power" that carries through the line of black female characters in the novel. Much of this power is dedicated to the prevention of Dianthe, Reuel, and Aubrey's incestuous relationships. Hannah attempts to eliminate the incest threat by revealing her family history to Dianthe, while her daughter Mira, whom Luciano describes as "the most powerful figure in the narrative," achieves nothing less than a return from the dead in order to warn her own children of their impending incest (179).

The redemption from a legacy of incest begins the very moment the incest legacy is revealed. During a seemingly chance reunion, Aunt Hannah, "moaning as though in physical pain," recounts the horrors of her life as a slave on the Livingston plantation to her long-lost granddaughter Dianthe (*One Blood* 175). Aunt Hannah laments what she modestly refers to as her "'relations with massa'"—repeated acts of rape by her master, "Ol' Marse," the patriarch of the white Livingston family—that resulted in the births of as many as ten children (175). Hannah was allowed to keep only one child, Mira, while "'all de res' were sold away to raise de mor'gage off de prop'rty'" (175). Hannah's daughter Mira suffers a fate worse than being sold; she becomes the sexual object of the master's only "legitimate" child (later known as Aubrey Livingston Sr.), who is also her half brother. Mira gives birth to three children—Reuel, Dianthe, and Aubrey—the novel's main characters. From Aunt Hannah's backstory, Dianthe thus learns that she is the descendant of slaves and that the two men with whom she has been romantically involved—Reuel Briggs and Aubrey Livingston—are both her own brothers. As offspring of the relationship between the black and white children of "Ol' Marse," Dianthe, Reuel, and Aubrey are heirs to what Wernor Sollors describes as an "intensely incestuous situation," and as shocking as the revelation of her siblinghood with Reuel and Aubrey may be for Dianthe, the doubly incestuous romantic triangle between her and her brothers actually extends a dark legacy of incestuous relationships between the black and white, enslaved and slaveholding lines of the Livingston family (304).

The problem of incest is thus imbricated in the racial and gendered power dynamics of American slavery. In one sense, Hannah's story is an indictment of the slaveholding fathers and male heirs of the Livingston family, whose unchecked legal powers over their female slaves provide the social license for their practices of miscegenous and incestuous sexual violation while sowing the seeds of their own family ruin in the process. The continuance of incest in the post-Reconstruction setting is the damning, unforeseen outcome of the master's exercise of unlimited racial power, and Hopkins's indictment of the slaveholding fathers demonstrates Werner Sollors's analysis of the "liberal-antislavery" ideology behind some narrative intertwinings of incest and miscegenation: "The tyrannical patriarch who does not stop short of incest signals the chaotic perversion of the whole system he embodies, putting his unacknowledged children into a problematic position as victims and possible rebels and setting into motion a chain of events that may end in the downfall of the house when the illegitimate and the legitimate families encounter each other" (319). Hopkins clearly suggests the culpability of Hannah's master and his heirs for their practice of the sexual abuses that eventually lead to Dianthe, Reuel, and Aubrey's intolerable predicament. In another context, Hopkins would similarly suggest the responsibility for miscegenation anxiety on the part of "Chivalrous Southern men" who took legal ownership rights as license for sexual domination and "desecrated the purity of the Southern home, and, incidentally, opened this question of racial purity" (*Primer* 28). The masters' disregard for incest as a deterrent to such relationships may reinforce the claim of total sexual license over their female slaves, but this attempt to negate the familial bonds between themselves and their own slave offspring only compounds the post-slavery anxieties of hidden racial genealogy by adding the specter of further, hidden incestuous ties.

But Aunt Hannah's story is also the confession of her own part in creating the circumstances for her grandchildren's incestuous romances. After all, it is Hannah who, motivated by the impending sale of her daughter Mira, secretly switches Mira's newborn son with her white mistress's dead baby, thus counterfeiting her own black grandson for the white male heir to the Livingston line. Exchanging the literally dead white child for the "socially dead" black slave child, Hannah intends to subvert her master's proprietary claims on her grandson and to circumvent the child's "natal alienation" as an heir to his mother's "black blood."[3] Here the form and function of what we might call "Hannah's plot," following Carolyn Porter, resonates with that of Twain's Roxana in *Pudd'nhead Wilson*. Like Hopkins's Aunt Hannah, Twain's Roxy makes a daring switch of the master's infant heir for a look-alike slave descendant. The plot delivers a delicious, black feminist revenge against slavery's natal alienation. The black matriarchs take full advantage of their dual responsibilities for rearing their own and the master's descendants by exchanging the dispossessed black child for the rightful heir of the master who, while justifying the variant destinies of his black and white offspring through claims of natural inferiority and superiority, cannot even tell them apart. As Carolyn Porter explains in her reading of *Pudd'nhead Wilson*, "Because this [antebellum slave] code observed the Roman rule of matrilineal descent, in which the child follows the 'condition' of the mother, no matter what the father's status, a slave mother, in giving birth, delivered her child into slavery. It is this rule, among other unwritten laws, that Roxana subverts when she inserts her son into the patrilineal, and patriarchal, system, in which he becomes the 'heir of the house'" (Porter 129).

If such a switch undermines the master's patrilineal power, it also provides the circumstances for the unwitting incest that occurs later when the supposedly white child (Aubrey Livingston) becomes involved with Mira's only daughter Dianthe, his unwitting sibling. By relating her experiences as a slave to her granddaughter, Aunt Hannah attempts to atone for her own feelings of guilt for committing the baby switch ("'Den I believe de debbil took possession of me body and soul") and to avert the unthinkable outcome of the plot she has initiated (*One Blood* 177). A deep irony emerges from this incestuous outcome in that, by creating the circumstances for incest within the Livingston family, Aunt Hannah ushers in the horrible achievement of the slavemaster's ultimate genealogical goals in his adamant disavowal of miscegenation. Rather than the preservation of an untainted "white" genealogical line, the master's "black" descendants achieve his desire for genealogical purity ironically and in excess. If the master's obsessive protection of racial purity is a desire for homogeneity, then the avoidance of unwanted difference is a muted desire, Hopkins suggests, for a degree of sameness made possible only through the profanation of incest.[4]

Hannah's switch employs the age-old incest plot device of infant or childhood separation that prevents nuclear family members from recognizing their shared kinship when reunited later in life. This unfortunate separation in the unwitting incest plot is, of course, as old as literary drama. But, as W. Daniel Wilson suggests in his study of incest plots in eighteenth-century literature, the modern incest plot develops the ancient form in the light of emerging scientific theories of the origins and purposes of incest aversion. Indeed, Wilson insists that an understanding of the "literary obsession with consummated unwitting incest" during the eighteenth century is "unthinkable" without considering the period's debate over the roots of the incest taboo in divine and natural law (254). In conjunction with Hopkins's appropriation of the Jamesian "new psychology" of her era, an equally important although relatively implicit appropriation of unorthodox scientific theories of the incest taboo informs the development and meaning of her sibling incest plot.

By the time Hopkins published *Of One Blood*, the literary narrative of infant separation leading to unwitting incest had found its anthropological corollary in Edward Westermarck's influential "proximity aversion theory," which he explains at length in his 1891 study *The History of Human Marriage*. Westermarck argues that childhood proximity dampens sexual attraction between siblings, effectively neutralizing their incestuous desire and creating an instinctual barrier to the development of such relationships. "What I maintain is, that there is an innate aversion to sexual intercourse between persons living very closely together from early youth, and that, as such persons are in most cases related, this feeling displays itself chiefly as a horror of intercourse between near kin" (320). Literary plots of separated siblings who later commit unwitting incest make implicit reference to such an aversion in their narrative circumvention of what would eventually become known as the "Westermarck effect."

But while the separation in such plots makes the incestuous aspect of the later relationship "unwitting" (thus absolving the incestuous pair of any immoral intent), the unusually strong and strangely natural feelings of attraction felt between the siblings upon their reunion only heighten the ambiguity regarding the appropriateness of the sibling desire itself. The moral ambiguities of the incest tragedy force the reader into a difficult judgment regarding the origin and meaning of this "power of sympathy," a choice between reading the attraction between the siblings as the overcoming of a Westmarckian natural aversion or the indulgence in a Freudian desire. An interpretation made under the principle of an instinctual aversion will view the sibling affinity as an innocent yet tragic error in which the vestigial feelings of a natural horror are misinterpreted as romantic or sexual attraction; an interpretation made under the principle of psychological attraction will view the relationship as the consummation of otherwise repressed desire.

Yet both cases presuppose what W. Daniel Wilson describes as "an ability to recognize or to sense intuitively consanguinity without having been acquainted with the relative" (255). From a scientific standpoint, the notion is perhaps (as Wilson calls it) "far-fetched," but as a literary conceit it is the compelling heart of the incest drama's ambiguity and a critical concept for Hopkins's reconceptualization of sibling affinity. "This intuition which could attract siblings to each other is a gold mine for myth and literature, and has come to be identified by the term 'voice of blood.'" As with the eighteenth-century authors in Wilson's study, Hopkins "neatly circumvented the Westermarck effect by having the fictional children raised separately," and rather than interpreting their revivified mutual feelings as instinctual warnings against incestuous union—that is, against deleterious and prohibited relations of "blood"—Reuel and Dianthe are drawn toward each other later in life by a critically different version of this "voice of blood" (255).

Hopkins's novel imagines new scientific and narrative possibilities for this preternatural intuition of sibling "consanguinity" by casting Reuel and Dianthe's mutual and seemingly uncontrollable "call" to each other as the function of a transcendent occult link rather than a merely biological kinship. The mechanism that facilitates Reuel and Dianthe's feelings of attraction is a metaphysical force that takes the place of tabooed "blood"—a force that is, significantly, first felt through the use of Dianthe's voice—and this transubstantiation of blood is the core of Hopkins's reconceptualization of kinship and sibling affinity. The new substance and tenor of this revised "voice of blood" calling Reuel and Dianthe together is not the deterministic germ plasm of nineteenth-century ethnology but rather a mystical "blood" of occult affinity.

As the force behind Reuel and Dianthe's sibling affinity, the occult "voice of blood" provides an alternative scientific and narrative context for the moral framing of incestuous desire, redeeming Reuel's solitary psyche even as it facilitates his saving Dianthe's life. When a train accident leaves Dianthe incapacitated, Reuel seizes the opportunity to put his occult research into dramatic practice by reviving the victim from seeming death. Reuel demonstrates his mastery over an ethereal substance that unites each with all and energizes the dormant feelings between him and his incapacitated sister. He explains to those gathered around Dianthe that, "The secret of life lies in what we call volatile magnetism—it exists in the free atmosphere," and that he has developed the power to manipulate this force (*One Blood* 32).

> "This subtile [*sic*] magnetic agent is constantly drawn into the body through the lungs, absorbed and held in bounds until chemical combination has occurred through the medium of mineral agents always present in normal animal tissue. When respiration ceases this magnetism cannot be drawn into the lungs. It must be artificially supplied. This, gentleman, is my discovery. I supply this magnetism. I have it here in the case Dr. Livingston has kindly brought me."[5] (*One Blood* 33)

The dramatic resuscitation of Dianthe from "seeming death" is also the reinvigoration of "blood" as a metaphor through the defamiliarizing science of an occult transfusion. Set against the biological determinism of blood in nineteenth-century racial science, Reuel's occultism offers what Nancy Stepan and Sander Gilman have described as an "alternative ideology" to orthodox science, a scientific practice that produces "a genuine oppositional discourse or set of discourses . . . by positing a radically different world view, with different perceptions of reality, goals, and points of reference" (99). Part bodily substance, part universal ether, Hopkins's "volatile magnetism" strikes a critical compromise between the physical-corporeal and the metaphysical, taking on the characteristic features of nineteenth-century "vital materialism," which, as scientific historian Kim Pelis explains, "located any potential 'vital principle' in the material of the living body" and "left open the working analogy between blood, electricity, and life" (181).

It is precisely the more orthodox scientific notions of the relationship between blood and the vital forces of organic life as they relate to racial identity that Hopkins's novel calls into question. Reuel's resuscitation of Dianthe reproduces the familiar scene of the male medical practitioner working over the body of the female patient, and the procedure by which Reuel saves Dianthe's life is reminiscent of a blood transfusion: "It may be artificially supplied. . . . I have it here in the case Dr. Livingston has kindly brought me." In this novel full of doubles, Reuel's volatile magnetism acts as a doppelganger of the substance of blood itself. The ethereal medium retains the life-sustaining function of blood but also transcends blood's biological limitations and, equally importantly, its attendant metaphorical associations. Redefining the possibilities of what it means to be "of one blood," Hopkins's volatile magnetism literally flows through all human beings, and by virtue of this substance, all human beings share a powerful unity that can never be achieved through the more limited biological or genealogical paraphrase of "one blood" as a figurative reference to the theory of monogenesis.

As an alternative science that fundamentally alters the associations between blood and kinship, occultism makes possible the redemption of sibling affinity and with it the meaning of "one blood." As siblings, Reuel and Dianthe are drawn to each other by this force that neither can wholly explain, even though Reuel's studies in "supernatural phenomena" prepare him for the reality of forces beyond the realm of orthodox science and common experience. Upon first encountering Dianthe during her performance with the Fisk Jubilee Singers, Reuel (without any knowledge of their siblinghood) feels awakened and deeply compelled by her presence. While her voice "awakened ringing harmonies in the heart of every listener," the effect of Dianthe's voice on Reuel is particularly powerful: "Reuel was carried out of himself; he leaned forward in eager contemplation of the artist; he grew cold with terror and fear" (*One Blood* 14, 15). Dianthe's voice lifts Reuel out of his depression and inward obsessions, into a consciousness transcending the narrowness of his individual psyche. Reuel begins the novel in suicidal despair, but the return of his sister into his life prompts him to reconsider the possibility of his own happiness, and after seeing Dianthe perform, Reuel expresses a new-found enthusiasm for female companionship. With the magnetic attraction he feels toward Dianthe confirming his emotional attraction for her, Reuel expresses his newly stirred romantic feelings in terms of his mesmeric research. "'I suppose there are plenty of men in the world as lonely as I am,' he mused; 'but I suppose it is my own fault. . . . The woman I marry must be to me a necessity, because I love her; because so loving her, "all the current of my being flows to her," and I feel she is my supreme need'" (23). Feeling "strangely happy," Reuel wonders "whether the spirit is sometimes mysteriously conscious of the nearness of its kindred spirit; and feels, in anticipation, the 'sweet unrest' of the master-passion that rules the world" (23).

As if to confirm these thoughts and their transpsychic implications, Dianthe appears to Reuel with "lovely features" in a supernatural vision. She promises that he will soon be able to help her and then vanishes, leaving Reuel feeling the "slave of a passion as sudden and romantic as that of Romeo for Juliet; with no more foundation than the 'presentments' in books which treat of the 'occult'" (25). This "'restless, unsatisfied longing' [that] rose again in his heart" upon seeing Dianthe's apparition is Reuel's unwitting desire for his own sister, couched in terms of an occult, transpsychic affinity (23). Later he will explain to Aubrey (who is simultaneously feeling his own inexplicable attraction for Dianthe) that "a mad desire seized me to find that face a living reality that I might love and worship it. Then I saw her . . . *in the flesh!* My desire was realized" (42–43). The psychologically salutary effect that attends the awakening of this unwitting sibling desire suggests a refashioning of the consequences of sibling affinity. Whereas orthodox scientific and cultural proscriptions against incest designate close family members as the least fit for biologically sound and morally sanctioned relationships, the occult forces behind sibling affinity in *Of One Blood* lead Reuel, in the throes of a "sweet unrest," to consider his sister as the singularly perfect mate and his "supreme need." Achieved by virtue of a mystical rather than a biological link, the return to incest with an occult difference, here and at the novel's end, provides the radical revision of deterministic conceptions of kinship and their attendant rhetoric of racial "blood."

Moreover, Reuel's unorthodox mastery of the metaphysical brings about the bold revision of "blood's" figuration, changing the meaning and the very nature of this term in incest and miscegenation rhetoric. As the fundamental substance of an altered physical and metaphysical state, Reuel's ethereal blood substitute opens new possibilities for altering the literal and figurative associations between the vehicle of "blood" and the tenors of life, character, and kinship. Redefining the force that draws Reuel and Dianthe together, Reuel's occult science reimagines the incestuous "voice of blood" in terms of a transcendent, metaphysical "power of sympathy," and provides the fictional corollary for the new linguistic and cognitive sympathies to be derived from a refashioning of racialism's figurative language of "blood."

The key to this radical revision lies in the idea of a connective substance that makes the psychic sympathies of Reuel's occultism and the conceptual sympathies of metaphor work. Roman Jakobson's discussion of the homologous action of totemic magic and figurative language is particularly useful here for demonstrating the resonance between Reuel's discovery of new physical and psychic dimensions and Hopkins's narrative reconfiguration of kinship discourse. In his influential discussion of metaphor and metonymy, Jakobson posits two types of conceptual relationships by which the terms of a discourse can be associated. "The development of a discourse may take place along two different semantic lines; one topic may lead to another either through their similarity or through their contiguity. The metaphoric way would be the most appropriate term for the first case and the metonymic way for the second, since they find their most condensed expression in metaphor and metonymy respectively" (129). Jakobson finds the same work of similarity and contiguity at play in Freudian dream work and an "illuminating" homology in the actions of anthropologist James George Frazer's twin branches of sympathetic magic: homoeopathic or imitative magic (operating by the law of similarity) and contagious magic (by law of contact).

This comparison between the operations of dream work, figurative language, and sympathetic magic highlights the creative process required to reconstruct what are essentially errors of association made in the linking of terms and ideas in each case. Jakobson's reference to totemic theory as an anthropological corollary to the element of creative error in the associative dynamics of his two "semantic lines" of figuration is supported by Frazer's own description in *The Golden Bough* of the two principles of "the magician's logic" as "two different misapplications of the association of ideas": "Homeopathic magic commits the mistake of assuming that things which resemble each other are the same: contagious magic commits the mistake of assuming that things which have once been in contact with each other are always in contact" (13). In all of these cases (Jakobson, Freud, and Frazer), an interpretation based on simple paraphrase is frustrated by the severely truncated or lost terms of the relationship between the manifest set of signs (the vehicle of the figurative expression, the dream content, the magic talisman) and their poetically, psychologically, or symbolically "hidden" referents.

With this homology between figuration and sympathetic magic in mind, we can see that the substitution of an occult substance for literal blood as the vehicle for kinship depicts the real and available possibility for a strategic refashioning of the figurative and conceptual relationship between blood and kinship, effectively altering the cultural and symbolic associations that the figure of "blood" infuses into this discourse. The metaphysical transfer of knowledge and power between human subjects and psyches in *Of One Blood*—made possible by Reuel's discovery of a connective synergy between a universal ethereal substance and "'the hidden self lying quiescent in every human soul'"—correlates with the semiotic transfer of associative concepts between terms in the action of metaphor (*One Blood* 7). Reuel's occult science suggests a change in the figurative meaning of "blood" by altering the very substance through which metaphysical and metaphorical sympathy is achieved. As Frazer explains:

> Both branches of magic, the homeopathic and the contagious, may conveniently be comprehended under the general name of Sympathetic Magic, since both assume that things act on each other at a distance through a secret sympathy, the impulse being transmitted from one to the other by means of what we may conceive as a kind of invisible ether, not unlike that which is postulated by modern science for a precisely similar purpose, namely, to explain how things can physically affect each other through a space which appears to be empty. (Frazer 14)

Reuel's discovery of a mystical blood substitute reveals the secret metaphysical sympathy between all things and alters the literal and figurative vehicle of the "secret sympathy" between Reuel and Dianthe, thus allowing for what would otherwise be impossible under the discourse of kinship figured through biological blood—the purity of sibling union. Occult science thus provides the new figurative and conceptual relationships between blood and kinship necessary for the novel's semiotic revision and cultural transvaluation of incest. Unorthodox science redeems monogenesis, and by ushering in the end of incest as the primary blood taboo, undermines the scientific and symbolic logic of all other related taboos against illicit crossings of blood.

In addition to the entailment of biological determinism, Hopkins's revision of incest discourse refutes the entailment of totemic blood's differential gender relations. In anthropological and psychoanalytic theories of the incest aversion derived from the principle of totemism, rituals of blood naturalize gender differences, as the fear of illicit contact with the feminine becomes the source of the kinship taboo. This is the case in Durkheim's *Incest: The Nature and Origin of the Taboo* (1898) (published four years before *Of One Blood*), where the incest taboo in "primitive" societies prevents contact with what is regarded as the recurring manifestation of impurity in the form of menstrual blood. "Thus the woman, in a rather chronic manner, is the theater of these bloody demonstrations. The feelings that the blood evokes are carried within her; we know in fact with what extraordinary facility the nature of the taboo is diffused" (85).

For Freud as for Durkheim, patriarchal anxieties over blood motivate the establishment of totemic kinship restrictions. In *Totem and Taboo*, the spilling of the father's blood by a "horde" of jealous sons creates feelings of communal remorse which, in turn, lead to the prohibition of violence against the totem animal, a stand-in for the father. The resultant power vacuum leaves the sons vying for the attention of the females in the community, and in order to ward off the fratricide that would result from the sons' battle for favor, the prohibition against incest is instituted: "[T]he brothers had no alternative, if they were to live together, but . . . to institute the law against incest, by which they all alike renounced the women whom they desired and who had been their chief motive for dispatching their father" (179). When the antifeminine underpinnings of some of the most influential scientific discourse on incest are taken into consideration, Hopkins's revisions of the scientific, cultural, and narrative implications of incest can be read as wholly consistent with the larger feminist politics guiding her political activism and her entire literary body of work.

Yet, for all of its interventions into the premises and implications of scientific discourse on incest, Hopkins's novel cannot easily put aside the troubling moral dimensions of its sibling romance plot. The revelation of these familial relationships becomes the moral nadir of the novel, a dark reversal of fortune in comparison to the standard reunion of ex-slave families in so many other racial melodramas of the period. When Dianthe learns of her relationships with her own brothers, she responds "with a look of utter horror that froze her blood. 'My brothers! both those men!'" (*One Blood* 177).

> Dianthe staggered as though buffeted in the face. Blindly, as if in some hideous trance, reeling and stumbling, she fell. Cold and white as marble, she lay in the old woman's [Aunt Hannah's] arms, who thought her dead. "Better so," she cried, and then laughed aloud, then kissed the poor, drawn face. But she was not dead.
>
> Time passed; the girl could not speak. The sacrilege of what had been done was too horrible. Such havoc is wrought by evil deeds. The first downward step of an individual or a nation, who can tell where it will end, through what dark and doleful shades of hell the soul must pass in travail? (177–78)

Whereas the occult blood transfusion performed by Reuel revives Dianthe from a state near death, the revelation of incest causes her to descend into a near-death state. Reuel may be destined to reestablish the glory of the ancient African civilization of Meroe, but for American subjects as supposedly for all in Western culture, the incest taboo is "commonly believed to represent a baseline in the definition of human morality," and so the siblings are fated outcasts (Arens ix).

Yet, even this notion of the incest prohibition as a litmus test for culture and morality is challenged in the novel's finale. The certainty of Dianthe's death near the end of the novel—"Dianthe was dead, poisoned; that was clear"—seems to suggest that she must pay the ultimate price in order to achieve a moral resolution to the problem of incest, as with her death goes the incest threat (190). The occult context alters the significance of Dianthe's *second* death (after her first "seeming" death resulting from the train accident), and the "ever-living faculty" that maintains her after natural death not only provides the alternative physical circumstances by which Dianthe cannot die, it also provides the thematic context within which Dianthe as the violator of double sibling incest *need* not die in order to bring about the moral resolution of the incest theme.

In several critical readings, the shift from the American to the African setting in the novel's final act has been considered a morally cleansing recontextualization because the change of venue leaves Dianthe behind (dead) and abandons the context of American slavery from which the incest problem stems. Gillman suggests that, "[O]nce we learn all about the characters' mysterious and intertwined pasts under slavery, this knowledge offers no possibility of restoring the American social and moral order" ("Mulatto" 232). For Eric Sundquist, the shift signals Reuel's immersion into the mysticism of his rediscovered African culture and his purified relationship with Queen Candace as antidotes to the problem of incest: "Sheared away in his return to African kingship, Briggs's white blood and skin, associated with slavery, incest, cruelty, and betrayal, are subordinated to his black lineage" (572). Similarly, Dana Luciano observes, "The tension between the endorsement of racial monogenism and the prohibition of familial incest is resolved, in the final pages of the novel, by Reuel's resettlement in Telassar, away from the potentially incestuous disarray of the American scene that is the legacy of slavery" (176).

But if the shift to the African setting solves the problem of incest, it does so not only through the evacuation of associations with American slavery, but also—with a second "resurrection" of Dianthe in the form of the ancient Ethiopian Queen Candace in the novel's finale—through a bold and ironic embrace of sibling affinity and a reappraisal of the sibling romance's "impurity." For in a final iteration of the novel's many doublings, the incestuous union between Reuel and Dianthe is repeated with a difference in the relationship between Reuel and yet another feminine figure of genealogical restoration. Reuel travels to Africa as part of an archaeological expedition and learns of his destiny to fulfill the long-awaited return of the Ethiopian King Ergamenes, ruler of the island capital of Meroe. Reuel weds the Ethiopian female monarch, Queen Candace, the "'virgin queen who waits the coming of Ergamenes to inaugurate a dynasty of kings'" (*One Blood* 130).[6]

If Dianthe's death and the change in venue from America to Africa are read as the turning away from sibling incest, it is more difficult to reconcile this rejection with the uncanny duplication of Dianthe in the figure of Candace and what must be understood as Reuel's persistently incestuous attraction to his sister's form. Captivated by Candace's beauty, grace, and majesty, Reuel is enthralled by her "flute-like voice," a "voice like unto silver chimes," the same feature that had enflamed his desire for his sister Dianthe: "Reuel started, for it seemed to him that Dianthe's own voice was breathing in his ears" (138, 136). If, as Sundquist argues, "the suggestion that Dianthe and Candace are part of the same 'personality' or 'soul' that lives beyond the confines of the physical body and its death empties consanguinity of any threat in the novel," the fact that Candace is not Dianthe "in the flesh" alone does not satisfactorily mitigate the problem of Reuel's "incestuous" desire for his sister Dianthe in the *form* of Candace (Sundquist 572). "She reminded him strongly of his beautiful Dianthe; in face, the resemblance was so striking that it was painful. . . . She was the same height as Dianthe, had the same well-developed shoulders and the same admirable bust" (*One Blood* 137). Candace is (as Sundquist suggests) a "more appropriate mate"—not because she is *not* Reuel's sister but, I would argue, because she is so much like her (Sundquist 572).

Reuel's desire for Queen Candace, rather than a departure from his incestuous relationship with Dianthe, is the consummation of that forbidden desire with a critical difference. It is, after all, the very power of a proxy sibling affinity that forges Reuel and Candace's relationship, and as Dianthe's double, Candace reinscribes even as she revises the incestuous implications of the siblings' relationship. The manner by which

Reuel surrogates Candace as the object of his incestuous desire for his sister (a sublimation that provokes Sundquist's description of Hopkins's plot as "proto-Faulknerian") allows him both to avoid and *engage* in the illicit union (572).[7] While Reuel's union of "one blood" with Dianthe results in a relationship that supposedly undermines culture itself and leaves sterile, genealogically corrupted offspring by anthropological and ethnological accounts, the union of "one blood" with Candace is a prophesy-fulfilling fertile union. Candace is described in terms anathema to the very etymological roots of incest in the sense of the "impure" and "unchaste," for in contrast to Dianthe's descent from a long line of slave women whose chastity had been repeatedly violated, Candace, as the Ethiopian guide Ai explains to Reuel, "'is a virgin queen'"; indeed, she seems "the embodiment of all chastity" (*One Blood* 130, 137). In the final embrace of sibling affinity, all of the received notions of incest discourse are reversed, and the "consanguineous" union that once threatened the entire culture—the union to which Dianthe responds with an "utter horror that froze her blood"—is transformed into a transcendent propinquity that now sets African blood in motion: "Yes; she was a Venus, a superb statue of bronze, moulded by a great sculptor; but an animated statue, in which one saw the blood circulate, and from which life flowed" (177, 137).

The strangely incestuous character of the union between Reuel and Candace should be understood as the thematic capstone of the cultural transvaluation and historiographic revision that is the very purpose of the African expedition. Reuel and Candace's wedding completes Reuel's return as the lost ruler of the ancient Ethiopian civilization of Meroe, capital of the Kingdom of Kush. The African archaeological expedition that comprises the novel's latter half—culminating in Reuel's union with Candace—rehearses nineteenth-century ethnological debates over racial castes in ancient Egypt and anthropological debates over ancient Egypt as the origin of Western civilization. The purpose of the expedition is to establish ancient Ethiopia as the wellspring of Western civilization. As leader of the expedition, Professor Stone explains, "'I know that in connecting Egypt with Ethiopia, one meets with most bitter denunciation from most modern scholars. Science has done its best to separate the race from Northern Africa, but the evidence is with the Ethiopians. If I mistake not, the ruins of Meroe will prove my words'" (99). The lineage of civilization that Professor Stone is determined to reestablish is outlined in an essay by Hopkins on black female educators published in *The Colored American Magazine* in 1902.

> Rome got her civilization from Greece; Greece borrowed hers from Egypt, thence she derived her science and beautiful mythology. Civilization descended the Nile and spread over the delta, as it came down from Thebes. Thebes was built and settled by the Ethiopians. As we ascend the Nile we come to Meroe the queen city of Ethiopia and the cradle of learning in to which all Africa poured its caravans. So we trace the light of civilization from Ethiopia to Egypt, to Greece, to Rome, and thence diffusing its radiance over the entire world. (qtd. in Carby 156)

In its dramatization of a grand cyclical return to African ascendance, the novel's conclusion reflects Hopkins's own Ethiopianist or pan-Africanist worldview, and with the installment of Reuel's Christianity in place of African spiritualist practices, there may be no reading that can completely redeem the cultural chauvinism and "civilizing mission" of Reuel's return.[8]

Yet taken within the context of the novel's theme of revising Western cultural genealogy, the suggestion of a vague incest desire in Reuel and Candace's relationship can be read as an oblique reference to the ancient north African practices of sibling incest that have challenged theories of a universal incest taboo and that undermine the notion of the taboo as a "litmus test of culture." Historically, ancient Egypt stands out among the handful of civilizations in which incestuous relationships, particularly between brother and sister, were practiced openly. For anthropologists and classical historians, ancient Egypt is exceptional even among the rare exceptions to the supposedly universal taboo. Remarking on the particularly unusual extension of the practice beyond royalty and the upper castes in this period, Lévi-Strauss considered ancient Egypt (along with Peru and Hawaii) as one of the "three classical exceptions" to the universality of the incest taboo (9). For anthropologist W. Arens, the "peculiar but well documented occurrence of incestuous marriages among a significant portion of the Egyptian middle class during the Roman era" constitutes a "particularly bedeviling instance, for—lacking other examples—it comprises a unique class and thus must be considered a legitimate ethnographic and historical oddity" (9). Similarly, historian Keith Hopkins suggests the significance of this "oddity" for undermining all totalizing claims of incest's cultural prohibition. "The Egyptian practice . . . constitutes not merely a unique case in world ethnography, an antiquarian curiosity, but also a challenge to the propositions put forward by leading anthropologists, psychologists and sociologists, who have assumed that the taboo on sexual relations, let alone marriage, between siblings was universal and have made the incest taboo a cornerstone of their theories" (303–4).

As the practice of incest in ancient Egypt challenges the universal claims of the incest prohibition, it serves as an anthropological parallel for the category-bending phenomena of occult science practiced by Reuel in *Of One Blood*. Incest in Egypt must either undermine the notion of the universality of the incest prohibition or be relegated to the margins beyond category, into a set of phenomena not unlike that described by the text Reuel reads in the novel's opening: "The Unclassified Residuum." Considering the novel's Ethiopianist historiographical revisions dedicated to the claim for Ethiopia's antedating of Egyptian civilization, the return to incestuous desire in Reuel and Candace's union reads as a bold reclamation of what is, for Hopkins's counter-metanarrative purposes, a rather pointedly *unsettling* aspect of ancient Egyptian culture.

While *Of One Blood* contains no explicit references to the Egyptian practice of incest, the novel is laced with partly veiled allusions to incestuous unions in Egyptian mythology (perhaps attributable to Hopkins's own study in Egyptology). The avaricious and insouciant playboy Charlie Vance is often referred to as "Adonis," a nickname that, as Marla Harris explains, serves as a subtle Egyptian mythological reference to the novel's incest theme. "Invoking the mythical Adonis, the product of incest between a father and his daughter Mirra (or Myrhha), Hopkins prepares us for her Mira, the mother of Aubrey, Reuel, and Dianthe in *Of One Blood*. Unlike the Myrrha of Ovid's *Metamorphoses*, whose lust for her father leads her to trick him into sex, Hopkins's Mira is raped by her white master/brother" (384). Reuel viewed a set of hieroglyphics upon entering the pyramids and "noticed particularly the figure of a queen attired in long robe, tight at neck and ankles, with closely fitted legs" (*One Blood* 104). The lotus flower image is the graphic citation of the lotus lily birthmark which, the reader learns, is given to all descendants of Ergamenes and serves as the device later used to identify Reuel as the lost king of Meroe. The image of Osiris suggests parallels between the Egyptian god and Hopkins's hero: just as Osiris battled with his brother (Seth), Reuel will do battle with the man revealed to be his own brother (Aubrey Livingston), and like Osiris, Reuel will be "resurrected" when he fulfills the prophesy of the return of the king. The lash of Osiris also presages the revelation of incest; like this god of the Egyptian underworld who ruled with his sister Isis, Reuel becomes involved in a relationship with his sister.

Reuel's fulfillment of the prophesied return of ancient Ethiopia's King Ergamenes also makes a historical reference to Egyptian incest. Ergamenes is the Ethiopian ruler whose reign coincided with the reign of Egypt's second Ptolemy, a fact that Professor Stone articulates in *Of One Blood* and that Hopkins repeats in her ethnological *Primer*. The concurrency of these Ethiopian and Egyptian kingships draws a subtle relationship between the Ethiopianist return to ascendancy and ancient Egypt's tolerance of sibling incest (both of which resound in Reuel and Candace's union) because the concurrency emphasizes Ergamenes as the Ethiopian king whose reign corresponds with the height of the practice of incest in Egypt. This Ptolemy was the second Greek king of Egypt who, quite contrary to repudiating incest, took up the practice and, according to Keith Hopkins, "divorced his wife who had borne him several children and married his full sister Arsinoe" (311–12).[9] As he carries his incestuous desire into the ancient African setting, Reuel conserves sibling affinity in the cultural syncretism between Egyptian and Greek civilization.

These references to mythological and historical incest are subtle, yet numerous enough to be viewed as deliberate, and considering the degree to which the practice of sibling incest violates modern Western norms,

Hopkins may not have been comfortable with representing the practice of incest in ancient Egyptian society more explicitly. Of course, she also runs the risk of suggesting the generally loathed practice is a feature of the African culture she hopes to valorize. Yet these many references to mythological and historical incest underscore the alternative cultural system of value that mitigates the abhorrence to being "one blood."

Before concluding with a discussion of this cultural revision, a final example of the novel's references to Egyptian incest mythology may help make the point that the relationship between Reuel and Candace should be interpreted as a repetition of (rather than a retreat from) the tabooed romance between Reuel and Dianthe, now divested of its immorality, not through elimination but through revision. This reconfiguration becomes evident by a comparison between the different responses elicited by the revelation of the symbolic lotus lily in two different contexts. The lotus lily birthmarks—shared by Reuel, Dianthe, and "'every descendant of the royal line'"—not only designate members of the Ethiopian royal family but also serve as bodily warnings against the consummation of incestuous unions between the flesh of those who bear the marks (102). In the event of physical intimacies between family members in this line, the recognition of the lotus lily birthmarks would be the last defense against (or final confirmation of) the commission of incest. Thus, just before she reveals Dianthe and Reuel's incestuous relationship, Aunt Hannah makes the somewhat cryptic exclamation, "My Mira's children, by de lotus-lily on each leetle breast I claim them for de great Osiris, mighty god'" (177). Hannah's evocation of Osiris links the siblings' bodily markings with the incestuous sibling relationship between Osiris and Isis. And when Dianthe asks, "'Did each of Mira's children have this mark?,'" Hannah's response explains what the mark signifies: "'Yes, honey; all of one blood!'" (177).

Dianthe's death prevents the unification of the lotus lily birthmarks in the flesh, that is, on the skin of the biological siblings, but the unification of the lilies as the symbolic parallel of incest does indeed take place at the end of the novel in a suggestive interaction between Reuel and Candace. Exclaiming triumphantly to Reuel that she has "prepared against this happy hour," the queen produces her prized possession, a "curious ring of dull gold, bearing one priceless gem cut in the form of a lotus lily" (140). Suggestively, the virgin queen slips the ring, which she has carefully preserved and protected in an "inlaid cabinet," onto Reuel's waiting finger. Perhaps for the peace of mind and larger good of the kingdom, the royal attendants look on, bearing witness to this digital consummation with all of its weighty implications for the continuation of the imperial dynasty. "The Sages had watched the actors in this life-drama with jealous eyes that noted every detail with satisfaction." Inspired by this mere prelude, Ai ushers everyone else out of the bedchamber. "'Let us hence, that the union may be speedily accomplished'" (140).

If the social and anthropological frameworks for incest and miscegenation taboos support political distinctions of genealogy and kinship augmented by culturally constructed fears of contamination and figured (prior to the advent of genetics) by blood, then in Hopkins's novel, the monogenetic decree of "one blood" carries what Marc Shell describes as a "trade-off for this universalist sentiment" that cannot be dismissed, "a characteristic psychological disquietude and political instability" (625). The great "horror" of the "one blood" decree is not merely the problem of unwitting incest within the nuclear family, but also the inevitable "carnal contagion" resulting from notions of kinship based on and articulated through a figure as polysemic as "blood." But, as Shell explains:

> [I]n the culturally vibrant terminology of kinship it is debatable which kind of kinship is the literal one. After all, the fundamental distinction between "real" kinship and "pseudo"-kinship—between literal and figural signification—is the topic of a still-unresolved debate about whether kinship is essentially a matter of biology (however understood) or of sociology. Which is fundamental in determining "literal" kinship, for example, my likeness to my supposed genitor or my likeness to God, who created me in his image? Which substance is fundamental: the genes I share with my genitor, the love between my adoptive parent and myself, the milk I sucked from my mother, the blood I commingled with my blood brother, the wafer and wine I shared at a communal feast, or the dust from which all things (including myself) are made? (Shell 638)

In *Of One Blood* Hopkins expresses just such deconstructive implications of incest for racial biologism in the narrator's commentary following the incest revelation in the novel:

> The slogan of the hour is "Keep the Negro down!" but who is clear enough in vision to decide who hath black blood and who hath it not? Can any one tell? No, not one; for in His own mysterious way He has united the white race and the black race in this new continent. By the transgression of the law He proves His own infallibility: "Of one blood have I made all nations of men to dwell upon the whole face of the earth," is as true today as when given to the inspired writers to be recorded. No man can draw the dividing line between the two races, for they are both of one blood! (178)

Ultimately, *Of One Blood* suggests that the cultural meaning of incest, like the meaning of miscegenation, is based upon constructed categories only taken as natural. Claude Lévi-Strauss describes the incest prohibition as "a rule which embraces that which in society is most foreign to it, but also a social rule which retains what in nature is most likely to go beyond it. The incest prohibition is at once on the threshold of culture, in culture, and in one sense . . . culture itself" (12). But when the differences that define the foreign and the unnatural are shown to be politically and historically contingent metaphors for conceptualizing and managing difference itself (here with respect to race and gender), then the broader meaning of incest and certainly the universalizing claim of a relationship between the incest prohibition and the maintenance or decline of culture become uncertain.

Formally homologous to the forbidden union between Reuel and his sister Dianthe, the final union between Reuel and Candace resolves incest's dialectic between the categories of the natural and unnatural, neutralizing incest's prescribed cultural and moral meanings. The union allows Reuel to respond to the "call of blood" from Dianthe without actually committing incest, but more radically, provides the possibility for a sanctioned and pure relationship between brother and sister. The relationship is formally endogamous yet it cannot be termed "incest" because incest is unchaste by definition. Thus the plot purifies the notion of "one blood" by separating the commitment of incest from the fulfillment of the Paulinian decree. Finally, rather than substituting incest for monogenism, Hopkins demonstrates that, ultimately, one cannot maintain "pure races" protected against miscegenation without an incestuous doctrine of blood purity, and yet one cannot celebrate the unity of a single human family without embracing familial or even sibling affinity. For the polygenesist, then, only the impurity of incest can maintain the distinct purity of the "bloodlines" of original and permanent races, while for the monogenesist incest is an etymological misnomer, for in a monogenetic world, all relations are "incestuous," which is to say that none of them are, and the impurity of incest has no meaning. Thus, as in Hopkins's novel, all roads lead to incest, and the only real choice is that between the open and the occult practice of incest, between the biblical imperative of brotherhood and the untenable nature of racial science's taxonomies, between a guiltless doctrine of "one blood" and the repressed desires of the hidden self.

CHAPTER 4

William Faulkner and the Color of Blood

As they invoke the material image of blood in support of an ideology of race that thrives upon visible criteria, racial blood metaphors make an implicit call for violence. In *Blood and Belief: The Circulation of a Symbol Between Jews and Christians* (2007), David Biale discusses the remarkable way in which "blood inhabits the imagination as both substance and symbol" (1). Racial blood metaphors work to make race seem more real by negotiating the thin difference between blood as symbol and blood as substance, a threshold that, when crossed, leads to the slippage from a discourse of difference to differentiating forms of violence against the racialized body that satisfy racialism's reliance upon visible criteria. Much to the threat of the ambiguous racial subject, while the figurative language of blood within racial discourse aids in discussing and legally codifying race, a visible blood—blood that can actually be seen—is ultimately required for the insatiable racial gaze to tell difference. In this chapter, through a reading of William Faulkner's *Light in August* (1932), I will argue that the use of blood imagery in racial rhetoric works to bridge the divide between blood as symbol of racial visibility and blood as the truly visible, racializing result of physical violence against ambiguously signifying bodies.

Blood is both the symbol of racial difference and the substance of racial violence, and if metaphors operate by drawing meaningful associations between terms, then the stakes of racial blood discourse—the stakes of speaking about race in terms of blood—include the threat of crossing this threshold between symbol and substance. To observe the dangerous proximity between a symbolic blood that figures race and a substantial blood whose visible flow enforces racial divisions, one need only recognize the slippage from symbol to substance intimated in some of the most enduring rhetorical images produced by turn-of-the-century antilynching discourse, from Ida B. Wells's *A Red Record* (1895) to James Weldon Johnson's description of the summer of 1919 as "Red Summer." Appealing to a universal response to the color of blood, these phrases employed by the period's antilynching crusaders subtly convey the shift from symbol to substance that racial blood rhetoric constantly threatens to bring into effect. In the discourse of lynching, a blood that once supposedly flowed latently and threateningly through black bodies now paints the landscape of the post-Reconstruction era in color, although neither black nor white, and the blood that was once considered the ultimate social and genealogical contaminant, the ultimate symbol of aversion and avoidance, quickly becomes the substance that the white supremacist imagination most desires to see and to touch. Ida B. Wells describes the manner in which lynching transubstantiates blood from a mere fantasy within the racial imagination to the real object before the racial gaze in the course of an 1893 lynching in Roanoke, Virginia, one of the many lynchings documented in *A Red Record*: "At once the old cry was sounded that the [white] woman had been assaulted, and in a few hours all the town was wild with people thirsting for the assailant's blood" (109).

The kind of racial violence Wells vehemently condemned is fueled by anxieties of visibility created by the tension between practices of seeing race and cultural meanings of seeing blood, and this space between the visibility of race and the visibility of blood constitutes a cognitive space that racial blood rhetoric works to close. Racial blood rhetoric strategically conflates the anxieties of seeing race with the anxiety of seeing blood, providing a conceptual common ground in which the metaphorical blood of racial discourse becomes conceptually, psychologically, and dramatically transubstantiated into the form of visible blood. Through this process, the image of blood in racial rhetoric works to construct a special practice of racial visibility, drawing from cultural meanings associated with the sight of blood and raising social anxieties over race that prompt the tilt toward violence.

This relationship between the project of racial determination and the enactment of racial violence emerges as a feature of William Faulkner's rural, early nineteenth-century South, as suggested in a scathing critique of southern culture written by one of the region's most vocal critics. In *Killers of the Dream* (1949), author and cultural critic Lillian Smith wholly rebuked southern life and values and characterized the region as one in which the regular sight of blood, a function of the region's hunting culture, supported the tolerance for blood spilled in another context: racial violence. "Blood-letting is a thing one gets used to in the country. Hog-killing . . . sticking a pig, hanging it up, listening to those human-like squeals, watching blood streak the flesh. . . . Negro-killing. . . . So strangely akin—in sick minds that hold no words to stop the deed" (161). For Smith, southern culture raises no barrier against the casual transition from animal slaughter to racial violence that would allow a viewer to tell the difference. Instead, hearing animal "squeals" and "watching blood streak the flesh" desensitizes the viewer to bloodletting such that animal slaughter and "Negro-killing" become "strangely akin." "Southern culture," Smith continues, "has put few words in the mind to make the difference between human and animal. The words in the white mind are words that turn the Negro into animal, words deliberately fed to people to place the Negro beneath the level of human, to make him not only animal but a 'menace'" (161). One of the words employed by racial discourse to close the "difference between human and animal" is "blood" itself, a word that when used in racial discourse helps to reify race not by suggestions of biological racial determinism but by creating an affinity between the visual determination of racial difference and the visual consumption of racial violence.

Smith's formulation suggests the racial imagination's appeal to blood as metaphor and sign of racial difference as a strategic capitalization upon the common emotional response to the sight of blood, which I argue works as a way of employing the image of blood to elicit the desire to make racial essences visible, moving racial blood from symbol to substance. Analyzing the relationship between race and blood in the construction of race as "man's most dangerous myth" during the mid-twentieth century, anthropologist Ashley Montagu explains that, "There are many words in our vocabulary that are characterized by an exaggerated emotional content; words distinguished by a high emotional and low rational quality. 'Race' is such a word; 'blood' is another" (360). As a particularly emotional and irrational form of imagination, racialism thrives upon the emotional content Montagu describes as being attached to the words it uses to "create ideas and stereotypes, which become our personal reality" (360). "The word and the emotion are often conflated, so that when the idea, word, or perception of race is presented, the emotion associated with it, especially in a racist society, is simultaneously aroused" (360).

As I will demonstrate through the following reading of *Light in August*, racial blood metaphors work to engender racial violence through the associations they make between the visibility of race and the response to the sight of blood. The violence suggested by racial blood metaphors is a function of the tension they create between what must be seen and what cannot be seen—between the visual demands of race as practice and the invisibility of the substance through which these metaphors claim race is carried. "Because race works through the domain of the visible," writes Linda Alcoff, "the experience of race is predicated first and foremost on the perception of race, a perception whose specific mode is a learned ability" ("Racial Embodiment" 20). Racialism's visual imperative not only detects signs of race as part of its categorizing project but also constructs an entire "visual registry" as part of the process by which "visible difference naturalizes racial meanings" (23).[1]

Racial blood discourse extends racialism's "domain of the visible" beyond that which can literally be seen. While the predominant discourse of race as color—a chromatic rhetoric of "blacks" and "whites" (as well as "red"s, "yellow"s, etc.)—is based on the perception of skin, the interrelated rhetoric of racial blood goes beneath the skin while rhetorically maintaining racialism's emphasis on epidermal color and visibility. Literally visible chromatics are projected as subcutaneous images of "black" and "white" blood. Meanwhile, the wholeness of the racialized body becomes at stake in the use and interpretation of such language, for by locating racial difference in a substance that ordinarily cannot be seen, racial blood metaphors raise a tension in the project of racial determination that can only be resolved by closing the gap between literal and figurative visibility. In *Black Skin, White Masks*, Frantz

Fanon describes the violence felt when a "racial epidermal schema" imposes upon and crumbles the more general "corporeal schema" of the body's visibility: "What else could it be for me but an amputation, an excision, a hemorrhage that spattered my whole body with black blood?" (112). As it calls upon blood to serve as the determining substance of a rigorously visible enterprise, the rhetoric of racial blood demands that blood become visible. This implicit violence that racial blood metaphors insinuate into the discourse of race constitutes one of the most operative and important differences between a rhetoric of race based on skin color and a rhetoric of race based on blood.

Through a reading of William Faulkner's *Light in August*, this chapter considers the implications of the kind of racial visibility constructed through the use of racial blood metaphors. Such analysis provides a more complete understanding of how the visuality entailed in racial blood metaphors contributes to the visual dimension of the practice of race itself, as well as a more complete understanding of what it means to see racial difference (as racial blood metaphors suggest it be seen) in terms of blood. When racial discourse turns from the skin to the blood, the differences between these two forms of visibility highlight the features of racial visibility most prized by the racialist gaze. Such analysis provides a view of the very constructedness of racial visibility itself and reveals how much of what we see when we "see" race is not physical but rather (like the race concept itself) narrative and cognitive. Although racial blood metaphors refer to a substance that cannot literally be seen, a latent visibility of blood works through these metaphors to energize racial aversion by an aversion to the sight of blood. Recognizing this function of racial blood metaphors is important for considering the effects of racial blood discourse beyond their suggestions of biological racial essentialism. For, although references to "black blood" and "white blood" clearly tread away from literalism, the form of visibility they borrow from blood imagery remains one of the most operative ideas about race that they instill, an idea that is not captured through the paraphrasing of racial blood metaphors as figurative claims to biological determinism.

The racializing work that racial blood metaphors perform through their violence-inducing rhetoric is dramatized in the plot of Faulkner's *Light in August* (1932). As perhaps Faulkner's most visual novel, *Light in August* is also his work most concerned with the ability to tell difference by sight, as it depicts the tragic experiences of a racially indeterminate character rejected by a southern culture characterized by a relentless racial awareness and an abrasive scrutiny of outsiders. As with so many other fictional racial passers, the ambiguity of Christmas's race is a function of the discrepancy between his near-white visible appearance and his suspected African American genealogy. Because his physical features display none of the supposedly telltale indicators of African American ancestry, Christmas's assumed "hidden" blackness is often expressed in terms of his possession of what cannot be seen, his "black" or "nigger blood." As Christmas says himself, "'I think I got some nigger blood in me. . . . 'I dont know. I believe I have'" (196–97). Through such language, the rhetoric of racial blood provides a discursive alternative to racialism's reliance upon visual determinants. With his racial identity shrouded in the obscure details of his illegitimate birth, Christmas spends his entire life wondering whether he possesses the figurative "black blood" that would define him racially in the novel's early twentieth-century Mississippi setting. The circulation of racial blood rhetoric may be inadequate to explain whether Joe Christmas is black or white, but this rhetoric nevertheless works effectively to racialize the way that Christmas is seen. Christmas and the residents of Faulkner's Yoknapatawpha county resort to the language of "black blood" in order to make Christmas's assumed blackness visible, if not literally then at least rhetorically.

Yet, as the metaphorical sign of a difference that cannot yet must be seen, Christmas's blood is forced into view through violence. The novel demonstrates the work that racial blood metaphors perform with respect to the construction of racial visibility and shows how racial blood metaphors mobilize the image of blood in order to incite and justify the desire for violence against the racialized body. Christmas's racial identity is systematically constructed through the image of blood until the violent desire of the racial gaze is finally excited into the fury of violence that ultimately destroys him.

Because the visibility of blood is an integral part of the process that makes Joe Christmas black, as the novel suggests over and over again, in order for Christmas to be made black, he must be made to bleed. In *Violence and the Sacred*, Rene Girard warns of the contagious nature of violence spurred on by the sight of the flow of blood: "When violence is unloosed . . . blood appears everywhere—on the ground, underfoot, forming great pools. Its very fluidity gives form to the contagious nature of violence. Its presence proclaims murder and announces new upheavals to come. Blood stains everything it touches the color of violence and death. Its very appearance seems, as the saying goes, to 'cry out for vengeance'" (34). Similarly, in *Light in August*, the sight of blood circulates a racial rhetoric that, in turn, demands blood become visible again. Racial blood metaphors make blood appear to the racial imagination, whetting the appetite for racial violence and begetting the spilling of literal blood. As I will argue, the spilling of Joe Christmas's blood is not a social punishment for his transgressive blackness but rather the act that makes him black. The novel's deployment of racial blood metaphors amidst images of literal blood demonstrates the necessary relationship between acts of racial determination, acts of looking, and acts of violence. *Light in August* dramatizes that blood is, after all, what the racial gaze is really and always looking for.

In conjunction with the novel's racial themes, there is a decidedly visual, even cinematic quality or texture to the descriptive language of *Light in August* as well as a sustained thematic emphasis on the social and psychological implications of acts of seeing.[2] Several Faulkner critics have discussed how a study of visibility develops integrally with the novel's treatment of the construction of racial difference. Patricia McKee, for example, identifies a racialized and gendered "visual economy of looks" governing the novel in which "it is white men who do the looking that constitutes public meaning" while African Americans and women serve as the objects of this white male gaze (124). Privileged as the agents of acts of looking "used as means of knowledge," white men become the center of the community's knowledge production. White men thus possess a certain collectivized power-knowledge that they wield in the novel that, when applied to newcomers like Christmas, acts as a culturally defensive social gaze identifying potential threats for isolation or elimination. In a similar line of thought, Peter Lurie employs film theory to analyze the aggressive force motivating what he describes as the "particularly visual form that interest acquires" in the novel, particularly the town's visual interest in Christmas, who is "defined by the activity of his being looked at by others—as well as by an aggressiveness behind such acts of looking (285).[3] The gaze in *Light in August* aggressively disseminates power; it is not only a gaze that consumes and assesses but a gaze capable of doing damage.

The novel's acts of looking, as pervasive acts of power and aggression, depict the look as an incisive racial practice. Indeed, the novel's emphasis on the probing eyes of the community underscores the visual practices endemic to racialism. As George Mosse states in his history of the development of European racism in *Toward the Final Solution*, "The importance of the emphasis upon the visual for racial thought cannot be overestimated" (24–25). More recently, Linda Alcoff, taking a phenomenological approach, also emphasizes the essential role played by visibility in racialist thought. "Inherent to the concept of race is the idea that it exists there on the body itself, not simply on its ornaments or in its behaviors" ("Habits" 31). An individual's racial identity may be "usually determined by ancestry," but the act of determining that ancestry always involves at least an attempt to read that ancestry through the application of a scrutinizing gaze. The practice of race is thus mobilized by an aggressive visual scrutiny in the service of the underlying belief "that identity is discernible if one peers long enough at, or observes carefully enough, the person's physical features and practiced mannerisms" (31). It is through the application of this scrutiny, Alcoff explains, that "the ideology of race asserts its impervious visibility, despite the fact that the two are not always in sync" (31). Racial subjects, even those visibly ambiguous ones like Faulkner's Joe Christmas, become racialized through such aggressive acts of looking as the racial gaze seeks to determine racial identity through the close scrutiny and measurement of viewable morphological features.

Alcoff's notion of an "impervious visibility" at the core of racialist thinking is particularly helpful for considering how racial blood rhetoric bridges practices of visible racial determination with acts of racial violence. As Alcoff suggests, racialism's demand for the visible will not be denied even when the facts of genealogical or legal racial identity go out of "sync" with the more readily perceived and thus more impressionable system of visible racial marks. Like Faulkner's Joe Christmas, individuals with indeterminate racial appearances may deceive the racial gaze in acts of deliberate or involuntary passing, but they cannot evade or escape the ideology of visibility mobilizing this gaze.

The passing subject relies upon racialism's insistence on visibility while simultaneously taking advantage of this visibility's unreliability, doing so with the understanding that his or her racial identity will be determined by sight, not based on whatever genealogical truths lie "beneath" skin color.[4] Ultimately, racialism's own reliance upon visible physical features creates the loophole through which the passing subject may pass. The miscategorization of the passer's genealogical or legal racial status does not undermine racialism's practice of visibility so much as it depends and plays upon it, as the willful or accidental misdirection of visible racial signs becomes an implicit concession to the visual demands of race. Werner Sollors thus considers racial passing as a particular example of a more broadly human tendency, the "camouflaging of aspects of one's identity" (247). Sollors insightfully explains passing as the product of "the widely shared social belief system, according to which certain descent characteristics, even invisible ones, were viewed as essential and more deeply defining than physical appearance, individual volition, and self-description, or social acceptance and economic success" (248). The phenomenon of passing, we might say, is constituted by the very idea that "certain descent characteristics" can be "invisible" even though these characteristics are (in Sollors's own suggestive metaphorical language) "viewed as essential and more deeply defining than physical appearance" (248).

Ultimately, if the visibility of racialism is truly "impervious" (as Alcoff contends), then rather than evading or thwarting the irrepressible scrutiny of the racial gaze, passing subjects, like Faulkner's Joc Christmas, actually invite it. In this sense, passing has existed in a reciprocal rather than antagonistic relationship with American racialist thought; American racialism enjoys the possibility of passing—the possibility for the evasion of racialism's own endemic visuality—as a rationale for its own ever-vigilant, aggressive, and intrusive acts of visible scrutiny. Passing may demonstrate the unreliability of visibly determining race in the American system of racial determination, but the phenomenon of passing also makes this visible determination more anxious, aggressive, and pervasive. As Walter Benn Michaels has written, "It is only because the thing itself [race] is invisible that everything can be imagined as a way of seeing it" (130). Instead of undermining the visible criteria of race, passing only strengthens it, for the very possibility of passing requires racialism's eye—its technologies of the visible—to work harder. The discourse of racial blood, a discourse that posits essential yet invisible racial determinants, connotes the physical aggression motivating American racialist thought in its suggestion of racialism's irreducible paradox of visibility.

Joel Williamson describes such a dynamic in his account of the anxieties over passing that contributed to the development of the so-called "one-drop rule." As a legal and social response to the problem of racial indeterminacy resulting from racial "intermixture" and the increasing presence of interracial offspring in America from the colonial era through the nineteenth century, the one-drop rule provided the impetus, according to Williamson, for an even more, not less, anxious scrutiny of racial bodies. The implementation of the rule made blackness legally legible and thus more trackable, but it could not make the blackness that it sought to codify any more literally visible. The rule could not satisfy the demands of race's visible practice. Although the rule was ostensibly designed to stabilize the category of blackness by defining subjects as black based on minimal genealogical requirements, one of the tangential effects of the rule was to raise the attention and deepen the intrusiveness of the racial gaze. Thus Williamson suggests that the rule's most significant effect may be that which it had outside of the law, where, by legally constructing a definition of blackness that could not be seen by the naked eye, the rule ratcheted up the level of racial fear in the day-to-day interactions through which race is practiced.

> It would seem that the definitiveness of the one-drop rule ought to have brought an end to Southern white difficulties in dealing with mulattoes. In actuality, it only raised another and more subtle range of difficulties around the central problem of "invisible blackness." Well before one was down to the single drop of African blood, that heritage was lost to sight. Centuries of miscegenation had produced thousands of mulattoes who had simply lost visibility, so much did color and features overlap between those who were mixed and those who were purely white. (98)

The one-drop rule does not override the visual imperative of race; instead, the very tension in the oxymoronic figuration "invisible blackness"—a blackness which cannot be seen—reveals the term's function as a metaphor for anxiety created by the law's inability to bypass the visual imperative of racial determination.

The imaging of blood in the language of the one-drop rule, then, increases rather than dissipates this anxiety, adding another level of insidiousness to the circulation of this racial rhetoric. As racial blood images a racial essence that cannot be seen—yet, because it is racial, must be seen—and metaphorically situates that racial essence in a substance that exists beneath the skin and out of sight, this rhetoric effectively appeals for a moment of violence that will make that substance viewable for the satisfaction of the irrepressible racial gaze. Encouraging the racial gaze to look deeper, to go beneath the skin, passing becomes not only what the racial subject does, but also what the racial gaze must do when it cannot be satisfied by what it finds on the surface. The gaze itself must probe the racial subject beneath his or her surfaces for what Sollors calls the "more deeply defining" characteristics of race existing below the level of "physical appearance" and "self-description."

Racial blood rhetoric invokes an image of what the racialist imagination wants, a racial essence that can be hidden so that it must be found. Moreover, by figuring this racial essence in terms of the very substance whose visibility marks the rupturing of the body, this rhetoric guarantees that this elusive racial essence will be found in ways that lead inevitably to the bodily destruction and thus the social elimination of the unwanted racial subject. The racialist imagination thus rationalizes its own need for a violence that eradicates the threat it has created itself. The very possibility of an "invisible blackness" carried in the blood gives license to the racial gaze to do whatever it can to get its view of that essence, even by penetrating beneath the skin that conceals it.

Racial blood rhetoric thus constructs a particularly violence-inducing kind of racial visibility, the aggressive nature of which emerges as a central theme of *Light in August*. The intent and aggressive acts of looking performed by members of the rural southern community depicted in Faulkner's novel constitute a cooperative project of racial determination that also sets the stage for aggressive acts of physical violence against Joe Christmas, a character whose ambiguous visible appearance incites such aggression by defying easy racial categorization. The aggressive acts of looking applied to Christmas and the subsequent acts of physical violence waged against him are functions of the language used to image his racial indeterminacy. The interrelationship between acts of looking, acts of racial determination, and acts of violence in the novel demonstrates how the rhetoric of racial blood, supposedly employed to address passing as a problem, actually whets individual and social appetites for racial violence.

A threatening racial gaze greets Joe Christmas immediately upon his arrival in Jefferson when, in his first dramatized act (related through the consciousness of Byron Bunch), Christmas engages the townspeople in a mutual act of visual appraisal. Arriving seemingly out of nowhere and looking for work, Christmas approaches a group of planing mill workers. "[T]he group of men at work in the planer shed looked up, and saw the stranger standing there, watching them" (31). While Christmas remains quiet and withdrawn, the mill workers actively scrutinize his body, making every effort to read his past and situate his identity through his physical features. "He did not talk to any of them at all. And none of them tried to talk to him. But they were all conscious of him, of the steady back . . . and arms" (34). Christmas enters a rural southern culture characterized by vigorous acts of visibility motivated by the belief that such scrutiny may reveal the narrative of his past. "He did not look like a professional hobo in his professional rags, but there was something definitely rootless about him, as though no town nor city was his, no street, no walls, no square of earth his home" (31).

Christmas's observers begin to racially construct him through a scouring visual interpretation of his physical features. The narrator's initial physical description of Christmas rakes his body with an abrasive scrutiny, fixing him through the use of descriptive terms suggestive of an ethnologically informed anatomy report. "His face was gaunt, the flesh a level dead parchment color. Not the skin: the flesh itself, as though the skull had been molded in a still and deadly regularity and then baked in a fierce oven" (34–35). Figuring Christmas as already dead, this description adumbrates the violence that will later be directed against him. This gaze immediately begins to probe beneath the surfaces of the stranger's body, peeling back his skin rhetorically and making clear that this gaze will not rest upon the supposed racial indicator most readily available to the eye, his skin, but rather seek below to "the flesh itself." Moreover, as it exposes and interprets the "deadly regularity" of Christmas's skull, the narrator's description speculates on the meaning behind the shape of Christmas's head in a manner reminiscent of the pseudoscientific cranial appraisals of eighteenth-century racial science.[5] Seemingly motivated by an excavating desire that wants to turn Christmas's body inside out in order to reveal something, anything, about his origins and character, this description of Christmas is at once subcutaneous, ethnological, and suggestively violent, complete with the image of Christmas's head being "baked in a fierce oven." As his racial identity becomes increasingly suspect during the course of the novel and as the ambiguity of this identity becomes increasingly intolerable within this community, this threateningly visual dressing-down will mount to physical threat as Christmas's racial ambiguity incites the desire for real violence against him.

Christmas thus becomes an object of violence from the moment he is seen. Indeed, these first views of Christmas constitute the first acts of violence against him, the first signs of his subjection to what Alcoff described as racialism's "impervious" visibility. His indefinite placement within this tightly knit community is enough to get the violence of the determining gaze working. And while suspicion of his blackness has not yet been raised, his racial identity is most certainly the implied object of this fixing gaze, for the scrutinizing looks applied to Christmas are clearly most frustrated by their inability to fix his identity and origins. He arrives in Jefferson looking "like a tramp, yet not like a tramp either" and with "something definitely rootless about him" (31). The planing mill workers take offense at Christmas's seemingly willful embrace of his own ambiguity. He appears to them "as though no town nor city was his, no street, no walls, no square of earth his home. And that he carried this knowledge with him always as though it were a banner, with a quality ruthless, lonely, and almost proud" (32).

As these scrutinizing looks remain unappeased by any knowledge of Christmas's background, the mill workers quickly become restless, and their growing anxiety over Christmas's presence becomes manifested in threats of violence against him. Unwilling to allow Christmas to exist in such an undefined state, the workers imagine violence as a way to eliminate Christmas's free-floating appearance, his insolent and resistant visibility. "'We ought to run him through the planer. . . . Maybe that will take that look off his face'" (32). This casual proposal of violence against Christmas's body is intended to restore the stability of the social order that Christmas's ambiguous presence has unsettled. The suggestion of resorting to violence by running Christmas's body "through the planer" as a way to define and control his visibility, to "take that look off his face," demonstrates the imminent translation of a racial gaze's frustration into the enactment of real violence. At first sight, the racial gaze begins its consideration of drawing blood.

We are examining the expectant rhetoric of violence greeting Joe Christmas because this form of abrasive scrutiny dramatizes one of the critical effects of blood metaphors in racial discourse beyond their suggestion of biological essentialism. The initial views that meet Christmas upon his arrival constitute the first steps in the process of Christmas's racialization, the first step in the blackening of Joe Christmas. Long before he becomes perceived as possibly being black, Christmas is viewed as unwanted and threatening. The novel dramatizes the process through which Christmas, the outsider, becomes racialized into Christmas the black threat to Jefferson's notions of race purity, particular its valuation of white southern femininity embodied in the woman he murders, Joanna Burden. The ongoing speculation over his "black blood" plays a role in this process, not only by figuring Christmas's hidden racial essence but by adumbrating and inciting the community's response to his presence. By making his blood the sought-after object of the community's racial gaze, the description of Christmas's racial identity in terms of blood engenders the narrative leading from his rejection as an outsider to his own bloody murder in the name of racial purity. The novel's symbolic racial economy demands the sight of blood as a condition of Christmas's racialization such that Christmas is not seen as black until he bleeds.

For, if there is a "visual economy of looks" in *Light in August* (as Patricia McKee suggests), there is also a concurrent economy of blood. Blood oscillates through forms seen and unseen, viewable and unviewable, between fact and fiction, substance and symbol, appearing now in reality coating Joe Christmas's hands after the grotesque ritual sacrifice of a sheep and then again as mere metaphor for a blackness that many, including Christmas himself, suspect but do not know whether he possesses. In this manner, blood circulates through *Light in August*, alternating between literal and figurative modes in an almost rhythmic fashion, seemingly replicating the systolic and diastolic rhythms of an underlying pulse. And like the alternating forms of arterial and venous blood that move in circulation, these oscillations of literal and metaphorical blood in the novel are inexorably interrelated; they are duplicitous manifestations of the same substance, constantly obfuscating yet defining each other by opposition.

What begins as a metaphor for the town's obsession with Christmas's indeterminate racial identity becomes manifested in the "periodic filth" of the menstrual cycle that sears Christmas's psychosexual development and interrupts his physical relationship with his prostitute girlfriend Bobby. When menstrual blood recedes during the onset of Joanna Burden's menopause, hastening the end of Christmas's tumultuous sexual relationship with her, it only returns again through her bloody death and then again in Christmas's own murder and castration at the hands of Percy Grimm. The image of blood seems to appear everywhere in the novel, so much so that, as Jay Watson has put it, "it might be apropos to describe *Light in August* as written with a pen dipped in blood" (77). Yet, these many scenes of blood are far from gratuitous, as they constitute one of the novel's central arguments about the construction of race: racial identity emerges as a function of this tense interplay between blood as matter and blood as metaphor, blood that can be seen and blood that cannot. By making blood visible in so many variations in the backdrop of its narrative of passing, the novel's many scenes of bloodletting demonstrate the construction of an alternative kind of racial visibility based on cultural responses to the sight of blood.

When considering the relationship between racial visibility and the sight of blood in the novel, we should recognize that the practices of racial visibility depicted in *Light in August* are substantially informed by Faulkner's own interest in the anthropological discourse of taboo formation. The blood saturating *Light in August* is not only the *in*visible blood of racial determinism, but also the visible blood at the origins of taboo. By synthesizing these forms of blood into its representation of race, *Light in August* infuses the visual project of racial determination with meanings of blood's visibility drawn from the process of taboo. While the biological discourse of racial blood has little to do with the sight of actual blood, the anthropological function of blood is rooted in blood's very image. Unlike the metaphorical references to black and white blood in biological race discourse (in which such chromatic designations actually make oblique reference to the visibility of skin color), the affiliations of identity effected by tabooed blood derive from the actual sight of blood itself.

This difference makes all the difference with respect to *Light in August*'s representation of racial construction. Faulkner's understanding and literary representation of racial blood in its tabooed form bypasses the biological meanings of blood underwriting nineteenth-century dramatizations of miscegenation. The form of blood in *Light in August* derives instead from Faulkner's study of the system of myths and mythmaking in the work of anthropologist Sir James Frazer. Frazer's influence on Faulkner's art can be seen throughout his body of work but, at least by one assessment, "Faulkner's most systematic infusion of material from Frazer is found in *Light in August*" (Hlavsa 153).[6] Some of the most formative events in Joe Christmas's experience, from the development of his childhood aversion for menstrual blood and his antidotal ritual sacrifice of a sheep to the vengeance enacted through his own murder, are rendered according to the logic of Frazer's analyses of how blood functions in totemic rituals and the arrangement of social hierarchies in "primitive" cultures described at length in *The Golden Bough*.[7]

As it interweaves scenes of arcane sacrificial blood rituals seemingly drawn from the pages of *The Golden Bough* with its thematization of the construction of race, the plot of *Light in August* suggests how a shared symbolic logic links such "primitive" beliefs about blood with the logic governing the more "modern" concept of racialization. Frazer explains the origin of blood taboos in "the common belief that the soul or spirit of the animal is in the blood"; thus members of cultures practicing the taboo "will not taste blood because they believe that it contains the animal's soul, which would enter the body of the person who tasted the blood" (265). In this context, blood's association with the crossing of the threshold between life and death, derives from the view of blood as a dangerous and unpredictable portal through which the tabooed subject might draw others unwillingly into an unwanted transition from life to death (or perhaps even vice versa). "As tabooed persons are believed to be in a perilous state—for example, the relations of the slain man are liable to the attacks of his indignant ghost—it is especially necessary to isolate them from contact with spirits; hence the prohibition against raw meat" (265). The threat of the tabooed subject lies in his or her power to negotiate the border between two radically different states, a threat that must be quarantined or somehow neutralized lest it engulf others.

In the racialist terms of Faulkner's novel, the threat of blood is also rendered as the threat of a permeable border between modes of identity. Faulkner's rural southern community is governed by a similar symbolic logic in which the spilling of literal blood connotes the crossing of racial and gender identities. Beginning during his own transition from childhood to adulthood, Christmas's lifelong engagement with blood starts with a series of episodes "during and after adolescence" when a group of young boys introduce him to the biological details of the female menstrual cycle. Providing his earliest understandings of gender difference, these crude adolescent conversations about menstruation constitute Christmas's first true experiences with and contemplations of the opposite sex. Raised by his adopted father McEachern, an evangelical Christian fundamentalist, Christmas has been conditioned to contain his own developing sexual urges and simply to ignore the female figures around him. McEachern's strict code of religious conduct prohibits Christmas from acknowledging any women he encounters outside of the context of religious worship: "They were associated with Sunday and with church. So he could not notice them. To do so would be, even to him, a retraction of his religious hatred" (184). Away from church, on Saturday afternoons spent hunting and fishing, Christmas becomes awakened to the knowledge of gender difference in a manner that completely overwhelms him. As they prepare to engage in unspecified sexual acts with a young "negro girl"—whose consent seems ambiguous and questionable at best (one boy, we are told, has "arranged" these encounters)—a group of boys first trade knowledge of menstruation, which they can only seem to conceive in terms of an incommoding reason why the female object of their desire might actually resist their sexual solicitations. "'They all want to,' [one] told the others. But sometimes they cant. . . . It's something that happens to them once a month'" (185). The boy proceeds to describe (what the narrator refers to as) "his idea of the physical ceremony," "the temporary and abject helplessness of that which tantalized and frustrated desire; the smooth and superior shape in which volition dwelled doomed to be at stated and inescapable intervals victims of periodical filth" (185).

Whether providing an excuse by which some of the boys can avert the anxious moment or, more disturbingly, a rationale for overcoming the girl's resistance to a sexual encounter, this misogynistic conception of women becoming "victims of periodic filth" during their menstrual cycle objectifies the female subject and divests her of any and all agency that might be resistant to the encounter. After all, the attitude of this description suggests, she is already considered the victim of her own inability to control (in the minds of these boys) an unwanted discharge of bodily fluid. In *Volatile Bodies: Toward a Corporeal Feminism*, Elizabeth Grosz observes that "there remains a broadly common coding of the female body as a body which leaks, which bleeds, which is at the mercy of hormonal and reproductive functions" (204). In the view of these adolescent male characters in Faulkner, what makes women weak (what makes them women in their view) is their tendency to bleed in this routine and uncontrollable manner. The image of menstrual blood thus constructs the terms of the binary difference between male and female, as a shared female victimization by blood places women in a category on the other side of the gender divide from the young male onlookers. In the context of Faulkner's southern gothic vision, the scene has to be considered, disturbingly, as a moment in Christmas's grotesque "coming-of-age," but it is also the moment that engenders the many negative attitudes toward women that Christmas holds throughout his life and that play a significant part in his own racialization.

This periodic flow of blood marks the otherwise ciphered "negro girl" as different in the consciousnesses of these young males. A visual imperative of blood plays a role in this process as the graphic narrative provided by one of the males serves to socialize the construction of female difference for those boys who have had no direct experience with the female figure's periodic bleeding. The central male speaker introduces Christmas (and the others) to menstruation through a verbal description using vivid visual imagery that allows Christmas to come to terms with the matter as he processes the description of the sight of blood into usable knowledge. "Perhaps he knew. Anyway he was graphic enough, convincing enough. If he had tried to describe it as a mental state, something which he only believed, they would not have listened. But he drew a picture, physical, actual, to be discerned by the sense of smell and even of sight" (185). Young Joe Christmas is "moved" along with the others as his knowledge of gender difference becomes mediated through the image of menstrual blood produced in his mind's eye, spurred by the vivid description given by his adolescent companion. "That was how the boy told it, with the other five listening quietly, looking at one another, questioning and secret" (185). Here the imaged "picture" of blood does its work in drawing the binary divide between male and female as one boy brings the image of blood to the imagination of the others, giving it vivid and tactile texture through graphic language. The narrated image of blood thus cements the other boys' fears of encountering real, literal blood and, by extension, the women who bleed.

This narrativized image of menstrual blood provides a focal point for Christmas's symbolic imagination through which he is able to cognitively construct and stabilize a binary distinction (between male and female) that becomes instrumental for his own processes of identity formation. By figuring the very threshold of difference through its associations with the ultimate and existential divide between life and death, the image of blood allows Christmas to tell the difference between himself and the feminized other. Here race and gender are mutually constructed, as the boys' fearsome experiences of the "mysteries" of female menstruation come within the context of their collective objectification of this nameless, bodiless abstraction of a "negro girl."

Keeping in mind George Mosse's assessment of the importance of "the visual for racial thought," we should recognize how the visual component of this scene's mobilization of psychological response to menstruation—"But he drew a picture, physical, actual, to be discerned by the sense of smell and even of sight"—speaks to an imperative of visibility shared between the construction of blood taboos (in this case, the menstrual taboo) and the construction of race (24–25). In *Light in August*, the thematic overlap between the operation of blood taboos and the operation of race demonstrates the mutual construction of these forms of visibility, focusing the reader on a conceptual overlap critical to racial blood rhetoric's production of meaning. The same substance symbolically drawing the line between male and female through the menstrual taboo provides the metaphorical image for the distinction between blackness and whiteness in racial blood rhetoric. The metaphoricity of the unseen blood of racial discourse—blood's ability to figure race—is underwritten by the substantiated, material, and, most importantly, visible form of blood at work in the practice of the menstrual taboo. Although the boys in the novel do not speak of the Negro girl in terms of having "black blood," it is clearly her menstrual blood that blackens her in their imagination, inasmuch as it is her menstrual blood that defines her as different, less than, dangerous, and untouchable. (Although, when one boy explains that "'They all want to . . . But sometimes they cant," there is no clear indication whether he's referring only to "negro girls.") The blood that genders this "negro girl" is the same blood that racializes her—and the same blood that will come to racialize Joe Christmas—a visible blood whose symbolism of the difference between life and death becomes reified into gender and racial difference. In this moment, the visibility of blood is thus part and parcel of its function and operation as a figure for racial difference.

Thus, while the development of Christmas's menstrual aversion may seem far removed from his journey toward discovering his racial identity, the experience implicitly demonstrates how the cultural response to literal blood underwrites the racial violence that will ultimately consume him. Christmas's experience with menstrual blood dramatizes how the image of blood works to provide the association between identity difference and socially sanctioned violence. Girard identifies an implication of violence in the formation of menstrual taboos: "We have conceded that menstrual blood has a direct relationship to sexuality; we also contend that its relationship to unleashed violence is even closer. [. . .] [T]o understand the impurity of menstrual blood we must trace its relationship to blood spilt by violence, as well as to sexuality. The fact that the sexual organs of women periodically emit a flow of blood has always made a great impression on men; it seems to confirm an affinity between sexuality and those diverse forms of violence that invariably lead to bloodshed (35). In Girard's account, the flow of blood from the "sexual organs of women" creates the cognitive relationship between violence and sexuality, between violence and gender difference through its associative "impression on men." The same blood that so often becomes visible when violence is wrought also becomes visible as a product of the biological function distinguishing women from men. Thus, through a kind of "sympathetic magic" of associations, blood "confirm[s] the affinity" between violence and difference.

Following this logic, it is only through the violent spilling of actual blood that Christmas can come to terms with the blood forming his consciousness of gender and racial difference. Sickened into a state of deep aversion by his new knowledge of menstruation, Christmas shuns what was once the socializing and normative fraternal contact with his male peers: "On the next Sunday Joe did not go hunting with them" (185). Taking the image of recurring menstrual bleeding as an indication of the feminine lack of bodily control and corporeal integrity that threatens to deprive him of his own physical and psychological wholeness, Christmas finds the knowledge of female menstruation impossible to abide. He cannot participate in the activities that previously forged bonds with the other boys until he finds some way to come to terms with this new paradigm of difference that now defines the bounds of that same fraternal relationship. After all, his own masculinity and perhaps his entire sense of self have now become mediated through the image of the blood spilled from the body of that once merely incidental and abstract "negro girl."

He confronts his own anxiety in isolation, but finds that he must engage directly with the literal and tactile form of the substance that has heretofore only appeared to him through mental image. This process of psychological atonement is anticipated by Girard's analysis of the logic of the blood ritual. "Does there exist some miraculous substance potent enough not only to resist infection but also to purify, if need be, the contaminated blood? Only blood itself, blood whose purity has been guaranteed by the performance of appropriate rites—the blood, in short, of sacrificial victims—can accomplish this feat" (36). Following a period of self-isolation, Christmas enacts just such a ritual following the symbolic logic of Girard's model of ritual sacrifice. He stalks and kills a sheep and covers himself with the blood of the sacrificed animal victim. "[H]e knelt, his hands in the yet warm blood of the dying beast, trembling, drymouthed, backglaring. Then he got over it, recovered" (185). Christmas overcomes his aversion to menstrual blood only by forestalling the feelings of "tantalized and frustrated desire" through his own sacrificial blood ritual (36). The movement from his consumption of one boy's narrative representation of blood to Christmas's own literal engagement with the substance of blood comprises the scene's significance: although he is first affected by the "graphic" verbal representation of menstrual blood provided by his adolescent companion, it is only contact with literal blood that allows Christmas to rid himself of the aversion produced by that representation. The image of blood in his male companion's sexist adolescent rhetoric precipitates the cutting of the sheep and the bringing of literal blood into view. Moreover, by depicting the symbolic logic by which Christmas's own psychic aversion to difference becomes ameliorated through the violent release of and intimate engagement with the sheep's blood, Christmas's bloody sacrifice of the sheep adumbrates his own murder and reveals the kind of blood symbology underlying the social processes governing Christmas's own process of racialization.

Thus, physical violence and the spilling of blood repeatedly accompany and usher in transitions of identity in *Light in August*. Christmas's turbulent sexual relationship with Joanna Burden, for example, begins as a relationship between two ambiguously raced figures and ends in events of bloodshed that define both of their racial statuses. Indeed it is the spilling of Joanna's blood through violence that revives her from a state of social dormancy, making her socially visible again and redefining her racially. When Christmas arrives at Joanna's large dark house near Jefferson, the forty-year-old "spinster" is living a life of near-solitude, secluded from the rest of the community (232). Looked after by neighboring "colored folks," Joanna lives enveloped within the "all-mother of obscurity and darkness" of her isolated estate. Although she lives only a short distance from Jefferson, the county's hub of activity, she remains separated from Jefferson's social life not so much by sheer geography as by an impassible length of social indifference to her. One of Joanna's African American neighbors and few social contacts tells Christmas upon his arrival at the Burden house, "'I reckon aint nobody round here going to do her no harm. She aint harmed nobody'" (227). Christmas learns that Joanna has for some time served as the financial benefactor and consultant for "a dozen negro schools and colleges through the south," and it is only then that he "understood the town's attitude toward her" (233, 234). Like Christmas, Joanna has lived a life of social and individual liminality, a figure of ambiguity in terms of her gender, race, even her age. While Christmas presumes to describe her as an "old woman," her neighbor corrects him: "'Miz Burden aint old. Aint young neither'" (227). Although a fixture within the town's collective memory, Burden is at once endemic to and completely alien from it, living much of her life ostracized from "the town in which she had been born and lived and died a foreigner, an outlander" (289). This paradoxical alienation results for her defiant, socially proscribed interactions with the black community with which she has become ambiguously identified.

Living in this way, Joanna Burden maintains only a tenuous grasp on her white femininity in Jefferson. Upon her murder, however, she effectively becomes fully vested of her whiteness once again. In its response to her murder, the community reacts to what is perceived as an assault on Burden's white femininity, and their response also becomes an element in the reconstruction of that white womanhood. For, despite her lengthy detachment from the town's affairs, all of Jefferson rises to avenge her murder at the hands of a supposedly black assailant. The spilling of her blood incites the community's racial imagination into a raging "emotional barbecue," as fierce as the fire that consumes her house after her murder (289). When the town finds Joanna's body nearly decapitated and wrapped in a sheet on her property, "they moiled and clotted, believing that the flames, the blood, the body that had died three years ago and had just now begun to live again, cried out for vengeance . . ." (289). Formerly indifferent to Joanna's existence, the white community encircles her, rallying around the cause of her death and taking action against her murderer. The spilling of Joanna's blood thus ushers her across a double threshold, transitioning her from life to death while also reviving her from a social death into a socially visible and socially meaningful white female figure once again.

Joseph Urgo once argued that, by murdering Joanna, Christmas takes command of his own sense of self by ending Joanna's awkward and unwanted efforts to define him racially and sexually. "Christmas is intent on killing Joanna because she blurs the racial and sexual differentiations on which his fragile identity rests" (400). In Urgo's reading, the spilling of Joanna's blood through her murder refeminizes her after the physiological change of menopause: "When Christmas kills Joanna he lets her blood flow again" (401). But while Joanna's bloody death may signal Christmas's own objectification of her as female by releasing through violence a form of blood that serves as her menses by proxy, Joanna's bleeding is also critical for the stabilization of her own whiteness. By spilling Joanna's blood through violence for the community's observance, Christmas reorients the community's regard for her and effectively whitens Joanna. The onlookers "believed aloud that it was an anonymous negro crime committed not by a negro but by Negro and . . . knew, believed, and hoped that she had been ravished too: at least once before her throat was cut and at least once afterward" (288). If the brutal nature of the crime inevitably mobilizes the community's imagination toward the construction of a beastly black perpetrator, Joanna's propensity to bleed at the hands of this unknown yet black killer (rather than through menstruation) redefines her as the very embodiment of white femininity and allows the community to reinstall her on the pedestal of white womanhood.

In the same moment that the discovery of the murder raises speculation about the blackness of the assailant, the community also constructs the whiteness of Joanna as victim. Joanna is granted the crossing of racial boundaries once proscribed to her once her blood "cries out," as a renewed affinity and empathy for her as a member of the larger white community resurges. After her death, the sheriff learns from his deputy that Joanna "'might have had niggers living in the house with her,'" a fact that before Joanna's death only contributed to her ostracism (291). "None of them had ever entered the house. While she was alive they would not have allowed their wives to call on her. When they were younger, children [. . .] had called after her on the street, 'Nigger lover! Nigger lover!'" (292). But upon Joanna's death, the "niggers" that were once viewed as the cohabitants of a confused and desperate spinster now transition in the community's imagination into the figures of a black threat against her. As the deputy himself muses, "'What I am surprised at is that it was this long before one them done for her" (291). And when the townspeople see the randomly selected "nigger" for which the sheriff calls in order to begin his investigation, they are already beginning to reconstruct the narrative of Joanna Burden as the white female victim of a black male monster: *"By god, if that's him, what are we doing, standing around here? Murdering a white woman the black son of a* ——" (291). Thus, despite being socially excluded due to her associations with the African American community for much of her life, Joanna's violent death brings her back into the fold of Jefferson's white community.

By becoming the victim of an unknown murderer, Joanna is cast within a narrative that effectively alters her constructed racial identity. In this social system in which her behavior (associating herself with the black community) undermines the whiteness indicated by her skin color, the spilling of Joanna's blood reestablishes this identity in a way that even her skin color could not. Once bled, Joanna becomes unquestionably white, so white that she becomes the embodiment of the community's collective pride in whiteness itself. The spilling of Joanna's blood abruptly transitions her from marginalized racial exile to the very axis of the community's sense of shared racial identity. The community's race pride now revolves around the nearly decapitated body of a woman who "had died three years ago and had just now begun to live again" (289).

This racializing effect of corporeal violence is a response to blood made visible and depends upon an underlying binarism associated with the sight of blood, a binarism that lies at the core of the process by which a new kind of racial visibility becomes constructed through the use of blood metaphors. Here we must consider the oblique meanings of blood that convey the concept of difference through connotations of visibility rather than through suggestions of blood as differentiating and determining racial essence. Beyond determinism, the image of blood constructs racial differentiation by virtue of its cultural symbolism as a substance whose moment of visibility indicates the crossing of a threshold from one (often mutually exclusive) state to another. That is, the image of blood connotes the concept of racial difference, not only through erroneous understandings of its role in inheritance, but also by virtue of the cultural and social meanings attached to experience when blood can be seen and when blood cannot be seen.

By virtue of blood's natural state lying out of sight (beneath the skin), the invisibility of the substance symbolizes desired states of integrity, purity, peace, and security. In *Juice of Life: The Symbolic and Magic Significance of Blood*, Piero Camporesi describes how the significance of blood's physical location beneath the skin and out of view frames the construction of transcultural beliefs in the substance's mystical embodiment of human consciousness. "Blood was the seat of the soul—that invisible, elusive principle (abstract, but not without its inexpressible physical concreteness)—that was deemed to ebb and flow in hiding, swelling and diffusing in the oily liquid of life" (32). For centuries and across cultures, blood has been regarded as the "ghost in the machine" of human animation and consciousness precisely because it normally cannot be seen, because its most natural state is to remain, quite literally, occult. Yet, unlike the occult "souls" or "ghosts" to which blood itself is sometimes figuratively compared, blood regularly becomes visible and even tangible, augmenting belief in the power of its latent presence. If the unbroken surface of the skin indicates a body whose integrity grounds metaphors of cultural, social, and psychological wholeness, then the sight of blood indicates that the body has been turned inside out and that the general peace has been broken along with the skin.

When blood is seen, the state of the bleeding body presages the radical transition from life to death. Tracing the belief in a relationship between blood and race in *Man's Most Dangerous Myth*, Ashley Montagu explains that because of the associations created by the simultaneous observance of death with "an appreciable loss of blood," the "identification of blood as vital to life, and its investment with special life-giving qualities, must have been almost inevitable steps in the process of endowing this essence with meaning" (360). While each culture attributes its own specific meanings to the spilling of blood, constant among these cultural interpretations is the investment of meaning in a supremely differentiating, existential transition that occurs when blood exits the bounds of the body.

Moreover, in his analysis of the logic of blood rituals in Christianity and Judaism, David Biale observes how "Blood arouses the powerful emotions that are harnessed by ritual, since, when it does become visible, it is often a sign that the body is no longer whole" (4). Anthropological studies of blood's symbolism similarly suggest how the movement of blood from its invisible place beneath the skin into the visible realm has been taken as a momentous and meaningful occasion marking radical divisions in individual, social, and even cultural time. Mino Gabriele explains the sight of blood's movement from inside to outside the body as a culturally transitional moment:

> Blood either flows through the body, where it is enclosed within the human or animal microcosm, or else it flows out of the body and spills elsewhere. It goes to meet other bodies, objects, and things. Here we have two fundamental ways of looking at blood, which also provide confirmation of its use and significance. On the one hand, blood is a warm liquid that moves and nourishes the body from within, filling it with life. On the other hand, however, if the blood flows out of the body, this heralds death.[8] (33)

This association of the sight of blood with the transitional moment between life and death establishes the image of blood as perhaps the most powerful and seemingly universal symbol of liminality and identity transformation. Considering these "two fundamental ways of looking at blood . . . [that] provide confirmation of its use and significance," it becomes clear that a concept of a visual binarism is endemic to the discourse of blood, deriving from the almost universal investment of meaning in the significant occasion of blood's visibility (Gabriele 33).

This binary of visibility is of particular significance in the use of blood as a metaphor in racial discourse. As a substance whose visibility marks such a shift in cultural norms and social relations "almost as if there were two parallel and symmetrical realities," the image of blood supports racialism's construction of a "scientifically" viable, politically actionable form of differential visibility, and blood emerges as the perfect substance for figuring the imperative visibility of "parallel and symmetrical realities" that supposedly characterize the two alternative realities of life on opposite sides of the invisible "color line" (33). The very sight of blood means difference, and in this way, the image of blood rhetorically lends its own imperative of visibility to the concept of race, as the rhetoric of racial blood casts the visibility of racial difference in blood's image.

In *Light in August*, the construction of race through this binary of blood's visibility is manifested in the racial imagination of Gavin Stevens. After Christmas's death, the town collectively wonders "why when free, [he] had taken refuge in the place which he did [the home of Reverend Hightower], where he must have known he would be certainly run to earth, and why when that occurred he neither surrendered nor resisted" (443). While some speculate that Christmas "had shown wisdom, since he would not have been suspected of being in the minister's house at all," Stevens, we are told, "had a different theory" (443, 444). Although not present during Christmas's final moments, the Harvard-educated country lawyer explains the motivations behind Christmas's last actions in terms of the oscillating influences of his black and white blood, which Stevens proceeds to narrate while riding on a train with one of his former Harvard classmates:

> It was the black blood which swept him by his own desire beyond the aid of any man, swept him up into that ecstasy out of a black jungle where life has already ceased before the heart stops and death is desire and fulfillment. And then the black blood failed him again, as it must have in crises all his life. He did not kill the minister. He merely struck him with the pistol and ran on and crouched behind that table and defied the black blood for the last time, as he had been defying it for thirty years. He crouched behind that overturned table and let them shoot him to death, with that loaded and unfired pistol in his hand. (449)

Stevens's racial fantasy has often been dismissed by readers and critics as the workings of an overactive racist imagination trading in the "warring blood" imagery of an earlier era. When asked in a 1957 interview whether readers should take Stevens's surmise as a "guess" or as "final knowledge" of Christmas's racial identity, Faulkner himself described the monologue as "an assumption, a rationalization which Stevens made" (Gwynn and Blotner 72). Nevertheless, the import of Stevens's imagination should not be disregarded. If race is indeed a construction of economic, psychological, legal, and historic contingencies and the languages used to express them, then even the most seemingly bizarre expressions of racial belief such as this one provided by Stevens should be closely examined and dissected, as they constitute the very stuff of which race is made.

Indeed, the terms of Stevens's racial fantasy are particularly helpful for understanding the function of blood in the operation of the racial imagination. Because Stevens speaks in terms of blood, an ostensibly biological term, it is easy to read his theory as a reactionary endorsement of biological racialism, and critics have seen fit to characterize Stevens's blood fantasy as such. Judith Wittenberg, for example, refers to Stevens's "biological explanation for Joe Christmas's unfortunate behavior" (147). But the blackness that Stevens imagines and constructs through this monologue is not one of biological essentialism, despite the theory's heavy reliance on the explanatory power and language of blood. Instead, what makes Stevens's explanation so revealing and meaningful is precisely the manner in which the explanation itself is so irrational and lacking in anything resembling any standard of reason, much less scientific backing. Stevens is by no means putting forth a systematic biological theory of race in this passage. Rather, the speculative terms that frame his narration of events—a bevy of assumptions about what Christmas "must" have done based on what Stevens "thinks" happened—suggest an awareness of the fragility of his own theory. "'I think I know why it was, why he ran into Hightower's house for refuge at the last,'" he says, but later in the monologue he admits, "I dont believe any man could reconstruct'" much of the material he nevertheless proceeds to narrate (445, 448). Particularly in this context, the prolific use of blood alone signals no appreciable effort toward racial scientific theory.

To the contrary, when interpreting passages like this one, it becomes even more important to bracket blood's biological associations in order to analyze the more ancillary concepts through which such rhetoric configures racial difference through the image of blood. Even in his own estimation, Stevens is not attempting an account of Christmas's biology. If anything, Stevens's theory demonstrates that for him, Christmas's blackness cannot simply be reduced to the mere possession of "black blood." He knows full well that attributing Christmas's racial motivations to such a deterministic influence of blood would be, as Wittenberg suggests, "simplistic, [and] inadequate to the nature of events and character as represented" (147).[9]

Instead, Stevens's monologue demonstrates the resiliency of blood as a metaphor for race in the absence of anything like an actual biological theory. Stevens can employ blood imagery to explain Christmas's supposedly racial motivations without any pretense toward biologism because Stevens is not articulating a racialist view based upon Christmas's biological blackness. Indeed, we might read the monologue as conveying a subject hopelessly *un*determined by blood as suggested by the speech's endless oscillations between blackness and whiteness: "'Because the black blood drove him first to the negro cabin. And then the white blood drove him out of there . . .'"

Stevens imagines a pitched battle between Christmas's "black" and "white blood," but the blackness that ultimately defines Christmas is not dependent upon which of these bloods prevails in a zero-sum game of mastery; it is not the dominance of Christmas's "black blood" that ultimately makes him black. Instead, for Stevens, Christmas's blackness is a function of his propensity for a divided psychology, his capacity to serve as the object of an uncontrollable oscillation between action and inaction, a will to live and a resignation to die.[10] Stevens blackens Christmas through his own imagination by figuring an irrepressible vacuum of ambiguity at Christmas's center through a language of blood (that simultaneously makes Christmas seem completely irrational).

Blood serves Stevens's purposes as the image of this ambiguity and precisely because of the cultural beliefs that attach to blood as an image that marks the crossing of a threshold between radically different states. As Stevens says, Christmas's blood "would not be either one or the other and let his body save itself" (449). By casting Christmas as a victim of an unstable binary of blood within him, Stevens describes him as the embodiment of liminality, helplessly teetering between agency and passivity, between a desperate grasping for God and an embrace of godlessness, between the choices he could make that would save his life and the choices he makes that guarantee his death. "And it was the white blood which sent him to the minister, which rising in him for the last and final time, sent him against all reason and all reality, into the embrace of a chimaera, a blind faith in something read in a printed Book" (449). Stevens blackens Christmas by imaginatively grounding his identity in a substance that symbolizes liminality itself. Here, this helpless fluidity of motivation and character is what the metaphor of blood is a metaphor for.

Through its stylized depiction of the binarism of Christmas's blood, Stevens's theory demonstrates how the racial imagination employs the rhetoric of blood to instill race with explanatory power beyond biological determinism. What racialist thinking gains from the image of blood in this instance is not only the suggestion of biologism, but also the suggestion of a binarism rooted in visibility. In this way, the image of blood divides black from white and "explains" Christmas's actions in a way that the indeterminate visible evidence of Christmas's skin color cannot. Here, by figuring Christmas's mental instability through the dichotomy of blood's binary visibility—its oscillation between black and white—the image of blood creates an illusion of discrete categories where none exist. The metaphor of blood thus provides the suggestion of a radical binarism that supports a notion of alteration between states, even when that difference cannot be seen. The radical alteration attendant upon the visibility of blood conveys a sense of radical difference as the rhetorical image of blood provides a proxy for the visible binary of race, taking the place of the sight of actual differential racial marks. When race cannot be differentiated or determined by seeing the body, the sight of blood helps to make the difference.

The moment Joanna's blood becomes visible, the novel is propelled toward its ultimate conclusion, as her death provides the final impetus for the community's desire to get through Christmas's skin. But Christmas's murder is only the culmination of a series of threats and acts of violence against him that systematically increase the imperative need for a view of his literal blood as evidence of his racial categorization. Throughout the novel, the desire to make Christmas bleed is used as a method for reading his racial identity. When he attempts to draw his girlfriend Bobbie away from her life as a prostitute, Bobbie's lover and pimp Max violently attacks Joe, using the knowledge of Christmas's confusion over his own racial identity as an ostensible motive for the desire to make Christmas bleed. "*We'll find out. We'll see if his blood is black*" (219). Max proceeds to beat Joe's prostrate body, saying, "*We'll need a little more blood to tell for sure*" (219). Max's sarcastic call for Christmas's blood here is merely a pretense to justify the use of violence against him as a way to deter Christmas's involvement in Bobbie and Max's affairs. While Max has little to no real interest in Christmas's actual racial status, his beating of Joe along with his stated intent to "see if his blood is black" literalizes the "black blood" metaphor as a pretense for violence. If Joe's skin will not reliably indicate his racial identity, and if this masked racial identity is indeed carried in Joe's blood, then the only way to be sure and to bring knowledge of Christmas's racial identity into alignment with the external and visible cues of race is to turn Christmas inside out.

Soon after Joanna's murder, Christmas is apprehended in nearby Mottstown and returned to Jefferson. Hearing that they have caught "'that nigger murderer. . . . Christmas,'" and fearing that the suspect may be her lost grandson, Mrs. Hines inquires about the man's appearance. One of the men who witnessed the manhunt reports, "'I never noticed much. . . . They had to bloody him up some, catching him. Young fellow. He dont look no more like a nigger than I do, either" (346). Despite the white skin that makes Christmas look no more like a "nigger" than the white townsman who describes him, the rumors of his involvement in Joanna's murder, coupled with the apparent sign of his guilt in the form of the retributive blood covering his face, are all the "evidence" that the townspeople need to be convinced that this is indeed the "nigger murderer" (346). Christmas is black by virtue of blood that can now be seen, rather than the blood that supposedly flows hidden in his veins. Thus when Halliday approaches Christmas in custody, Halliday "'hit the nigger a couple of times in the face, and the nigger act-ing like a nigger for the first time and taking it, not saying anything: just bleeding sullen and quiet'" (350). Joe's passive subjection and the release of his blood simultaneously satisfy the need for evidence of both his blackness and his guilt. Like the "negro girl" whose difference is defined for the male imagination by her periodic bleeding, Christmas becomes black in the collective consciousness of the community because of his own propensity to bleed.

As he is being transferred from his prison cell to the courthouse for his appearance before a grand jury, Christmas breaks from the sheriff's custody and flees. He escapes to Reverend Hightower's house where he is run down by Percy Grimm, captain of the state national guard. Earlier, Grimm had insisted on the preservation of order and seemed intent on protecting Christmas from the growing mob of townspeople threatening to lynch him. "'We must let the law take its course,'" Grimm insists. "'The law, the nation. It is the right of no civilian to sentence a man to death. And we, the soldiers in Jefferson, are the ones to see to that'" (452). But instead of returning Christmas to the confines of the law, Grimm carries out his own act of extralegal retribution. "When the others reached the kitchen they saw the table flung aside now and Grimm stooping over the body. When they approached to see what he was about, they saw that the man was not dead yet. . . . Then Grimm too sprang back, flinging behind him the bloody butcher knife" (464). While Grimm has no more evidence of Christmas's black racial identity than the speculative rumors of Christmas's "black blood" circulating through the community, upon killing and castrating Christmas, Grimm makes the pronouncement that claims justification for the act in the crime with which Christmas is accused, the rape and murder of Joanna Burden: "'Now you'll let white women alone, even in hell'" (464).

Christmas's racial identity does not exist apart from his bloody death; instead, his racial identity is a function of his manner of death. While Christmas's racial status remains indeterminate for the reader, the bleeding of Joe Christmas effectively blackens him. Christmas becomes black in this moment by virtue of the community's aggressive response to the sight of Joanna's spilled "white" blood. Upon Grimm's pronouncement that Christmas will "leave white women alone," Christmas *is* black—not because of the color or essential characteristics of his own blood but rather because of the social function of Joanna's, or to be more precise, because of the view that the community has been given of her literal blood spilled through the violence of her murder.

We have already seen how Joanna's whiteness, once diminished in the eyes of the community, emerges redefined and strengthened as a function of the community's response to her murder. In the understanding of the Jefferson community, only a "nigger" would rape and murder a white woman in such a manner, and so Joanna's death itself stands as proof of Christmas's blackness. As he stands with his hands covered in Christmas's blood (just as Christmas once warmed his hands in the blood of the sacrificial sheep), Grimm's statement that Christmas will now "'let white women alone, even in hell'" speaks to his own sense of vengeance for Joanna Burden's murder and his charge as one of the community's defenders of white femininity against black animalistic aggression (464). The impetus for this violence is not any existence of Christmas's figurative "black blood" but rather the sight of the literal blood for which Christmas's murder and concomitant racialization as black are meant to atone, the blood of Joanna Burden, the figure of white southern femininity whom Christmas is accused of murdering. Christmas's bloody death in Joanna's name determines and constructs his blackness in turn. The sight of Joanna's spilled "white" blood, not the figurative color of his blood, ultimately makes Christmas black.

Thus, the literary and cultural functions of Christmas's spilled blood, particularly with respect to the novel's racial themes, can only completely be understood in relation to Joanna's. But while the reader may be willing to accept the analytical proposition that Joe and Joanna's blood mutually construct each other, the characters in the world of the novel must instead strive to keep separate the respective functions of their supposedly racially distinct bloods, so that the two forms of spilled blood do not become (we might say) conceptually miscegenated. With two figures whose racial identities had been considered ambiguous (albeit for different reasons) both now lying dead through bloody acts of violence, the community's response becomes burdened with the high stakes of differentiating what their deaths have meant and will mean.

In particular, the function of Christmas's death must be differentiated from Joanna's. On pain of an intolerable moral equation between the death of the white woman and the death of her black murderer, neither Joanna's death nor the violence of it can be considered parallel to what has happened to Christmas. Almost immediately after Joe's murder, the process begins by which the community seeks to distinguish between the functions of their deaths, between the work performed by Joanna's blood and the work performed by Christmas's. Through this process, Christmas's death will be justified by attributing his behavior to his unstable and threatening blood (as in Gavin Stevens's theory of Christmas's "warring blood"). And while Joanna's blood will be regarded as the blood spilled unjustly by a black murderer, Christmas's blood becomes elevated to the realm of pure fantasy.

This differential is registered in the narrator's depiction of Christmas's death, where, although the literal color of Christmas's blood carries no evidence to determine Christmas's blackness or whiteness, the narrator fixates upon the image of his spilled blood. "For a long moment he looked up at them with peaceful and unfathomable and unbearable eyes. Then his face, body, all seemed to collapse, to fall in upon itself, and from out the slashed garments about his hips and loins the pent black blood seemed to rush like a released breath" (464–65). When reading this scene for its racial thematics, it is important to keep in mind that *Light in August* continually (and seemingly deliberately) blurs the line between the narration of "factual" events and events conjured almost entirely out of whole cloth by the narrative imagination of its characters (as in other of Faulkner's works, particularly *Absalom, Absalom!*). Given all of the language indicative of the scene as a product of the collective thoughts and emotions of the townspeople (Christmas's body "seemed to collapse" and his blood "seemed to rush"), it becomes impossible to determine whether this description of Christmas's death (already told in one version by Gavin Stevens) conforms to any standard of veracity.

Much critical commentary on this moment, perhaps the most discussed moment in *Light in August*, has focused on the description of Christmas's "pent black blood." James Snead has suggested that, with the narrator's description of Joe's death, "the various fatal ambiguities concerning 'white' and 'black' blood come to a head, without being at all resolved," because "whether 'black' is here a 'figurative' or 'literal' term is crucial, but impossible to determine" (166–67).

But the question of whether the description of the color of Christmas's blood here is literal or figurative has no bearing on the matter of Christmas's racial identity (no more so than Gavin Stevens's fantasy of warring black and white blood helps to explain the motivations behind Christmas's final moments). Christmas's blood might certainly appear dark or literally black in color, but whether the narrator actually "sees" a black fluid coming out of Christmas's body—or instead chooses to describe a presumably red blood as figuratively "black"—means nothing with respect to the question of Christmas's race. Whether Christmas's blood really appears black in this moment or not, the color of his blood still bears no relation to his racial status, even if the narrator, Percy Grimm, everyone in Jefferson—or even the reader, for that matter—thinks that it does. So, while Snead suggests that the narrator's use of the term "black" does not settle the question because the literalness or figurativeness of "black" is "impossible to determine," in actuality, the converse is true: the question of whether "black" is here a figurative or a literal term is quite possible to determine, but, as far as Christmas's racial identity is concerned, not crucial at all (167).

For contrary to Snead's suggestion that the literalness of Christmas's "pent black blood" remains indeterminate, the narration of the passage does help the reader make such a determination. An element of this description that makes clear that the narrator has not described what actually happens when Percy Grimm cuts Joe's body is the incongruity between the color and the action of Joe's blood. The narrator's vivid description of how "from out of the slashed garments about his hips and loins the pent black blood seemed to rush like a released breath" notably conflates the characteristics of literally "pent" blood (blood under pressure) and darkly colored or "black blood." That is, the description conflates the action of arterial blood—which due to its pressurization can actually spurt from the body when an artery is cut—with the dark color of deoxygenated venous blood, which is depressurized and therefore more likely to ooze or seep from cut veins rather than "rush." (While bright red oxygenated blood flows pressurized from the heart through the arteries, dark blood travels back to the heart through the veins under very little pressure.) Christmas's blood may literally appear dark in color, even black, but only if this blood were deoxygenated venous blood, which does appear dark in contrast with arterial blood, which appears bright red due to the oxygenation of the iron-carrying pigment hemoglobin. So, in order for Grimm to release a store of "pent" blood from Christmas's body, he would need to cut an artery, a pressurized blood vessel, rather than a vein; but if he were to do so, the blood released would not be dark in color. The release of blood described by the narrator may either be arterial, pressurized, and released in a "rush" of bright red color, or it may be venous, unpressurized, and released in a seep of dark fluid, but it cannot be both "pent" and "black." We can know that the narrator's description is not literal, then, because it describes something that does not, cannot exist.

This is not to insist that the narration adhere to a realistic or scientifically accurate description but rather (quite the opposite) to put aside any consideration of a literal reading in order to place more focus on drawing out the literary meaning of the scene as it deliberately diverges from the credibility of realistic expectation, particularly since that expectation has hinged on the color, sight, and action of Christmas's blood. In "Writing Blood: The Art of the Literal in *Light in August*," one of the most rigorous readings of the relationship between literal and figurative blood in the novel, Faulkner critic Jay Watson describes the final violent bleeding of Joe Christmas as a moment in which the metaphor of "black blood" is, like Christmas's own body, violently defigured. Watson argues that when literal blood becomes visible, the fact that this blood is not literally white or black becomes most evident and thus, "As the body leaks blood, 'blood' leaks as well, cracks open; the solidity and cohesion of the cultural concept is shaken with the return of the literal and the somatic" (88).

But the reader can hardly feel assured that the narrator's description entails such a "return to the literal and the somatic." Christmas would, of course, bleed profusely when castrated, but the narrator apparently never describes that bleeding (at least not literally). Instead, the narrator provides only an impressionistic description of what the bleeding of Joe Christmas "seemed" like to the community in the world of the novel.

> It seemed to rush out of his pale body like a rush of sparks from a rising rocket; upon that black blast the man seemed to rise soaring into their memories forever and ever. They are not to lose it, in whatever peaceful valleys, beside whatever placid and reassuring streams of old age, in the mirroring faces of whatever children they will contemplate old disasters and newer hopes. (465)

Like so many other critical moments in Faulknerian drama, the actual spilling of Christmas's blood goes unnarrated, a narrative omission that remains in keeping with the novel's thematics of race. The image of that literal blood would, after all, say very little about the meanings of Christmas's tortured life and death. It is only in the context of the narrator's symbolic rendering of Joe's death or in the fictional community's understanding of it that Christmas's blood can rush from his body both black in color and "like a released breath."

And so while the narrator's description of the color of Christmas's blood provides no insight into Christmas's racial identity, the discrepancy between the color and the action of his blood that characterizes the narration conveys (more accurately we might say) the meaning that Christmas's bloody death holds with regard to his racialization. This discrepancy is partly what makes the narrator's description of Christmas's death seem so unnatural, a difference between the literal and the figurative that the reader can feel. The unnatural flow of black blood in this scene from *Light in August* reminds the reader that "black blood" is simply not real. Christmas dies in an unnatural way in the name of the unnatural concept of race and so his blood flows accordingly.

To more accurately convey the meaning of Christmas's death, the narrator describes the spilling of a blood that behaves more closely to the manner in which the "black blood" of racial blood rhetoric performs, which is say, not like blood at all. When Joe Christmas finally bleeds out, his actual blood is narratively elided, and what emerges instead, so unnaturally, is the actual substance of what has determined his life. Instead of performing like literal blood, Christmas's blood performs like the "blood" of the discourse that has racially (and rhetorically) defined him. That is, his blood emerges from his body behaving like the kind of blood that it would have to be if it were to actually do the things that blood does in racial discourse. It takes on the characteristics of the underlying ideas about blood that have shaped its use as a metaphor for racial difference. Christmas's blood thus performs less like actual blood and more like air, releasing from his body "like a breath." By depicting a blood that behaves more like air, the scene implies how Joe's literal blood has been replaced in the social imagination with the blood of an ancient cosmology, a blood that gestures backward toward the ancient beliefs about blood that underwrite the racial blood discourse that has defined Christmas throughout his life.

This final release of Christmas's blood like a "breath" culminates a series of scenes in the novel in which blackness behaves like air, in which an ethereal synthesis of blood and air serves as the carrier of racial essence. During several moments, Christmas's attempts to come to terms with his racial identity are characterized by his inhaling or exhaling of racial essences in the air, including disturbing descriptions of racial smells. As he runs through the black section of Jefferson known as Freedman Town during one of several episodes of years of aimless wandering, his heart pounds as he leaves behind "the cold hard air of white people" and enters the space of a "negro smell" (115). In Freedman Town he is accosted by "the summer smell and the summer voices of invisible negroes" where it was "as if the black life, the black breathing had compounded the substance of breath so that not only voices but moving bodies and light itself must become fluid and accrete slowly from particle to particle, of and with the now ponderable night inseparable and one" (114). During fourteen years of aimless travel after leaving Jefferson, Christmas settles briefly in the North to live "as man and wife with a woman who resembled an ebony carving" (225). During one of their intimate encounters, Christmas attempts to inhale her racial essence, apparently hoping to define his blackness once and for all.

> At night he would lie in bed beside her, sleepless, beginning to breathe deep and hard. He would do it deliberately, feeling, even watching, his white chest arch deeper and deeper within his ribcage, trying to breathe into himself the dark odor, the dark and inscrutable thinking and being of negroes, with each suspiration trying to expel from himself the white blood and the white thinking and being. And all the while his nostrils at the odor which he was trying to make his own would whiten and tauten, his whole being writhe and strain with physical outrage and spiritual denial. (225–26).

This description of Christmas's encounter with a black female character comes in the context of his perpetual fears of an existential threat from the conglomerate "womanshenegro," and as Beth Widmaier observes, "Of all the sensory perceptions, it is the intangible sense of smell that marks Faulkner's black women rather than the more obvious visual demarcation of skin color" (26).

Such scenes in which air carries essences in *Light in August* convey how prescientific notions of blood remain resonant in post-Enlightenment racialist thought and discourse and how these ancient ideas contribute to the construction of modern racialism and racism. In a novel seemingly fixated on blood as the essence of race and identity, such a scene in which Christmas tries to breathe in the essence of blackness conveys an alternative cosmology, one in which air, not blood, acts as the elemental vehicle of blackness and identity.

The imbrication of themes of racial determination with themes of visibility in *Light in August* reminds us that race, as a metaphor, is also a way of seeing. Like language itself, the discourse of racialism is ultimately a way of cognitively filtering, sorting, and ordering experience in order to impose a particular meaning. Such cognitive filtering is the very function of metaphor, the borrowing of meaning from one context in order to use that meaning as a lens for seeing a second subject in a new light. It is no wonder that so many explanations and models, provided by metaphor theorists to explain how metaphors work, themselves resort to metaphors of vision. "Suppose I look at the night sky through a piece of heavily smoked glass on which certain lines have been left clear," writes Max Black in *Models and Metaphors* (1962). "Then I shall see only the stars that can be made to lie on the lines previously prepared upon the screen, and the stars I do see will be seen as organized by the screen's structure. We can think of metaphor as such a screen. . . . We can say that the principal subject is 'seen through' the metaphorical expression—or, if we prefer, that the principal subject is 'projected upon' the field of the subsidiary subject" (41). For Black, metaphors filter thought the way a screen filters vision, providing a partial view of the subject through the form or terms of an imposed apparatus (the "vehicle" of the metaphor). Metaphors invite the interpreter to see a rearranged or selected impression of an old idea. Using similarly visual language, metaphor theorist George Lakoff describes how metaphors operate "through a coherent network of entailments that highlight some features of reality and hide others" (158). In this sense, race as one of culture's most powerful and pervading metaphors can be thought of as one of culture's most powerful and pervading filters of human experience, a deeply ingrained and very "heavily smoked glass" through which only certain details can be made out while other aspects of reality remain hidden.

Faulkner's *Light in August* provides a meditation on race as metaphor, race as a way of seeing. Yet the novel also demonstrates how race is one of culture's most prevalent ideological origins of violence. Metaphors are by nature violent forms of figuration despite their acts of poetic and artistic distortion. And as it imposes an ideological filter to sift our views of human bodies—our views of each other—the racial gaze gives rise to a violent form of thought, constricting and distorting human beings into creatures they simply are not. The figure of "blood" in racial blood metaphors registers this violent action of racial thinking.

In Faulkner's novel, Joe Christmas's destructive process of racialization dramatizes the violence that always threatens to become manifest when the racial gaze is motivated by racial blood metaphors. Guilty of murder yet denied trial, Christmas is ultimately a victim of a violence sanctioned by the very language used to describe his experience and the community's experience of him. By figuring race in terms of blood, racial blood metaphors issue a call to action, a call for violence. Lakoff and Johnson have observed how metaphors "may create realities for us, especially social realities. A metaphor may thus be a guide for future action. Such actions will, of course, fit the metaphor. This will, in turn, reinforce the power of the metaphor to make experience coherent. In this sense metaphors can be self-fulfilling prophecies" (156). The reality created by racial blood metaphors is a reality in which the color of blood matters, and the bleeding of Joe Christmas in conjunction with his process of racial becoming reminds us of just what is at stake when social forces conspire under the demand that the reality of race "fit the metaphor" of racial blood in order to "reinforce the power of the metaphor to make experience coherent."

AFTERWORD

Like all metaphors, racial blood metaphors perform their work through substitution. In the legal, scientific, literary, and popular discourses of human difference, racial blood metaphors substitute more direct references to race with an image whose symbolic richness transcends cultures. Racial blood metaphors call upon the image of blood to perform work that race cannot perform for itself. These metaphors thus make it possible to imagine race and to talk about race doing what it cannot do for itself.

Blood Work has examined the ways that racial blood metaphors perform this work as exemplified by certain literary and legal acts of the American racial imagination. Building upon previous work detailing the cultural and intellectual histories of both race and blood, I have argued that the reifying work performed by blood in the American racial imagination extends well beyond blood's suggestions of biologism, and that the meaning of blood in American racial rhetoric is a function of the particular cultural, legal, and political needs of American racialism at the moment and the cultural history of occasions in which blood has become visible in the development of American racialism. I have sought to demonstrate blood's critical yet often under-examined nonbiological associations at work in the plots of selected works of American literature, texts that have made the relationship between blood and race a central thematic concern.

Through their various literary tensions and resolutions, these plots demonstrate how metaphors of blood contort and construct racial reality. While all of these novels—Mark Twain's *Pudd'nhead Wilson*, Frances Harper's *Iola Leroy*, Pauline Hopkins's *Of One Blood*, and William Faulkner's *Light in August*—have been read by other scholars as texts that attempt to deconstruct the biological race concept, I have sought to demonstrate how each text also reinstates an alternative relationship between blood and racial identity that allows race to become reconstituted and practiced in nonbiological terms for nondeterministic purposes. Thus, although these texts do reveal the contradictions inherent in theories of biological racialism, they do not suggest that race becomes a moot concept once its biological basis in blood proves untenable.

Instead, as my readings of these novels suggest, the cultural, theological, and psychological associations of blood perform some of the most important work of race. The broad range of blood's cultural symbolism and associations helps to construct a race concept that performs much more fluidly than the biological definition, and the plots of these texts ultimately demonstrate that a key source of the persistence and flexibility of the race concept lies in this critical malleability of blood's signification. Mark Twain's *Pudd'nhead Wilson* dramatizes the strategic turn to blood's materiality in American legal discourse as the law appropriates scientific racialism's nonsensible idioms of racial blood proportions to codify race for the purpose of legislating property inheritance. To track race as property, the diluting properties of racial blood imagined by biological racialism are brought to a halt; legal discourse effectively stops racial mixture conceptually by figuring race through a form of blood that marks rather than a blood that dilutes indefinitely. In *Iola Leroy*, Frances Harper refigures biological racial blood as the blood of Christian sacrifice, providing her heroine and "race woman" with a substance through which to figure her edifying and self-actualizing dedication to her people. While Iola's racial identity is not determined by blood in a mechanical fashion, she can nevertheless remain committed to her "African blood" as she comes to understand her blackness as a function of her self-effacing refusal to turn away from her community in pursuit of the social benefits offered by whiteness in nineteenth-century America. Pauline Hopkins's *Of One Blood* imagines an occult form of blood shorn of biological determinism but reinvested with a universalizing redemptive power previously unachievable under the terms in which blood functions in the construction of the incest taboo. Hopkins's novel dramatizes the racial imagination's retreat from miscegenation as a drive toward incest, which the novel's plot dares to suggest as the site upon which an alternative, nonbiological form of racial identity might be reconstructed. Finally, while Joe Christmas's interstitial racial career in William Faulkner's *Light in August* suggests the indeterminacy of biological race categories, the novel also demonstrates the power of racial violence and the spilling of real blood to perform the categorizing work of race itself.

Blood Work has examined this particular network of metaphors with an eye toward understanding how racial discourse benefits from metaphoric expression; in this sense, the claims of *Blood Work* come within the context of larger questions about how metaphors make meaning. I have therefore attempted to bridge concepts from metaphor theory with theories suggesting race itself as a kind of metaphor and applied these theories to my readings of American literature. Approaching the problem of race from the perspective of metaphor theory helps to illuminate the more complete range of associations through which blood conveys meaning to race by virtue of their figurative relationship. When blood's numerous nonbiological associations are taken into account, it becomes clear that the practice of race, particularly with respect to American racialism, has been supported substantially by concepts associated with blood well beyond the biological. The literary, cultural, and political narratives premised by the conceptualization of race as blood are governed by logics deriving from blood's place as the preeminent substance in theological, anthropological, occult, and psychological contexts. The application of metaphor theory provides insight into the ways the language of race shapes thought, which in turn shapes action and social reality.

To view race as metaphor is to view race as a function inseparable from the particular contexts in which it is mobilized and to understand that, while the now-defunct biological relationship between blood and race was instrumental in constructing what race once was, blood's nonbiological associations continue to play a central role in the work that race continues to do. Blood as a multivalent concept continues to perform the work of race long after the biological race concept has been rejected and disproven. The literary readings and cultural analysis performed in *Blood Work* have thus been motivated by a desire to understand more fully the role of literature and language in the persistence of the race concept. One of the implications of *Blood Work* is that the effort to undermine racialist thinking must continue to include a robust literary front. Racialist thinking cannot be combated with scientific facts alone; the battle against it must also take into account the vehicles of language through which racialism is disseminated.

In its focus on language as a way of addressing real-world implications, *Blood Work* takes up one of the lines of attack against racialism pursued by Ashley Montagu, the leading popularizer of antiracialist science and thought of the early and mid-twentieth century. A British-born naturalized U.S. citizen, Montagu insisted on the dissemination of scientific facts about race as a necessary strategy for countering racism in all its forms, particularly during the violent moment of the early 1940s. "In our time the problem of *race* has assumed an alarmingly exaggerated importance. Alarming, because racial dogmas have been made the basis for an inhumanly brutal political philosophy which has already resulted in the death or social disenfranchisement of millions of innocent individuals," he writes in 1942 (*Man's Most Dangerous Myth* (1942) ix).

As his part in exposing the gross misconceptions fueling racial atrocities, Montagu dedicated himself to a public education campaign on race, providing extensive scientific evidence against the concept through his many publications (including more than fifty books) and through his work with the United Nations Educational, Scientific and Cultural Organization. "It is highly desirable," Montagu writes, "that the facts about 'race' as science has come to know them should be widely disseminated and clearly understood" (ix). With *Man's Most Dangerous Myth: The Fallacy of Race* (updated through six editions over fifty years), Montagu collected the most current scientific research that would disabuse the reading public of the race myth, systematically laying out all of the misunderstandings that have allowed the concept to endure despite the prevailing scientific evidence of race's nonvalidity.

With respect to the arguments made in *Blood Work*, a salient moment in Montagu's project of public education comes in one of the additions made to post–World War II editions of *Man's Most Dangerous Myth* reflecting the anthropologist's postwar reflections on the persistence and perniciousness of race in light of the horrors of Nazi scientific racism. Along with a chapter dedicated to the question of "Are the Jews a 'Race'?" (which he answers in the negative),[1] Montagu adds a chapter on the problematic relationship perceived between "Race and Blood," a chapter intended to address the claims of Aryan blood purity propagated by Nazi rhetoric. Montagu explains that misconceptions about the relationship between blood and racial identity are not only the substance of national socialist propaganda but also of seemingly less insidious, everyday uses of language: he indicts the use of such terms as "blood royal," "full blood," "blood relationship," and "consanguinity." Through such terms, Montagu writes, "the words 'race' and 'blood' have come to be used as synonyms" (*Man's Most Dangerous Myth* (1964) 283).

To demonstrate how far such common figurative expressions misconstrue scientific fact, Montagu proceeds to explain the actual physiological functions of literal blood, emphasizing the distinction between this fluid substance that distributes oxygen to the body's tissues and the site of actual genetic material in the chromosomes. "Blood," Montagu states emphatically, "has nothing whatever to do with heredity, either biologically, sociologically, or in any other manner"; hereditary characteristics, he explains forcefully, are transmitted through the genes "*and nothing else*" (268, 286). But while Montagu attempts to clarify the true biological functions of blood by presenting scientific facts, he also acknowledges that such facts have long been understood but nevertheless "did not in the least deter Nazi propagandists from using the 'blood' myths to set human beings against one another" (286, 288). Here the anthropologist concedes the limitations of increased scientific knowledge to counteract racial thinking; the horrors carried out by the Nazis in the name of blood purity speak less to scientific misunderstanding and more to the enactment of ideological, political, and emotion-laden beliefs and negative fantasies about the "Other."

To fight a full-ranging battle against racialist thinking, then, part of the responsibility falls beyond the jurisdiction of scientific argument. Montagu thus takes a somewhat unexpected diversion from the text's presentation of scientific facts, turning the reader's attention away from the operation of genes and toward the operation of metaphors. "I suggest, with most students of language, that names are words and that words rule our lives; that in this sense words are among the most important things we have to deal with in the course of our lives," he writes (280). Amid many chapters devoted to compiling scientific evidence, this chapter on "Race and Blood" takes a literary turn, complete with allusions to Henry James, Francis Bacon, Goethe, and citations from the *Oxford English Dictionary* and contemporary studies of semantics. But this discussion is nevertheless part and parcel of Montagu's efforts to rout scientific racism. If the aim is to counteract the belief in race, the scientist must also become a student of language, as the inhumane tyrannies carried out in the name of race find their conceptual support in a tyranny of language: "Words fashion the thoughts of men, and most men become the puppets of their vocabularies," Montagu writes (281). In such a world in which subjects submit to words, the project of changing minds, attitudes, policies, and behaviors about race must involve a rhetorical as well as scientific reeducation campaign. The presentation of rationally argued scientific facts may clarify the realities of biological science, but "names, words, not only serve to describe, but also often serve to create ideas and stereotypes" with "serious consequences" (established by the field of what Montagu calls "semantogenetics") (281).

Montagu thus calls for more attention to the work of metaphorical language in the maintenance of racialism. His considerations of the power of metaphor to shape "personal reality" actually anticipate claims made later by metaphor theorists George Lakoff and Mark Johnson, as in their description from *Metaphors We Live By* of how metaphors "create new meaning, create similarities, and thereby define a new reality" (Lakoff and Johnson 158). Montagu warns his readers (quoting Goethe) that, "'Where an idea is wanting a word can always be found to take its place,'" and his chapter on "Race and Blood" argues (like *Blood Work*) that "blood" has been the proxy word of choice where "race" comes up short (281). He even describes the emotional rather than pseudoscientific content conveyed through racial blood metaphors as perhaps their "most dangerous" element. "There are many words in our vocabulary that are characterized by an exaggerated emotional content; words distinguished by a high emotional and low rational quality. 'Race' is such a word; 'blood' is another" (281). In this sense, Montagu's emphasis on the emotional content embedded in racial blood rhetoric takes into account the nonbiological, nonscientific meanings of blood that have likewise been the subject of the present study (359). The anthropologist's uncharacteristic foray into metaphor theory accords with one of the arguments made throughout *Blood Work*: that rational arguments (such as those arguments made against the absurdity of the one-drop rule) are ironically of little use when marshalled against the belief in racial blood, since the very purpose of racial blood as a concept and as a language of race is to appeal to the more irrational needs of the racial imagination.

The practices of American racialism during Montagu's time provide plentiful examples of the real-world implications of such irrationality spawned from the volatile emotional synthesis of "blood" and "race." In 1942 (the same year as publication of the first edition of *Man's Most Dangerous Myth*), America witnessed a sad and dramatic example of the tyranny of words described by Montagu and the power of emotional beliefs about blood and race to shut out scientific knowledge when the American Red Cross consented to segregate "black" and "white" blood donations despite the prevalence of scientific evidence (well known within the organization) showing no biological differences between them. This infamous episode in the history of one of the nation's leading humanitarian organizations speaks to the power of racial blood rhetoric to dominate public imagination and the relatively limited power of scientific information to ameliorate widespread fears about the consequences of racial blood mixture.

If written as a novel, the events surrounding the institution of the ARC's policy of blood segregation would make a fine addition to the fictional plots analyzed in *Blood Work*. The episode is all too real in demonstrating precisely how blood symbolism works to construct race through nonbiological means. Although the American Red Cross originally committed to accepting blood from both black and white donors during its earliest civilian blood donor programs (conducted in the South in the late 1930s), the organization, responding to the directives of the U.S. military, excluded African American donors from the collection program as the nation moved toward its involvement in World War II (Love 141, 144–45).[2] When the attack on Pearl Harbor precipitated the need for massive blood donations to support the U.S. war effort, the Red Cross struck a compromise and "persuaded the military to liberalize [by] accepting blood from black citizens, and then labeling and processing it separately" (Starr 108).

While some management, medical staff, and advisors within the organization fought the policy and were well aware that there existed no differences between the blood of black and white donors, the organization's leadership found it impossible to eradicate long-standing public misconceptions and fervent emotions about the supposedly harmful effects to come from mixing blood interracially. In the end, such emotional, nonscientific, racialist thinking trumped the rational science upon which the Red Cross had prided itself in its national and international relief efforts.[3] In January 1942, National Director of Blood Donor Services Dr. G. Canby Robinson issued the organization's new policy to all blood donor centers and plasma processing labs: "In deference to the wishes of those for whom the plasma is being provided, the blood will be processed separately so that those receiving transfusions may be given plasma from blood of their own race" (ARC "Statement of Policy" 1).

Because the Red Cross provided blood supplies in auxiliary support of the military, the organization pleaded its deference to military leadership in formulating the uneasy compromise. Nevertheless the policy's logic and language both hearkened back to the prosegregation arguments made in the *Plessy v. Ferguson* case. Like Justice Brown's eschewal that the Supreme Court was "powerless to eradicate racial instincts or to abolish distinctions based upon physical differences" or to put a race deemed socially inferior "upon the same plane," Red Cross officials maintained that the organization's chartered responsibilities simply did not include confronting the larger problems of race besetting America. In a written response to one religious leader's protest of the policy, Chairman Norman Davis pleaded that the Red Cross was indeed devoted to the emergency relief of "people in distress without regard to race, religion, or color" but that this charge was not tantamount to a mandate for solving America's racial strife. "While the pursuit of such a policy should help to break down race and religious prejudices," wrote Chairman Davis, "it is not the job of the Red Cross to try to settle racial controversies or to take sides in such controversies" (Davis 2).

The issuance of the policy initiated an avalanche of protest; the Red Cross was inundated with criticism and demands for the policy to be reversed from scientific observers, civil rights and religious leaders, labor unions, local Red Cross chapter chairpersons, and concerned citizens. In a letter to Davis, NAACP Secretary Walter White chided the ARC and articulated the NAACP's extreme disappointment that "a great humanitarian organization has morally surrendered to a racial prejudice for which there is justification neither in science nor practicality" (White 1). Public animosity over the policy would mar the Red Cross's reputation, particularly within the African American community, for many years. When Dr. Charles Drew, the African American Columbia-educated pioneer of the Red Cross's Plasma for Britain campaign, received the NAACP's Spingarn Medal for his work in plasma research in 1944, he used the occasion to continue the lament: "'It is unfortunate that such a worthwhile and scientific bit of work should have been hampered by such stupidity'" (*qtd. in* Love 158).

Many of the letters of objection the Red Cross received pointed out the jarring contradiction between the organization's mission; its public rhetoric, which was heavy with Americanist imagery advocating nationalistic and moral imperatives for donating blood; and the blood segregation policy's implicit support of the same kind of racialist practices the nation was supposedly at war against in Europe. Looking back (in the 1964 edition of *Man's Most Dangerous Myth*), Montagu himself would unforgivingly consider the episode as evidence that "the myth of 'blood' seems almost as strongly entrenched in this country as it was among the Nazis" (289). (The Red Cross would continue the practice of labeling blood by race until the late 1960s (Starr 170).) Ultimately, the inability of one of the world's leading organizational authorities in rapidly developing blood technology to conduct its donor operations free of prejudices born from erroneous and harmful public misperceptions speaks volumes, not only about the Red Cross of the 1940s, but also about the continuing power of the popular imagination of blood to shape and sustain American racialism.

While providing *Blood Work* with a pertinent historical coda, the episode remains a salient example of the persistent work of blood in American racialism. The arguments made in this book cannot, of course, do much to suspend the use of "blood" as a metaphor for race, nor are they intended to. I only hope that the readings in *Blood Work* help to explain in a fuller scope the work that the figure of "blood" performs for race and further illuminate the role played by the analysis of literature and metaphors in the fight against forms of racialism perpetuated through language.

NOTES

INTRODUCTION

1. Metaphor remains one of the least understood rhetorical devices, or, if not, there remains little consensus on the question of how metaphors convey meaning despite the dozens of theories that have been proposed. Nevertheless, the core principle of Aristotle's thought on metaphor remains dominant in theoretical approaches. Most theories continue to rest upon Aristotle's classical definition of metaphor in the *Poetics* (c. 330 BC) as "the transference of a name from the object to which it has a natural application" (Richter 74). Even such recent theories as the cognitive theory of metaphor advanced by George Lakoff and Mark Johnson (*Metaphors We Live By* (1980)) and Johnson (*Body in the Mind: The Bodily Basis of Meaning, Imagination, and Reason* (1987)) contend that the "essence of metaphor" remains "understanding and experiencing one kind of thing in terms of another" (Lakoff and Johnson 5). Misnaming is decidedly the essential work of metaphor: revising, reforming, reconstructing that which it renames. To conceive of race as metaphor, then, is to approach the problem of race as a problem of misnaming and substitution, an approach that significantly resituates the terms and strategies for reforming or eradicating racial thinking. As Anthony Appiah suggests, if race is an effect of metaphorical language and metaphorical thought, then racialism is to some extent "a cognitive rather than a moral problem" (Appiah, *In My Father's House* 13).

2. In describing the implications of their influential theory of racial formation, Michael Omi and Howard Winant concede that the theory actually reconceptualizes and thus conserves rather than dismisses the race concept. They argue that race theory must "avoid both the utopian framework which sees race as an illusion we can somehow 'get beyond,' and also the essentialist formulation which sees race as something objective and fixed, a biological datum" (55). The race concept may be "nebulous" and deeply problematic as an ideological source of social strife, they argue, but "it is rather difficult to jettison widely held beliefs, beliefs which moreover are central to everyone's identity and understanding of the social world. So the attempt to banish the concept as an archaism is at best counterintuitive" (55).

3. Furthermore, for Omi and Winant race is "*a concept which signifies and symbolizes social conflicts and interests by referring to different types of human bodies*. Although the concept of race invokes biologically based human characteristics (so-called 'phenotypes'), selection of these particular human features for purposes of racial signification is always and necessarily a social and historical process. In contrast to the other major distinction of this type,

that of gender, there is no biological basis for distinguishing among human groups along the lines of race. Indeed, the categories employed to differentiate among human groups along racial lines reveal themselves, upon serious examination, to be at best imprecise, and at worst completely arbitrary" (55).

4. Mosse identifies the sixteenth-century Spanish concept of "purity of blood" as one of the earliest manifestations of biological racism, although he notes that this policy "faded with time and did not constitute a viable precedent for the rest of Europe" (xv). For critical turning points in the conceptualization of the relationship between blood and race in European history and thought, see Ivan Hannaford, *Race: The History of an Idea in the West*. On purity of blood, see Hannaford 122–23. For a discussion of Niebuhr's historiographical naturalization of the wisdom of the ancient Greeks as a function of "kindred blood and colour," see Hannaford 238–40. On Count Arthur de Gobineau's contributions to racist thought through his emphasis on internal constitution and racial degeneration in *The Inequality of the Human Races* (1853), a landmark text in the development of European thought on the relationship between race and blood, see Hannaford 264–72.

5. Saidiya Hartman has perceptively observed that, "Under slavery, such intimacy extended the power and domination of the master since black captive bodies were the literal and figurative appendages of the master's body and the 'sign and surrogate' of his power. Thus this proximity did not imperil the racial order, for this intercourse was in the service of black subordination and white enjoyment" (186). On the violence latent in American slavery's intimate system of paternalism, see Book I, Part 2 of Eugene D. Genovese, *Roll, Jordan, Roll: The World the Slaves Made* (New York: Vintage, 1976), particularly 146–47.

6. In an interview, "Toni Morrison: The Art of Fiction" (first published in *Paris Review*), Morrison discusses her fascination with how "white writers imagine black people" (she names Hemingway, Flannery O'Connor, Faulkner, Fitzgerald, and Twain) and the influence of these authors' characteristically evasive narrative approaches to race on the elliptical structure of her own plots: "What is exciting about American literature is that business of how writers say things under, beneath and around their stories. Think of *Pudd'nhead Wilson* and all these inversions of what race is, how sometimes nobody can tell, or the thrill of discovery? Faulkner in *Absalom, Absalom!* spends the entire book tracing race, and you can't find it. No one can see it, even the character who *is* black can't see it. . . . Do you know how hard it is to withhold that kind of information but hinting, pointing all of the time? And then to reveal it in order to say that it is *not* the point anyway?" (74).

7. In *West Chester and Philadelphia Railroad Company v. Miles* (1867), for example, the case that "produced the earliest regularly reported judicial endorsement of the separate-but-equal doctrine in transportation law," the Pennsylvania State Supreme Court decided that the West Chester and Philadelphia Railroad Company could require segregated seating (Lofgren 118). In this case, State Supreme Court Justice Daniel Agnew argued that, while the railroad company could not exclude black passengers based solely on race, it could segregate both races with equal consequences based upon the "reasonable" assumption of the natural aversion between races and the presumption of social disturbance that forced interracial proximity would create. "The danger to the peace engendered by the feelings of aversion between individuals of the different races cannot be denied," wrote Agnew in his decision. Thus the transportation company could require the seating of passengers

"so as to preserve order and decorum, and to prevent contacts and collisions arising from natural or well-known repugnancies, which are likely to breed disturbances by a promiscuous sitting" (*qtd. in* Lofgren 119). "By 1890," writes Lofgren, "state and federal courts had extensively cited, quoted, and paraphrased *Miles* in the course of implanting the separate-but-equal doctrine into the common law of carriers of passengers. What proved especially serviceable were Agnew's comments about inherent race instinct, differences, and repugnancies, which so nicely harmonized with 'scientific' theories about race" (121). When the issue reached the Supreme Court, Justice Henry Billings Brown's majority opinion in *Plessy* rehearsed the same logic and language from such lower-court decisions in its treatment of private transportation companies under the "common law of common carriers," ruling that modes of private transportation were also "quasi-public" and thus "subject to judicial supervision on behalf of the entire community" (Lofgren 117).

8. Addressing the argument made by Plessy's counsel that "the enforced separation of the two races" was tantamount to an extension of the ideology of natural inferiority upon which American slavery had been based (if not an extension of slavery itself) because segregation "stamps the colored race with a badge of inferiority," Brown dismisses what he found to be an "underlying fallacy." "If this be so," argues Brown, "it is not by reason of anything found in the act, but solely because the colored race chooses to put that construction upon it" (*qtd. in* Lofgren 166).

9. The approach to race as a device for orchestrating the inheritance of property extends to nonbiological reformulations discussed in whiteness studies. George Lipsitz in *The Possessive Investment in Whiteness* (Philadelphia: Temple University Press, 2006), for example, concedes that "whiteness is . . . a delusion, a scientific and cultural fiction that like all racial identities has no valid foundation in biology or anthropology. Whiteness is, however, a social fact, an identity created and continued with all-too-real consequences for the distribution of wealth, prestige, and opportunity" (236, vii). He argues that, above and beyond the value of property inherited by specific individuals, "[w]hiteness has a cash value," returned in ways seen and unseen from the long-term effects of housing discrimination, educational discrimination, and "intergenerational transfers of inherited wealth that pass on the spoils of discrimination to succeeding generations" (vii). Thus, "[w]hiteness has more to do with property than with pigment" (236).

10. For a more charitable reading of Du Bois on the relationship between race and culture (one that also addresses Appiah's objections to Du Bois's references to "common blood"), see Bernard R. Boxill, "Du Bois on Cultural Pluralism" in *W.E.B. Du Bois on Race and Culture*, 57–85. In the same volume, Lucius Outlaw provides perhaps the most comprehensive rebuttal to Appiah's "serious misreading of Du Bois" (23) in "Conserve Races? In Defense of W.E.B. Du Bois" in *W.E.B. Du Bois on Race and Culture*, 15–37. For a summary and insightful commentary on the debate between Appiah and Outlaw, see Robert Gooding-Williams, "Outlaw, Appiah, and Du Bois's 'The Conservation of Races,'" in *W.E.B. Du Bois on Race and Culture*, 39–56.

11. Following the definition of "romantic racialism" provided by George M. Fredrickson in *The Black Image in the White Mind: The Debate on Afro-American Character and Destiny*, Nancy Stepan and Sander Gilman apply the term to Du Bois's strategy for a "transvaluation" of racial distinctiveness yet one that is "grounded in idioms of science" (93). For

a rigorous critique of the essentialist notions he views as embedded within and logically necessary for any such "antiracist culturalism," see Walter Benn Michaels, *Our America: Nativism, Modernism, and Pluralism* (Durham, NC: Duke University Press, 1995), 123–42.

CHAPTER ONE

1. In his brief before the court in *Plessy*, Albion Tourgée argues that, in the context of post-emancipation American racial discrimination aligning access to economic resources with color, whiteness remained "the most valuable sort of property, being the master-key that unlocks the golden door of opportunity" (Olsen 83). Tourgée thus contends that segregation, particularly when enforced erroneously, threatens this individual right to property in whiteness itself, that "in any mixed community, the reputation of belonging to the dominant race, in this instance the white race, is *property*, in the same sense that a right of action or of inheritance is *property;* and that the provisions of the act in question which authorize an officer of a railroad company to assign a person to a car set apart for a particular race, enables such officer to deprive him, to a certain extent at least, of this property—this reputation which has an actual pecuniary value 'without due process of law'—and are, therefore, in violation of the Second restrictive clause of the first section of the XIVth Amendment of the Constitution of the United States" (83).

2. This disproportionate accounting of ancestral inheritance, figured through the one-drop rule's disproportionate power of dissemination afforded to the "one drop," also serves as the rule's moment of catachresis, the moment (described in the metaphor theory of Monroe Beardsley) "when a term is combined with others in such a way that there would be a logical opposition between its central meaning and that of the other terms," thus triggering "that shift from central to marginal meaning which shows us the word is to be taken in a metaphorical way" (112).

3. This was the case at the rule's legal origin in the 1656 case in Virginia, *In Re Mulatto*, that legal scholar Christine Hickman identifies as the "first judicial expression of the rule of hypodescent" (1174). Colonial lawmakers ruled that the mulatto plaintiff in the case would be categorized as a slave rather than a free white person. "Implicit in its opinion is the finding that the litigant was of both African and European descent, but the court found that the European ancestry made no legally significant difference at all, and the holding is likely to have severed whatever ties this racial hybrid had with his European ancestry. In fact, it was the African ancestry that both defined his status and determined his fate" (1174). By defining the mulatto plaintiff as black (rather than of mixed race), the ruling was not blind to the evidence of the plaintiff's racial mixture, nor did the ruling depart from any available literal interpretation of the plaintiff's racial makeup. The ruling codified the plaintiff's race into legal discourse as blackness, not by departing from a recognition of a literal mixture that was "naturally" there, but rather by voiding the mulatto's race mixture in the only place that it actually existed, in the language.

4. Hartman perceptively describes the ironic reasoning behind the typical antimiscegenation statute in that "while it claims to protect nature's boundaries with the force

of positive law, it exposes the laws of nature as rather enfeebled. Despite assertions of omnipotence and divine sanctioning, the laws of nature require state protection and intervention in order to prevent unnatural and expressly repugnant practices from proliferating. Unmistakably, it is the fear of blacks infiltrating the perhaps permeable border between the races that fosters these statutes; in fact, they are instituted to police these awaited infractions" (189).

5. On the "American School of Ethnology" (Josiah Nott, Samuel George Morton, George R. Gliddon, and Ephraim G. Squier), which, through a series of texts published from the late 1830s through the 1850s, provided the "authoritative foundation" of antimiscegenation, see Reginald Horsman, *Race and Manifest Destiny: The Origins of American Racial Anglo-Saxonism* (Cambridge: Harvard University Press, 1990), 125–38.

6. We should also recognize that Nott's mulatto hybridity and the tragic mulatto's "warring blood" are manifestations of a line of racial blood discourse stemming from an ancient belief in blood as a carrier of character and the "mixed" blood offspring as the exhibit of a combination of the characters inherited from ancestors. Nott argued that the mulatto would suffer from the detrimental effects of a contradictory racial mixture because the figure was doomed to possess the qualities of both races since, whether white or black, "the parent will transmit to the child . . . his expression, external form, character, temperament, &c. . . ." (256). Nott's theory here is not so much pregenetic as it is neohumoral, tracing back to the ancient cosmology in which bodily harmony could be achieved through the balancing of the humors and their associated personality types: sanguine, melancholic, and phlegmatic. "Within this mechanism of sensations based entirely on analogy, blood plays a major role, because not only the individual's perception of reality but also his temperament and lesser or greater degree of intelligence depend on the mixture of elements inside his body. In particular, it is blood that represents the principle of thought" (Conticelli 56–57). The tragic mulatto's character is a latter-day version of humoral imbalance. Oddly enough, because the blood of the psychological discourse of racial character is based on this notion of humoral balancing, blood does indeed act more "naturally" here in the sense that blood does mix, although often with tragic effects.

7. If anything, the potency of white blood in the tragic mulatto formulation is more powerful than black blood, for there, writes Brown, "The logic runs that even inheriting the worst from white is sufficient for achieving among Negroes" (73).

8. This is not to say that a legal adherence to the one-drop rule led to the effective marshalling of the color line in reality but only that the mixture of whiteness and blackness was disallowed in the rhetoric of the rule. In "Crossing the Color Line: Racial Migration and the One-Drop Rule, 1600–1860," Daniel Sharfstein persuasively demonstrates the ineffectiveness of the one-drop rule for preventing actual mixed-race subjects from migrating into whiteness. But while mulattoes may have evaded the strictest applications of the rule, the law itself imagined no space between whiteness and blackness. Some mixed-race individuals may have become white, but there remained no such legal category in which an individual could be considered both legally black and legally white at the same time. Even those who "crossed the color line" did so as a transition from one binary racial status to another. Thus while "An over emphasis on the mechanics of *partus sequitur ven-*

trem or the judge-made and legislative rules of race obscures the reality that people were continually jumping the color line," the binarism of the one-drop rule is nevertheless observed in the breach (Sharfstein 656).

9. Tom and Chambers are thus conditioned by the social treatment prescribed for their counterpart: "Tom got all the petting. Chambers got none. Tom got all the delicacies, Chambers got mush and milk. . . . In consequence, Tom was a sickly child, and Chambers wasn't. Tom was 'fractious' . . . and overbearing. Chambers was meek and docile" (18–19).

10. Lee Clark Mitchell reads the moment as evidence that, "Even Roxy shares in the racism that oppresses her. . . . The biological logic of 'blood' is exposed as fully here as anywhere . . ." (301). For similarly critical readings of the scene, see Barbara Chellis, "Those Extraordinary Twins: Negroes and Whites," *American Quarterly* 21.1 (1969): 103. See also Nancy Fredricks, "Twain's Indelible Twins," *Nineteenth-Century Literature* 43.4 (1989): 498; and Michael Rogin, "Francis Galton and Mark Twain: The Natal Autograph in *Pudd'nhead Wilson*," in *Mark Twain's Pudd'nhead Wilson: Race, Conflict, and Culture*, ed. Susan Gillman and Forrest G. Robinson (Durham, NC: Duke University Press, 1990), 74.

11. Twain would describe his interested reading of Galton's work as the moment that "changed the whole plot & plan" of the novel (*qtd. in* Emerson 194).

12. On Galton's development of fingerprinting science, see Michael Bulmer, "The Development of Francis Galton's Ideas on the Mechanism of Heredity," *Journal of the History of Biology* 32 (1999): 35; and Martin Brookes, *Extreme Measures: The Dark Visions and Bright Ideas of Francis Galton* (New York: Bloomsbury, 2004), 242–58.

13. See particularly Susan Gillman, "'Sure Identifiers': Race, Science, and the Law in *Pudd'nhead Wilson*," in *Mark Twain's Pudd'nhead Wilson: Race, Conflict, and Culture*, 86–104; Michael Rogin, "Francis Galton and Mark Twain: The Natal Autograph in *Pudd'nhead Wilson*," 73–85; Simon Cole, "Twins, Twain, Galton, and Gilman: Fingerprinting, Individualization, Brotherhood, and Race in *Pudd'nhead Wilson*," *Configurations* 15 (2009): 227–65; and Anne P. Wigger, "The Source of Fingerprint Material in Mark Twain's Pudd'nhead *Wilson* and Those Extraordinary Twins," *American Literature* 28.4 (1957), 517–20.

CHAPTER TWO

1. In "Mother's Milk: Frances Harper and the Circulation of Blood," Geoffrey Sanborn situates the play of visible blood in the faces of Harper's characters within the context of a nineteenth-century racial aesthetics that privileged the alternating shades of the blush as "a distinctly feminine and white manifestation of sensibility, indicating that one was highly attuned to social and moral codes of behavior," as opposed to the static visage that supposedly revealed the lethargic social emotions of dark-skinned people (694). Sanborn argues that Harper's mixed-race characters tend, instead, to "flush," exhibiting the manifestation of a "cardiovascular event, a rise in the rate and pressure of the blood's circulation . . . prompted not by one's thoughts about what others might be thinking, but by a sudden and overwhelming passion, like anger or joy or sexual arousal," which in characters such as Iola Leroy "indicates attributes like a desire for independence. That idiom is, for Harper, distinctly black" (695).

2. Frederick Hoffman was chosen by the Prudential Life Insurance Company to write the report despite having "no formal scientific or statistical training" (Wolff 89). His professional profile had been elevated with the recent publication of an article in the journal *Arena*, one of the first empirical studies of African American vital statistics, in which Hoffman "displayed unusual actuarial talent and opinions on the Negro Problem conveniently well matched to those of Prudential" (89). Hoffman also touted his status as a German immigrant as a guarantee of his impartiality on the American race question and as an attribute that "however spuriously . . . suggested arithmetical expertise, as Germany was the world seat of statistical development in the late 19th century" (89). (A shorter version of Hoffman's argument was published as "Vital Statistics of the Negro" four years earlier in 1892, the same year of publication as *Iola Leroy*.)

3. Anthony Appiah charges W.E.B. Du Bois with falling back into biological essentialism while attempting a sociohistorical definition of race in Du Bois's 1897 essay "The Conservation of Races." Appiah bases his critique partly on Du Bois's use of blood rhetoric ("The Uncompleted Argument: Du Bois and the Illusion of Race" in *"Race," Writing, and Difference*, 21–37). Lucius Outlaw comes to Du Bois's defense in "Conserve Races? In Defense of W.E.B. Du Bois," in *W.E.B. Du Bois on Race and Culture*, 15–37. For a summary and commentary on the debate between Appiah and Outlaw, see Robert Gooding-Williams, "Outlaw, Appiah, and Du Bois's 'The Conservation of Races,'" in *W.E.B. Du Bois on Race and Culture*, 39–56.

4. Harriet Beecher Stowe lost four of her seven children between 1849 and 1887, the first and most devastating loss being that of her son Samuel Charles, who died of cholera at age one. Stowe would later attribute her sympathy for the maternal loss experienced by slave mothers during the sale of their children to her own grief over the death of this infant son. See Joan Hedrick, *Harriet Beecher Stowe: A Life* (New York: Oxford University Press, 1995), 193.

5. In her influential formulation, Jane Tompkins explains how "The power of the dead or the dying to redeem the unregenerate is a major theme of nineteenth-century popular fiction and religious literature" (128). Through its own kind of metaphorical transference, Tompkins's sentimental power mediates the psychic energy of death's transformation through the Christological narrative of martyrdom and into the energy of political change. "Stories like the death of little Eva are compelling for the same reason that the story of Christ's death is compelling; they enact a philosophy, as much political as religious, in which the pure and powerless die to save the powerful and corrupt, and thereby show themselves more powerful than those they save" (128).

6. John Brown began his final court speech by insisting that the intent behind his raid remained the same as it had been in all of his previous activist efforts, "to free the slaves" and make "a clean thing of that matter." "I never did intend murder, or treason, or the destruction of property, or to excite or incite slaves to rebellion, or to make insurrection" (Ruchames 125, 126).

CHAPTER THREE

1. While Harris identifies an "unreconciled antipathy" between earlier African American writers and the subject of incest, the theme does occur—although rarely and

discreetly—in African American literature before the 1970s (495). Indeed Hopkins broached the subject herself in a muted fashion in her first novel *Contending Forces* (1900), where the black heroine Sappho Clark disassociates herself from her past violation by a white half-uncle. Incest, of course, has been a theme in American literature since the publication of William Hill Brown's *The Power of Sympathy: Or, The Triumph of Nature, Founded in Truth* (1789), recognized as the first American novel. For critical discussions of literary incest as a register of social and political anxieties in early and nineteenth-century American literature and culture, see James D. Wilson, "Incest and American Romantic Fiction," *Studies in the Literary Imagination* 7 (1974): 31–50; Anne Dalke, "Original Vice: The Political Implications of Incest in the Early American Novel," *Early American Literature* 23.2 (1988): 188–201; Karen Sanchez-Eppler, "Temperance in the Bed of a Child: Incest and Social Order in Nineteenth-Century America," in Elizabeth Barnes, ed., *Incest and the Literary Imagination* (Gainesville: University Press of Florida, 2002); and Elizabeth Barnes, "Natural and National Unions: Incest and Sympathy in the Early Republic," also in Barnes, ed., *Incest and the Literary Imagination.*

2. Taken from Luke's account of Paul the Apostle's travels in Acts 17:26, the phrase "of one blood" recurs throughout American antislavery writing, appearing as early as 1700 in Samuel Sewall's *The Selling of Joseph* as a biblical endorsement of universal brotherhood and sisterhood. Werner Sollors traces the notion of "one blood" in the construction of ethnic American identity through various texts in *Beyond Ethnicity: Consent and Descent in American Culture* (New York: Oxford University Press), 60–64. For a discussion of the phrase's uses and development in the African American oral tradition, see Benjamin E. Mays, *The Negro's God as Reflected in His Literature* (Boston: Chapman & Grimes, Inc., 1938), 41, 162–88.

3. "Natal alienation" is Orlando Patterson's term for the slave's "loss of ties of birth in both ascending and descending generations. . . . It was this alienation of the slave from all formal, legally enforceable ties of 'blood,' and from any attachment to groups of localities other than those chosen for him by the master, that gave the relation of slavery its peculiar value to the master" (7).

4. Here I am trying to emphasize the important ideological and political critique of slavery effected by the plot's conflation and conceptual exchange *between* miscegenation and incest. Werner Sollors identifies this conflation as a broader strategy of antislavery and antisegregation writing. He writes, "Whereas miscegenation might look like a safe way of avoiding incest, it often turns out to *be* incest in liberal antislavery writing. The very fact that an interracial relationship can still also be described as incestuous suggests that there is a deeper collision between the system of maternal descent that sustains hereditary slavery and the patriarchal belief that kinship is established through the father. And for the antislavery and antisegregationist writers this collision provided a crack in the system of racial domination into which they could drive a wedge" (318).

5. Reuel's description of this "volatile magnetism" combines both orthodox and occult science. The term obviously evokes Franz Anton Mesmer's theory of "animal magnetism," which was influential in the nineteenth-century American spiritualist movement. Mesmer's animal magnetism was "a universal substance linking together every orderly process throughout nature," an "etheric medium through which sensations of every kind—light, heat, magnetism, electricity—were able to pass from one physical object to another"

(Fuller 2). But while Reuel's "volatile magnetism" is similar to Mesmer's "animal magnetism," the two exhibit significant differences. Reuel's substance is more materially stable while Mesmer's is only physically intermediary, and unlike Mesmer's substance, which must be manipulated by magnets due to its energetic properties, Reuel's "volatile magnetism" is described as having enough materiality that it can be contained in a case and physically handled quite easily.

6. In ancient Meroe, "Candace"—a Latin derivative of a Meroitic word meaning "queen" or "queen mother"—was not the name of a single figure but rather the title given to as many as five members of "a remarkable line of Ethiopian queens in Meroitic Cush" that ruled between 160 B.C. and 15 A.D. (see Fage 115; Williams and Finch 13). The appearance of this ancient African figure of feminine power in Hopkins's novel is a historical reference with considerable thematic significance. The reigns of the Candaces in ancient Ethiopia demonstrate a practice of feminine political empowerment to rival even that of Egypt. "These queens ran the civil administration, led armies against military foes, promoted long-distance commerce and diplomatic relations, and engaged in massive building programs. In every way, they exercised the full prerogatives and powers of rulership. Such independent female rulers are found throughout Africa in time and space and . . . this relative frequency of the queenship—compared to other parts of the world—reflected the persistent matriarchal patterns in Africa through the course of history" (Williams and Finch 16). In the context of the novel's Afrocentric political philosophy and historiography, the figure of Candace serves to associate feminine independence and empowerment with the Ethiopianist tenet of a future, cyclical revival of culture emanating from ancient Africa and extending to the Western world.

7. In Faulkner's *Absalom, Absalom!* (1936), the narrator muses over Henry Sutpen's desire for his half brother Charles Bon as the indulgence in a "pure and perfect incest," the surrogated desire for their sister Judith (77).

8. For readings critical of the novel's civilizationist and colonialist implications, see Kevin Gaines, "Black Americans' Racial Uplift Ideology as 'Civilizing Mission': Pauline E. Hopkins on Race and Imperialism," in Amy Kaplan and Donald Pease, eds., *Cultures of United States Imperialism* (Durham, NC: Duke University Press, 1993), 433–55, and Martin Japtok, "Pauline Hopkins's *Of One Blood*, Africa, and the 'Darwinist Trap,'" *African American Review* 36.3 (2002): 403–15.

9. Alan B. Lloyd disputes the notion that royal brother-sister marriage in the Ptolemaic line "evolved on the basis of Egyptian historical precedent, a notion that has persisted into recent literature, despite the total lack of reliable pharaonic evidence that full brother-sister marriage was ever practiced by Egyptian kings" (408). Instead, Lloyd points to the "obvious Greek mythological prototype in the marriage of Zeus and Hera, which was easy to invoke for a family that claimed Zeus as an ancestor," and raises the possibility of a "severely practical" goal in Ptolemy II's marriage to his own sister, that of neutralizing the powerful Arsinoe as a rival to the throne (410). Nevertheless, Ergamenes's reign in Ethiopia corresponds with what Lloyd describes as the "very remarkable . . . establishment of full brother-sister marriage as a recurrent, though not consistent, practice" in ancient Egypt (408). Indeed, seven of the next eleven Greek kings of Egypt after Ptolemy II also married their sisters. See Keith Hopkins 312.

CHAPTER FOUR

1. Alcoff explains that, "The criteria thought to determine racial identity have ranged from ancestry, experience, self-understanding, to habits and practices, yet these sources are coded through visible inscriptions on the body. The processes by which racial identities are produced work through the shapes and shades of human morphology, the size and shape of the nose, the breadth of the cheekbones, the texture of the hair, and the intensity of pigment, and these subordinate other markers such as dress, customs and practices. And the visual registry thus produced has been correlated with rational capacity, epistemic reliability, moral condition, and, of course, aesthetic status" ("Racial Embodiment" 23).

2. The very title of *Light in August* references a visible phenomenon. Asked about the title during an interview at the University of Virginia, Faulkner dismissed assumptions that the title referred to Lena Grove's pregnancy and explained that he chose the phrase "because in my country in August there's a peculiar quality of light and that's what that title means. It has in a sense nothing to do with the book at all, the story at all" (Gwynn 74).

3. Given the focus of the visual and the cinematic in *Light in August*, it is somewhat ironic that Faulkner's financial troubles in 1932 and his failure to secure payment for a serialized version of the novel necessitated his very reluctant move west to Hollywood to pursue more lucrative screenwriting. See David Minter, *William Faulkner: His Life and Work* (Baltimore: Johns Hopkins University Press, 1997), 139; and Joseph Blotner, *Faulkner: A Biography* (New York: Random House, 1974), 300–303.

4. In Alcoff's view, the visual demands of passing thus indicate one of the critical differences between race and both ethnicity and culture. The visual asynchronicity required by the act of passing indicates how "race operates differently from ethnic or cultural identities, which can be transcended, with enough effort" ("Habits" 31). Racial passing indicates racialism's visual imperative in that the act of passing itself requires the passer to become conscious of and take advantage of or manipulate societal assumptions about his or her visible morphology.

5. On the pseudoscience of measuring heads and the use of craniometry in the development of phrenology and the polygenetic theories of Josiah Nott, Samuel Morton, Louis Agassiz, and the "American School of Ethnology," see Stephen Jay Gould, *The Mismeasure of Man* (New York: Norton & Company, 1981), 30–112. For a discussion of the visual racial aesthetics in the work of Swiss physiognomist Johann Caspar Lavater and Dutch anatomist and craniometrist Pieter Camper, see David Bindman, *Ape to Apollo: Aesthetics and the Idea of Race in the 18th Century* (Ithaca, NY: Cornell University Press, 2002), 92–123, 190–221.

6. On the influence of *The Golden Bough* on Faulkner's work with an emphasis on the composition of *Light in August*, see Hlavsa's entry on "The Golden Bough" in *A William Faulkner Encyclopedia* (Westport, CT: Greenwood, 1999), 152–54; and Hlavsa, "St. John and Frazer in *Light in August*: Biblical Form and Mythic Function," *Bulletin of Research in Humanities* 83 (1980): 9–26. Sir James Frazer's anthropological compilation of folk mythologies was published in twelve volumes between 1890 and 1915, with the publication of an abridged version coinciding with the beginning of Faulkner's novelistic career in the mid-1920s. The considerable influence of Frazer on Faulkner's thought and work has been documented by Faulkner's biographers. Biographer Joseph Blotner documents Faulkner's

reading of Frazer as early as 1925 during the composition of his second novel *Mosquitoes* (1927). On Faulkner's reading of Frazer, see David Minter, *William Faulkner: His Life and Work* (Baltimore: Johns Hopkins University Press, 1997), 122; and Joseph Blotner, *Faulkner: A Biography* (New York: Random House, 1974), 138, 234. Among many other borrowings, Faulkner would name his home in Oxford, Rowan Oak, "from the rowan tree, which Frazer describes in *The Golden Bough* as symbolic of peace and security and as indigenous to Scotland, the land Faulkner thought of as his ancestral home" (Minter 122).

7. Even the initial apprehension meeting Christmas upon arrival in Jefferson finds its corollary in Frazer's commentary in *The Golden Bough* on "Taboos on Intercourse with Strangers." Frazer's conglomerate figure of the "savage," protective of his homeland's territorial ruler, remains perpetually suspicious of outsiders for he "suspects all strangers of practising" the "black arts" of "magic and witchcraft" (Frazer 226). In Frazer's analysis, native inhabitants establish elaborate procedural gateways, initiations, and ceremonies "for the purpose of disarming the strangers of their magical powers, of counteracting the baneful influence which is believed to emanate from them, or of disinfecting, so to speak, the tainted atmosphere by which they are supposed to be surrounded" (226). Faulkner's adaptation of Frazer's model of xenophobic anxieties can be witnessed in the narrative of Christmas, the outsider who comes to seek his own marginal place in a community that remains similarly suspicious of "something definitely rootless about him, as though no town nor city was his, no street, no walls, no square of earth his home" (31). Before being accepted into this community, Christmas must undergo certain probing initiative "ceremonies" as Frazer describes; his past associations must be assessed and publicized. The novel's narrative structure, which flashes through Christmas's backstory, gradually reveals to the reader that Christmas may indeed carry with him just the kind of viral past, his past indulgence in the "black arts" as it were, that the community's defenses are designed to guard against. Frazer's description of the taboo on intercourse with strangers becomes substantiated in Faulkner's novel through Jefferson's fear "that a man who has been on a journey may have contracted some magic evil from the strangers with whom he has associated" (Frazer 229).

8. Similarly, Rene Girard, discussing the origins of aversions related to menstruation, explains that the "universal attribution of impurity to spilt blood" derives from the radical divide between the state of social affairs when blood is visible and when it is not. "When men are enjoying peace and security, blood is a rare sight. When violence is unloosed, however, blood appears everywhere—on the ground, underfoot, forming great pools. Its very fluidity gives form to the contagious nature of violence. Its presence proclaims murder and announces new upheavals to come" (34).

9. If Stevens wanted to attribute Christmas's actions to a blackness derived from such a facile equation, he might have simply said as much and dispensed with narrating the elaborate series of events that precede the rise of Christmas's blood, his account of Mrs. Hines's visits to her grandson's cell, for example, during which she supposedly expressed her wish that he "die 'decent'" and then later "'told him about Hightower, that Hightower would save him, was going to save him'" (447–48).

10. In *Black Image in the White Mind*, George Fredrickson observes that the "concept of the duality or instability of Negro character was in fact one of the most important contri-

butions made by Southern proslavery propagandists to the racist imagery that outlasted slavery" (53). Such potential for a duplicity of character became one of the most efficacious and enduring concepts employed by white sociologists and racial scientists as a tool for raising anxiety over the dangers supposedly posed by African Americans during the nineteenth century, particularly in response to such events as the 1831 Nat Turner uprising, as the slavery establishment began to regard the stereotype of the inept and docile slave as an oversimplification unworkable for the purposes of antiblack propaganda. Thus, the stereotype of black submission was increasingly replaced by a model of the black psyche that included the latent capability for severe violence. "In moments of candor," Fredrickson writes, "Southerners admitted their suspicion that duplicity, opportunism, and potential rebelliousness lurked behind the mask of Negro affability" (53). The result was an image of blackness that made "the Negro character seem almost infinitely plastic" (53).

AFTERWORD

1. Montagu bases this conclusion on descriptions of "intermixture" with other peoples as described in the Old Testament ("the sole authority for the early physical history of the Jews") and subsequent records of "intermixture with every people among whom they have lived and continue to live" (318, 337). In response to the question, "Do the Jews possess a community of physical characteristics which serves to distinguish them as a distinct ethnic group among the people of mankind?," Montagu says that science must answer with "an unequivocal 'No'" (318). He concludes that, as a group, Jews are distinguishable based not upon ethnicity but "upon cultural grounds, and upon cultural grounds alone" (318), while recognizing the group exhibits a "quasi-national character" (330).

2. Devoted primarily to the care of wounded soldiers and peacetime disaster relief since its founding in 1881, the American Red Cross only began limited, donor-to-donor blood donor and transfusion services in 1937 in Georgia, other southern states in 1938, and selected cities across the nation by 1940 (Love 144). In 1940, the New York chapter of the Red Cross, in conjunction with the city's Blood Transfusion Betterment Association, initiated the pioneering Blood for Britain campaign, famously supervised by the renowned African American surgeon and blood researcher Dr. Charles Drew. This operation supplied much-needed plasma for the Allies and laid the groundwork for what would become the Red Cross's national blood collection program (Love 146–47). On the implementation of the ARC's blood segregation policy, see Love 155–60, 187–201; and Starr 108–9, 169–70.

3. Stating his agreement with the policy in 1941, Red Cross National Blood Program director G. Canby Robinson admitted that "'The reason for the policy is the opinion that there are so many people who would disapprove of having the plasma from colored blood used indiscriminately with that of white blood that it would jeopardize the project'" (*qtd. in* Love 195). Spencie Love records that Red Cross Chairman Norman H. Davis also publicly admitted "that the policy was based solely on emotion" (Love 195). On the influence of social science on the Red Cross's philosophy and practices of humanitarian relief, see Julia F. Irwin, *Making the World Safe: The American Red Cross and a Nation's Humanitarian Awakening* (Oxford: Oxford University Press, 2013), 32–33.

WORKS CITED

Ahlstrom, Sydney E. *A Religious History of the American People*. New Haven, CT: Yale University Press, 1972.

Alcoff, Linda Martin. "Habits of Hostility: On Seeing Race." *Philosophy Today* 44 (2000): 30–40.

———. "Towards a Phenomenology of Racial Embodiment." *Radical Philosophy* 95 (1999): 15–26.

American Red Cross. "American Red Cross Statement of Policy Regarding Negro Blood Donors," Jan. 21, 1942; Negro Blood, 1944–46; Records of the American National Red Cross; National Archives Gift Collection; National Archives and Records Administration, College Park, MD.

Appiah, Anthony. *In My Father's House: Africa in the Philosophy of Culture*. New York: Oxford University Press, 1992.

———. "The Uncompleted Argument: Du Bois and the Illusion of Race." *"Race," Writing, and Difference*. Ed. Henry Louis Gates Jr. Chicago: University of Chicago Press, 1985. 21–37.

Arens, W. *The Original Sin: Incest and Its Meaning*. New York: Oxford University Press, 1986.

Aristotle. "Poetics." *The Critical Tradition: Classic Texts and Contemporary Trends*. Ed. David Richter. 3rd ed. New York: Bedford/St. Martin's Press, 2007. 59–81.

Barnes, Elizabeth. "Introduction." *Incest and the Literary Imagination*. Gainesville: University Press of Florida, 2002. 1–13.

Beardsley, Monroe. "The Metaphorical Twist." *Philosophical Perspectives on Metaphor*. Ed. Mark Johnson. Minneapolis: University of Minnesota Press, 1981. 105–22.

Benn Michaels, Walter. "Autobiography of an Ex-White Man." *Transition* 73 (1997): 122–43.

Biale, David. *Blood and Belief: The Circulation of a Symbol between Jews and Christians*. Berkeley: University of California Press, 2007.

Black, Max. *Models and Metaphors: Studies in Language and Philosophy*. Ithaca, NY: Cornell University Press, 1962.

Borgstrom, Michael. "Face Value: Ambivalent Citizenship in *Iola Leroy*." *African American Review* 40.4 (2006): 779–93.

Boyd, Melba Joyce. *Discarded Legacy: Politics and Poetics in the Life of Frances E.W. Harper, 1825–1911*. Detroit: Wayne State University Press, 1994.

Brown, Sterling. "Negro Characters as Seen by White Authors." *African American Literary Criticism, 1773–2000*. Ed. Hazel Arnett Ervin. New York: Twayne Publishers, 1999. 55–81.

Camporesi, Piero. *Juice of Life: The Symbolic and Magic Significance of Blood*. New York: Continuum, 1995.

Carby, Hazel. *Reconstructing Womanhood: The Emergence of the Afro-American Woman Novelist*. New York: Oxford University Press, 1987.

Castronovo, Russ. *Fathering the Nation: American Genealogies of Slavery and Freedom*. Berkeley: University of California Press, 1995.

Cole, Simon A. *Suspect Identities: A History of Fingerprinting and Criminal Identification*. Cambridge, MA: Harvard University Press, 2001.

Conticelli, Valentina. "Sanguis Suavis: Blood between Microcosm and Macrocosm." *Blood: Art, Power, Politics, and Pathology*. Ed. James M. Bradburne. Munich: Prestel, 2002. 55–63.

Croly, David Goodman, and George Wakeman. *Miscegenation: The Theory of the Blending of the Races, Applied to the American White Man and Negro*. New York: H. Dexter, Hamilton & Co., 1864.

Davidson, Donald. "What Metaphors Mean." *Critical Inquiry* 5 (1978): 31–47.

Davis, Norman H., Chairman, American Red Cross, to Dr. Henry Smith Leiper, Secretary in America, World Council of Churches, New York, Jan. 27, 1942; Negro Blood 1941–43; Records of the American National Red Cross; National Archives Gift Collection; National Archives and Records Administration, College Park, MD.

Douglass, Frederick. "John Brown: An Address at the Fourteenth Anniversary of Storer College." *Blacks on John Brown*. 1881. Ed. Benjamin Quarles. Urbana: University of Illinois Press, 1972. 54–66.

Du Bois, W.E.B. *The Souls of Black Folk*. 1903. Ed. Henry Louis Gates and Terri Hume Oliver. New York: W.W. Norton & Company, 1999.

Durkheim, Emile. *Incest: The Nature and Origin of the Taboo*. 1898. Trans. Edward Sagarin. New York: Lyle Stuart, Inc., 1963.

Emerson, Everett. *Mark Twain: A Literary Life*. Philadelphia: University of Pennsylvania Press, 1999.

Erkkila, Betsy. *Mixed Bloods and Other Crosses: Rethinking American Literature from the Revolution to the Culture Wars*. Philadelphia: University of Pennsylvania Press, 2005.

Fage, J.D. *The History of Africa*. London and New York: Routledge, 2002.

Fanon, Frantz. *Black Skin, White Masks*. Trans. Charles Lam Markmann. New York: Grove Press, 1967.

Faulkner, William. *Absalom, Absalom!* 1936. New York: Vintage International, 1986.

———. *Light in August*. 1932. New York: Vintage International, 1990.

Foster, Frances Smith, ed. *A Brighter Coming Day: A Frances Ellen Watkins Harper Reader*. New York: Feminist Press, 1990.

Franklin, John Hope, and Alfred A. Moss. *From Slavery to Freedom: A History of African Americans*. 8th ed. New York: Alfred A. Knopf, 2003.

Frazer, James George. *The Golden Bough: A Study in Magic and Religion*. 1922. Abridged ed. New York: Touchstone, 1996.

Fredrickson, George M. *The Black Image in the White Mind: The Debate on Afro-American Character and Destiny, 1817–1914*. Middletown, CT: Wesleyan University Press, 1987.

Freud, Sigmund. *Totem and Taboo*. 1950. Ed. James Strachey. New York: W.W. Norton & Co., 1989.

Fuller, Robert C. *Mesmerism and the American Cure of Souls*. Philadelphia: University of Pennsylvania Press, 1982.

Gabriele, Mino. "Magia Sanguinis: Blood and Magic in Classical Antiquity." *Blood: Art, Power, Politics, and Pathology*. Ed. James M. Bradburne. Munich: Prestel, 2002. 33–39.

Galton, Francis. *Finger Prints*. 1892. Buffalo: William S. Hein & Co., Inc., 2003.

Gates, Henry Louis. "Writing 'Race' and the Difference It Makes." *"Race," Writing, and Difference*. Ed. Henry Louis Gates Jr. Chicago: University of Chicago Press, 1985. 1–20.

Gillman, Susan. *Blood Talk: American Race Melodrama and the Culture of the Occult*. Chicago: University of Chicago Press, 2003.

———. "The Mulatto, Tragic or Triumphant? The Nineteenth-Century American Race Melodrama." *The Culture of Sentiment: Race, Gender and Sentimentality in Nineteenth-Century America*. Ed. Shirley Samuels. New York: Oxford University Press, 1992. 221–43.

———. "Pauline Hopkins and the Occult: African-American Revisions of Nineteenth-Century Sciences." *American Literary History* 8.1 (1996): 57–82.

Girard, René. *Violence and the Sacred*. Trans. Patrick Gregory. Baltimore: Johns Hopkins University Press, 1977.

Goldberg, David Theo. *Racist Culture: Philosophy and the Politics of Meaning*. Cambridge, MA: Blackwell, 1993.

Gross, Ariela J. "Litigating Whiteness: Trials of Racial Determination in the Nineteenth-Century South." *Yale Law Journal* 108.1 (1998): 109–85.

Grosz, Elizabeth. *Volatile Bodies: Toward a Corporeal Feminism*. Bloomington: Indiana University Press, 1994.

Guillaumin, Colette. *Racism, Sexism, Power, and Ideology*. New York: Routledge, 1995.

Gwynn, Frederick L., and Joseph L. Blotner, eds. *Faulkner in the University*. Charlottesville and London: University Press of Virginia, 1995.

Hannaford, Ivan. *Race: The History of an Idea in the West*. Baltimore: Johns Hopkins University Press, 1996.

Harper, Frances. "Be Active." *A Brighter Coming Day: A Frances Ellen Watkins Harper Reader*. Ed. Frances Smith Foster. New York: Feminist Press, 1990. 76–77.

———. "Christianity." *A Brighter Coming Day: A Frances Ellen Watkins Harper Reader*. Ed. Frances Smith Foster. New York: Feminist Press, 1990. 96–98.

———. "Christ's Entry into Jerusalem." *A Brighter Coming Day: A Frances Ellen Watkins Harper Reader*. Ed. Frances Smith Foster. New York: Feminist Press, 1990. 330–31.

———. "Enlightened Motherhood." *A Brighter Coming Day: A Frances Ellen Watkins Harper Reader*. Ed. Frances Smith Foster. New York: Feminist Press, 1990. 285–95.

———. "A Factor in Human Progress." *A Brighter Coming Day: A Frances Ellen Watkins Harper Reader*. Ed. Frances Smith Foster. New York: Feminist Press, 1990. 275–80.

———. "Farmer Centre Ohio November 14 1859 [Letter to Mary Brown]." *A Brighter Coming Day: A Frances Ellen Watkins Harper Reader*. Ed. Frances Smith Foster. New York: Feminist Press, 1990. 48–49.

———. "The Great Problem to Be Solved." *A Brighter Coming Day: A Frances Ellen Watkins Harper Reader*. Ed. Frances Smith Foster. New York: Feminist Press, 1990. 219–23.

———. *Iola Leroy; or, Shadows Uplifted*. 1892. Boston: Beacon Press, 1987.

———. "Moses: A Story of the Nile." *A Brighter Coming Day: A Frances Ellen Watkins Harper Reader*. Ed. Frances Smith Foster. New York: Feminist Press, 1990. 139–66.

———. "A Mother's Heroism." *A Brighter Coming Day: A Frances Ellen Watkins Harper Reader*. Ed. Frances Smith Foster. New York: Feminist Press, 1990. 71–72.

———. "Our Greatest Want." *A Brighter Coming Day: A Frances Ellen Watkins Harper Reader*. Ed. Frances Smith Foster. New York: Feminist Press, 1990. 102–5.

———. "The Resurrection of Jesus." *A Brighter Coming Day: A Frances Ellen Watkins Harper Reader*. Ed. Frances Smith Foster. New York: Feminist Press, 1990. 331–33.

———. "The Two Offers." *A Brighter Coming Day: A Frances Ellen Watkins Harper Reader*. Ed. Frances Smith Foster. New York: Feminist Press, 1990. 105–14.

———. "We Are All Bound up Together." *A Brighter Coming Day: A Frances Ellen Watkins Harper Reader*. Ed. Frances Smith Foster. New York: Feminist Press, 1990. 217–18.

Harris, Marla. "Not Black and/or White: Reading Racial Difference in Heliodorus's *Ethiopica* and Pauline Hopkins's *Of One Blood*." *African American Review* 35.3 (2001): 375–90.

Harris, Marvin. *Patterns of Race in the Americas*. New York: Walker and Company, 1964.

Harris, Trudier. "Tiptoeing through Taboo: Incest in 'The Child Who Favored Daughter.'" *Modern Fiction Studies* 28.3 (1982): 495–505.

Hartman, Saidiya. *Scenes of Subjection: Terror, Slavery, and Self-Making in Nineteenth-Century America*. New York: Oxford University Press, 1997.

Henle, Paul. "Metaphor." *Philosophical Perspectives on Metaphor*. Ed. Mark Johnson. Minneapolis: University of Minnesota Press, 1981. 83–104.

Hickman, Christine. "The Devil and the One Drop Rule: Racial Categories, African Americans, and the U.S. Census." *Michigan Law Review* 95.5 (1997): 1161–265.

Higginbotham, A. Leon. *Shades of Freedom: Racial Politics and Presumptions of the American Legal Process*. New York: Oxford University Press, 1996.

Hoffman, Frederick L. "Race Traits and Tendencies of the American Negro." *Publications of the American Economic Association* 11.1–3 (1896): 1–329.

Holtorf, Christian. "My Blood for Thee." *Blood: Art, Power, Politics, and Pathology*. Ed. James M. Bradburne. Munich: Prestel, 2002. 21–30.

Hopkins, Keith. "Brother-Sister Marriage in Roman Egypt." *Comparative Studies in Society and History* 22.3 (1980): 303–54.

Hopkins, Pauline. "The Dark Races of the Twentieth Century." *Voice of the Negro* 2.3 (1905): 187–91.

———. *Of One Blood: Or, the Hidden Self*. New York: Washington Square Press, 2004.

———. *A Primer of Facts Pertaining to the Early Greatness of the African Race and the Possibility of Restoration by Its Descendants—with Epilogue*. Cambridge, MA: P.E. Hopkins and Co., 1905.

Jakobson, Roman. *On Language*. Ed. Linda R. Waugh and Monique Monville-Bursten. Cambridge, MA: Harvard University Press, 1990.

Johnson, Mark. *Body in the Mind: The Bodily Basis of Meaning, Imagination, and Reason*. Chicago: University of Chicago Press, 1987.

Jones, D. Marvin. "Darkness Made Visible: Law, Metaphor, and the Racial Self." *Georgetown Law Journal* 82.437 (1993): 437–511.

Jordan, Winthrop D. *White over Black: American Attitudes toward the Negro, 1550–1812*. Chapel Hill: University of North Carolina Press, 1968.

Lakoff, George, and Mark Johnson. *Metaphors We Live By*. Chicago: University of Chicago Press, 1980.

Lévi-Strauss, Claude. *The Elementary Structures of Kinship*. 1949. Trans. James Harle Bell, John Richard von Sturmer, and Rodney Needham. Ed. Rodney Needham. Revised ed. Boston: Beacon Press, 1969.

Linke, Uli. *Blood and Nation: The European Aesthetics of Race*. Philadelphia: University of Pennsylvania Press, 1999.

Lloyd, Alan B. "The Ptolemaic Period (332–30 B.C.)." *The Oxford History of Ancient Egypt*. Ed. Ian Shaw. Oxford: Oxford University Press, 2000. 395–421.

Lofgren, Charles A. *The Plessy Case: A Legal-Historical Interpretation*. New York: Oxford University Press, 1987.

Love, Spencie. *One Blood: The Death and Resurrection of Charles R. Drew*. Chapel Hill: University of North Carolina Press, 1996.

Luciano, Dana. "Passing Shadows: Melancholic Nationality and Black Critical Publicity in Pauline E. Hopkins's *Of One Blood*." *Loss: The Politics of Mourning*. Ed. David L. Eng and David Kazanjian. Berkeley: University of California Press, 2003. 148–87.

Lurie, Peter. "Cinematic Fascination in *Light in August*." *A Companion to William Faulkner*. Ed. Richard C. Moreland. Malden, MA: Blackwell Publishing, 2007. 284–300.

McKee, Patricia. *Producing American Races: Henry James, William Faulkner, Toni Morrison*. Durham, NC: Duke University Press, 1999.

Mills, Charles. *The Racial Contract*. Ithaca, NY: Cornell University Press, 1997.

Mitchell, Lee Clark. "'De Nigger in You': Race or Training in *Pudd'nhead Wilson*?" *Nineteenth-Century Literature* 42.3 (1987): 295–312.

Montagu, Ashley. *Man's Most Dangerous Myth: The Fallacy of Race*. 4th ed. Cleveland: World Publishing Company, 1964.

Montagu, M.F. Ashley. *Man's Most Dangerous Myth: The Fallacy of Race*. New York: Columbia University Press, 1942.

Morrison, Toni. "Toni Morrison: The Art of Fiction." *Toni Morrison: Conversations*. Ed. Elissa Schappell. Literary Conversations Series. Jackson: University Press of Mississippi, 2008. 62–90.

Mosse, George L. *Toward the Final Solution: A History of European Racism*. New York: Howard Fertig, 1978.

Nott, Josiah. "The Mulatto a Hybrid—Probable Extermination of the Two Races If the Whites and Blacks Are Allowed to Intermarry." *American Journal of Medical Sciences* 66 (1843).

Nudelman, Franny. *John Brown's Body: Slavery, Violence, and the Culture of War*. Chapel Hill: University of North Carolina Press, 2004.

Olsen, Otto H., ed. *The Thin Disguise: Turning Point in Negro History—Plessy v. Ferguson—a Documentary Presentation, 1864–1896*. New York: Humanities Press, 1967.

Omi, Michael, and Howard Winant. *Racial Formation in the United States*. New York: Routledge, 1994.

Outlaw, Lucius. "Conserve Races?: In Defense of W.E.B. Du Bois." *W.E.B. Du Bois on Race and Culture*. Ed. Bernard Bell, Emily Grosholz, and James B. Stewart. New York: Routledge, 1996. 15–37.

Patterson, Orlando. *Slavery and Social Death: A Comparative Study*. Cambridge, MA, and London: Harvard University Press, 1982.

Pelis, Kim. "Transfusion, with Teeth." *Blood: Art, Power, Politics, and Pathology*. Ed. James M. Bradburne. Munich: Prestel, 2002. 175–90.

Porter, Carolyn. "Roxana's Plot." *Mark Twain's Pudd'nhead Wilson: Race, Conflict, and Culture*. Ed. Susan Gillman and Forrest G. Robinson. Durham, NC: Duke University Press, 1990. 121–36.

Reynolds, David. *John Brown, Abolitionist: The Man Who Killed Slavery, Sparked the Civil War, and Seeded Civil Rights*. New York: Alfred A. Knopf, 2005.

Richter, David, ed. *The Critical Tradition: Classic Texts and Contemporary Trends*. 3rd ed. Boston: Bedford/St. Martin's, 2007.

Rubin, Miri. "Blood: Sacrifice and Redemption in Christian Iconography." *Blood: Art, Power, Politics, and Pathology*. Ed. James M. Bradburne. Munich: Prestel, 2002. 89–99.

Ruchames, Louis, ed. *A John Brown Reader*. London: Abelard-Schuman, 1959.

Saks, Eva. "Representing Miscegenation Law." *Raritan* 8.2 (1988): 39–69.

Sanborn, Geoffrey. "Mother's Milk: Frances Harper and the Circulation of Blood." *English Literary History* 72.3 (2005): 691–715.

Sharfstein, Daniel J. "Crossing the Color Line: Racial Migration and the One-Drop Rule, 1600–1860." *Minnesota Law Review* 91.3 (2007): 592–656.

Shell, Marc. "The Want of Incest in the Human Family; or, Kin and Kind in Christian Thought." *Journal of the Academy of Religion* 62.3 (1995): 625–50.

Smith, Lillian. *Killers of the Dream*. 1949. New York: W.W. Norton & Co., 1961.

Snead, James. *Figures of Division: William Faulkner's Major Novels*. New York: Methuen, 1986.

Sollors, Werner. *Neither Black nor White yet Both: Thematic Explorations of Interracial Literature*. Cambridge, MA: Harvard University Press, 1997.

Stancliff, Michael. *Frances Ellen Watkins Harper: African American Reform Rhetoric and the Rise of a Modern Nation State*. New York: Routledge, 2011.

Starr, Douglas. *Blood: An Epic History of Medicine and Commerce*. New York: Alfred A. Knopf, 1998.

Stepan, Nancy Leys, and Sander L. Gilman. "Appropriating the Idioms of Science: The Rejection of Scientific Racism." *The Bounds of Race: Perspectives on Hegemony and Resistance*. Ed. Dominick LaCapra. Ithaca, NY: Cornell University Press, 1991. 72–103.

Still, William. *The Underground Railroad*. 1872. New York: Arno Press, 1968.

Sundquist, Eric J. *To Wake the Nations: Race in the Making of American Literature*. Cambridge, MA: Harvard University Press, 1994.

Tompkins, Jane. *Sensational Designs: The Cultural Work of American Fiction, 1790–1860*. New York: Oxford University Press, 1985.

Twain, Mark. *Pudd'nhead Wilson and Those Extraordinary Twins*. 1894. New York: W.W. Norton & Company, 1980.

Urgo, Joseph. "Menstrual Blood and 'Nigger' Blood: Joe Christmas and the Ideology of Sex and Race." *Mississippi Quarterly: The Journal of Southern Culture* 41.3 (1988): 391–401.

Watson, Jay. "Writing Blood: The Art of the Literal in *Light in August*." *Faulkner and the Natural World: Faulkner and Yoknapatawpha*. Ed. Donald Kartiganer. Jackson: University Press of Mississippi, 1996. 66–97.

Wells, Ida B. *Southern Horrors and Other Writings: The Anti-Lynching Campaign of Ida B. Wells, 1892–1900*. Bedford Series in History and Culture. Ed. Jacqueline Jones Roster. Boston: Bedford/St. Martin's, 1997.

Westermarck, Edward. *The History of Human Marriage*. London: MacMillan and Co., 1891.

White, Walter, Secretary, National Association for the Advancement of Colored People, to Norman H. Davis, Chairman, American Red Cross, Washington, D.C., Jan. 27, 1942; Negro Blood 1941–43; Records of the American National Red Cross; National Archives Gift Collection; National Archives and Records Administration, College Park, MD.

Williams, Larry, and Charles S. Finch. "The Great Queens of Ethiopia." *Journal of African Civilizations* 6.1 (1984): 12–35.

Williamson, Joel. *New People: Miscegenation and Mulattoes in the United States*. Baton Rouge: Louisiana State University Press, 1995.

Wilson, W. Daniel. "Science, Natural Law, and Unwitting Sibling Incest in Eighteenth-Century Literature." *Studies in Eighteenth-Century Culture* 13 (1984): 249–70.

Wittenberg, Judith Bryant. "Race in *Light in August*: Wordsymbols and Obverse Reflections." *The Cambridge Companion to William Faulkner*. Ed. Philip M. Weinstein. Cambridge, UK: Cambridge University Press, 1995. 146–67.

Wolff, Megan J. "The Myth of the Actuary: Life Insurance and Frederick L. Hoffman's *Race Traits and Tendencies of the American Negro*." *Public Health Reports* 121.1 (2006): 84–91.

INDEX